Sovereignty at Bay

BASIC BOOKS

IN

The Harvard Multinational Enterprise Series

EDITED BY RAYMOND VERNON

SOVEREIGNTY AT BAY

The Multinational Spread of U.S. Enterprises

BY

RAYMOND VERNON

BASIC BOOKS, INC.

Publishers

NEW YORK / LONDON

For my second platoon,
Gruschenka and Nif.

© 1971 by Basic Books
Library of Congress Catalog Card Number: 73–167766
SBN 465–08096–0
Manufactured in the United States of America
DESIGNED BY THE INKWELL STUDIO
74 75 76   10 9 8 7 6

Preface

THIS book is no more than the tip of an iceberg. It was prepared as part of Harvard's Multinational Enterprise Project, a large-scale study that has been going on at the university since 1965. Other products of the study have already appeared in various forms: in a dozen doctoral theses, in two-score journal articles, and in a 500-page book of tables. However, this publication does mark a new phase in the study: It is the first of five volumes whose purpose is to present the project's main results. It is our hope that all five volumes will be published within the next eighteen months.

My role in this project has been that of general coordinator. In practice, this role has meant little in the way of coordination, but a great deal in terms of easy access to the exciting ideas and output of a group of hard-working colleagues. The imprint of their ideas is strong throughout the book. I have tried to acknowledge these ideas explicitly, but there must surely be cases in which they were unconsciously borrowed without attribution. In any event, I am in no position to make the usual disclaimer: Both the credit and the blame for this book are collective.

The main financial support for the study came from the Ford Foundation, in three grants to the Harvard Business School. Harvard's Center for International Affairs also dipped into a scarce supply of research funds to provide indispensable support for the study of a number of important issues. The

Federal College Work-Study Program underwrote most of the costs of the platoon of students who did much of the arduous library research.

James W. Vaupel and my research assistant, Joan P. Curhan, labored hard not only in the preparation of this book but in the construction of the study's statistical infrastructure, from which all the study's participants have profited. Apart from her professional contributions, Mrs. Curhan also managed the complex administrative and financial arrangements of the study. Mr. Vaupel's duties, which he discharged with unlimited ingenuity and good will, required him to produce an endless string of small miracles out of a laggard and resistant computer.

I was delighted by the brilliance and energy of a succession of young researchers who were recruited from various schools at Harvard to assist with this book: George Annas, Melvin Blanke, Michael Denger, Alexander Field, John Minervini, and Steven Simons among others.

Then, of course, there was the usual distinctive contribution of my friend, Max Hall, whose extraordinary capacity for gentle incisive criticism has left a deep imprint on every book I have published in recent years. Marina Finkelstein helped me polish the later drafts, adding considerably to their readability.

The making of any book takes its greatest toll, however, of the indispensable coproducer, the author's secretary. This book was a particularly nasty job, demanding more than the usual commitment of intelligence, energy, and aplomb. I was lucky to have Claudette Manancourt-Dubin in that role.

RAYMOND VERNON

Cambridge, Massachusetts
June 1971

Contents

Tables

Sovereignty at Bay

[**1**]

Multinational Enterprises: A View from Outside

SUDDENLY, it seems, the sovereign states are feeling naked. Concepts such as national sovereignty and national economic strength appear curiously drained of meaning. Germany sees itself as buffeted by a flood of dollars; yet it only takes some cautious and inhibited measures at its borders. France feels oppressed by the presence of foreign-owned subsidiaries; yet its response is limited and restrained.

Though the sense of nakedness and dependence has produced only inhibited responses so far, it has focused the world's interest on the institutions that are thought to be the main agents of the change. One of these is the multinational enterprise. In only a few years, there have been scores of books and hundreds of articles about corporations that are "global" or "transnational" or "international" or "multinational," according to the semantical preferences of the writer. In just as brief a span, governments have begun to ask how these entities were affecting their national interests and what policies were needed to deal with them.

Defining the Target

Exactly which enterprises are the object of this heightened interest? One way to define them is by induction and inference, that is, by developing a list of the "multinational" companies that governments profess to be worrying about and asking what they have in common. Each entry on a list of this sort generally turns out to be a parent company that controls a large cluster of corporations of various nationalities. The corporations that make up each cluster appear to have access to a common pool of human and financial resources and seem responsive to elements of a common strategy. Size is important as well; a cluster of this sort with less than $100 million in sales rarely merits much attention. Moreover, the nature of the group's activities outside its home country is relevant; mere exporters, even exporters with well-established sales subsidiaries abroad, are unlikely to draw much attention, and mere licensers of technology are just as rarely mentioned. Finally, the enterprises involved generally have a certain amount of geographical spread; a parent with a stake in only a country or two outside its home base is not often found on the list.

As a rule, multinational enterprises exude an aura of strength and flexibility. These attributes seem to come partly from the fact that the constituent parts of the multinational enterprise generally consist of corporations, that those corporations are of different nationalities, and that their assets are located in a number of national jurisdictions.

To muse over the power of the corporate form in the latter decades of the twentieth century may seem a bit quaint and anachronistic. Yet one should recall that barely 100 years have passed since corporations first acquired some of their extraordinary modern powers—not a very long time in the evolution of so fundamental an institution. What are their attributes?

Multinational Enterprises: A View from Outside

First, though corporations are endowed with some of the rights of natural persons, such as the right to own and owe and the right to sue and be sued, they are not constrained by the prescribed three score years and ten. Second, corporations manage to avoid another frustrating human constraint, that of a single, explicit, unambiguous identity. A corporation can create offspring without limit, generate siblings as needed, even experience death and reincarnation.

Though the corporation's attributes of unlimited life and multiple identity are revolutionary, its ability easily to acquire different nationalities for its offspring and siblings is even more so. There may be some limitations on the power of a U.S. corporation to create or acquire a French or Brazilian or Togolese corporate offspring; but these limitations are not usually prohibitive. Accordingly, though the parent of the multinational enterprise may be American, its offspring may take on many other nationalities.

Though multinational enterprises existed here and there for almost as long as the modern corporation itself, they have appeared in considerable numbers only during the past few decades. In terms of what they were created to do—to make and sell goods and services more effectively—there is not much doubt of their utility. At the same time, however, they sit uncomfortably in the structure of long-established political and social institutions. They sprawl across national boundaries, linking the assets and activities of different national jurisdictions with an intimacy that seems to threaten the concept of the nation as an integral unit. Accordingly, they stir uneasy questions in the minds of men. Is the multinational enterprise undermining the capacity of nations to work for the welfare of their people? Is the multinational enterprise being used by a dominant power (read "United States") as a means of penetrating and controlling the economies of other countries? Whatever the answers to these questions may be, is the political and economic power of the multinational enterprise "excessive"?

These questions, of course, have relevance only to the extent that the constituent parts of such enterprises respond to a common strategy and draw on a common pool of resources. What do concepts of this sort mean? Economists, as a rule, have no trouble with such abstractions; the idea of the firm, singlemindedly devoted to maximizing its profits, fits neatly into the framework of economic theory. Practically everyone else, however, will recognize that an institution as complex and diverse as a multinational enterprise cannot be said to have a clear, unambiguous will. Such an enterprise represents a coalition of interests, sometimes collaborating over the achievement of a common objective, sometimes warring over conflicting priorities. In some multinational enterprises the sense of common objectives and common identity is strong; in others it is much less so. If the objectives of the constituent parts are sufficiently unrelated or antagonistic, can one say meaningfully that he is dealing with a single "enterprise"? This is a problem familiar to those who try to understand the operations of large, complex organizations, whether these are national or multinational, public or private.

For anyone trying to comprehend the purposes and strategies of multinational enterprises, the problem is compounded by another kind of difficulty. There is always the possibility that differences in national origin and industry structure may breed distinctive types of multinational enterprise, with different goals and patterns of operation. In this book, the response to that difficulty has been a compromise of sorts. In the interest of exploring a manageable set of ideas, the book deals with those multinational enterprises that are controlled by U.S. parent companies. From time to time, it is true, references appear to multinational enterprises whose parents have headquarters in other countries, but these references are generally for purposes of comparison or contrast rather than of broadening the field of study. Moreover, some industries have been omitted from the main body of the study, notably banking, trade, and transportation. To phrase these limitations the other way around, the bulk of the study has to do with understanding multinational enterprises in the manufacturing and extractive industries that are managed by U.S. parent companies.

Even with those delimitations, however, one dare not pretend that the field of study is tidily confined to a well-delineated group of homogeneous organizations. On first impression, the manufacturing and extractive industries are a motley group, a group whose members appear to exhibit more differences than similarities. The challenge has been to develop a frame of analysis that explains both the common elements and the differences.

How can these enterprises be identified more precisely? Throughout most discussions of the problems of multinationality, the question of sheer size has constantly been in the fore. General Motors' $25 billion in annual sales is, it is noted with concern, larger than the gross national product of about 130 countries. Size, it is presumed, means power. And power lies somewhere near the heart of the problem.

Even if the tie between the problems of corporate multinationality and the phenomenon of corporate size had not been so commonly taken for granted, other indications would have focused the search on the largest U.S. corporations. A relatively few large U.S. corporations account for most of the foreign direct investment of the U.S. economy, a higher proportion in fact than their share of U.S. industry itself.[1] With the emphasis on size, therefore, the search turned to the usual group that epitomizes U.S. industrial giants: *Fortune*'s list of 500 U.S. industrial firms.

Large size is a necessary but not sufficient condition for including an enterprise in the ambit of this study. A few industrial giants are not engaged in manufacturing, for example, airlines and public utilities; these were passed over. Moreover, some giants fail to venture abroad in spite of their size;

TABLE 1-1

Key Characteristics of 187 U.S.-controlled Multinational Enterprises and of Other U.S. Enterprises

CHARACTERISTIC[a]	FORTUNE'S 500 ENTERPRISES		U.S. MANUFACTU-RING ENTERPRISES NOT ON FORTUNE'S 500[c]	ALL U.S. MANU-FACTURING ENTERPRISES
	187 MULTINA-TIONAL ENTERPRISES	REMAINDER OF FORTUNE'S 500 ENTERPRISES[b]		
Size Measures				
Sales per enterprise, 1964, in millions of dollars	927.3	283.2	1.0[d]	2.4[d]
Employees per enterprise, 1964	35,800	11,500	38[d]	93[d]
Plants in U.S. per enter-prise, 1965	76	34	1.5[d]	1.6[d]
Profitability Measures				
After-tax earnings as percent of sales, 1964	7.2	5.9	3.1	5.2
After-tax earnings as percent of investment, 1964	13.3	11.1	9.1	11.6
R & D Advertising Measures				
Corporate funded R & D as percent of sales, 1964[e]	2.48	1.85	c	1.29

TABLE 1-1 (continued)

CHARACTERISTIC[a]	FORTUNE'S 500 ENTERPRISES		U.S. MANUFACTU-RING ENTERPRISES NOT ON FORTUNE'S 500[c]	ALL U.S. MANU-FACTURING ENTERPRISES
	187 MULTINA-TIONAL ENTERPRISES	REMAINDER OF FORTUNE'S 500 ENTERPRISES[b]		
Scientists and engineers as percent of labor force, estimated from industry patterns, 1962[f]	6.72	5.15	c	3.64
Scientists and engineers in R & D as percent of labor force, estimated from industry patterns, 1962[f]	2.33	1.89	c	1.33
Advertising expenditures as percent of sales, 1965[g]	2.57	2.39	c	1.46
Advertising expenditures as percent of sales, esti-mated from industry patterns, 1965[f]	1.58	1.27	c	1.42

(footnotes follow on page 10)

TABLE 1-1

ᵃSales, earnings, employment, and investment for *Fortune's 500* enterprises are based on consolidated returns. For implications, see p. 11.

ᵇOnly 304 enterprises, not 313, owing to incomplete data.

ᶜFigures in this column are obtained by subtraction and therefore contain the residual errors of all estimates in the other columns. Entries have not been made where the possibility of error is sufficiently large as to be substantially misleading.

ᵈThe number of enterprises used in calculating these figures was based on U.S. income tax returns for corporations.

ᵉThe coverage of the 187 enterprises and the rest of *Fortune's 500* is incomplete, only 90 enterprises in the first, 101 in the second.

ᶠEstimated for each of *Fortune's 500* enterprises, by assuming for each enterprise (1) that the sales of the enterprise for each product in its mix was in the same proportion to its other products as aggregate U.S. sales in that product were to aggregate U.S. sales in the other products of the enterprise and (2) that the ratio of R & D expenditures to sales of the enterprise in each product was the same as for the U.S. industry. Estimates for "scientists and engineers," and for "advertising expenditures," when estimated from industry patterns, are based on the same type of assumptions.

ᵍThe coverage of the 187 enterprises and the rest of *Fortune's 500* is incomplete: only 103 enterprises in the first, 91 in the second.

Sources: Sales, employment, earnings, and investment for all manufacturing are from Council of Economic Advisers, *Economic Report of the President, 1969* (Washington, D.C.: Government Printing Office, 1969), pp. 258 and 309; tables B-27 and B-71; *Fortune's 500*, *Fortune*, July 1964, pp. 149-167. The number of firms for all manufacturing is from U.S. Internal Revenue Service, *Statistics of Income 1964: Corporate Income Tax Returns* (Washington, D.C.: Government Printing Office, 1968), table 6 and from the 1969 report, table 5. Corporate-funded R & D for all manufacturing is from U.S. National Science Foundation, *Basic Research, Applied Research and Development in Industry, 1964* (Washington, D.C.: Government Printing Office, 1968), table 12. Corporate-funded R & D for individual enterprises is from "Corporate Funded R & D Expenditure by Industry," *News Front*, pt. 1, November 1965, p. 16; pt. 2, January 1966, p. 37; pt. 3, February 1966, p. 40. Concentration indexes are from U.S. Bureau of the Census, *Concentration Ratios in Manufacturing Industry, 1963* (Washington, D.C.: Government Printing Office, 1967), pt. 2, table 27. Advertising expenditures for all manufacturing are from "Estimated Annual U.S. Advertising Expenditures 1947-1966," *Advertising Age*, June 19, 1967, p. 88. Advertising expenditures for individual enterprises are from "U.S. Industry's Ad Budget," *News Front*, March 1966, pp. 40-43. Advertising statistics for industry patterns are from "Percentage of Sales Invested in Advertising in 1965-1966," *Advertising Age*, November 4, 1968, p. 77. The number of R & D workers is from U.S. Bureau of Labor Statistics, *Employment of Scientific and Technical Personnel in Industry, 1962* (Washington, D.C.: Government Printing Office, 1964), B.L.S. bulletin no. 1418, tables A-10, A-16.

about one quarter of *Fortune*'s 500 in 1964, for instance, had no overseas manufacturing subsidiaries at all. In addition to size, therefore, a second criterion of selection was needed, reflecting the propensity of the large corporation to venture widely abroad.

As it turns out, most of the foreign manufacturing subsidiaries of the *Fortune*'s group of 500 are controlled by a relatively few enterprises. For instance, during 1967, 180 enterprises on the *Fortune* list had manufacturing subsidiaries in six or more countries, and this group alone accounted for more than 2,000 of the 2,500 "subsidiary countries," of the entire *Fortune* group; these 180 accordingly seemed presumptively entitled to the "multinational enterprise" label.* Seven more enterprises on the *Fortune* list had once controlled manufacturing subsidiaries in six or more countries; these were added to the 180 to produce a total of 187. The 187 companies, as it developed, contained not only the best-known manufacturing enterprises with major overseas interests but also practically all the major U.S.-controlled raw material producers with such interests. Indeed, on scanning the list of 187, the selection criteria seem to have identified quite adequately the manufacturing and extractive enterprises that are generally thought of as multinational.

One Hundred Eighty-seven Multinational Enterprises

The 187 enterprises prove to be an extraordinary group, quite distinct in many respects from the rest of the U.S. corporate economy. The figures in Table 1–1 suggest the nature of some

---

* The enterprises examined were those that appeared on *Fortune*'s 500 list in either 1963 or 1964; enterprises that were the subsidiaries of foreign parents were omitted and those that were merged by 1967 were counted as one.

of those distinctions.[2] They portray a group of enterprises of extraordinary size and high profitability, committed to activities that involve the relatively heavy use of skilled manpower and of advertising outlays—in short, a group of enterprises bearing the characteristics usually associated with oligopoly.[3]

The supergiantism of the 187 is especially striking. Measured by sales or employees per firm, these enterprises are in a class by themselves.* The profitability data suggest that the 187 have an edge in this respect, when compared with either *Fortune*'s 500 or the economy as a whole. However, the underlying data for this sort of measure are fairly soft; the differences portrayed may not be wholly reliable.

The emphasis among the 187 on relatively extensive use of skilled technical manpower and relatively heavy expenditures for advertising can be detected in various ways: partly inductively, from the characteristics of the industries in which they specialize; partly directly, from data that cover only a part of the *Fortune*'s 500 group. But the signals from the different sources are consistent. Though the 187 enterprises tended to concentrate their activities in industries bearing the signs usually associated with oligopoly, they also displayed a strong tendency to spread their activities across many industries.[4] Their outstanding size, it was apparent, was owing in part to the unusual spread of their activities.

Not only were the number of products of the 187 larger in relation to the rest of *Fortune*'s 500; they were also less closely related to one another. Some kinds of items are generally produced together in the same firm because of various production and marketing affinities, such as steel rods and steel wire; and some are not, such as canned pineapple and aluminum siding. A complex measure designed to register such associations indi-

* Corporate sales figures suffer from many shortcomings, owing notably to the differences in reporting practices among enterprises. Consolidation practices, for instance, vary widely, affecting the extent to which the sales of foreign subsidiaries are included. In general, the tendency is to exclude foreign, more readily than domestic, sales, which would bias the figures for the 187 downward.

cated that the products of the 187 enterprises showed much more heterogeneity and variety than did the rest of the *Fortune* list.[5]

In Table 1–2 the 187 enterprises are identified by their primary industries and are compared with all U.S. enterprises in those industries. The industries in which the 187 are most prominent offer no surprises, in view of their heavy emphasis on skilled manpower and on advertising. At the low end of the scale are textiles and steel; at the high end motor vehicles, fabricated metals, petroleum, drugs, and other chemicals. One might perhaps have expected the tobacco and the aircraft industries to appear higher on the list; but otherwise the picture that emerges is very much according to expectations.

Table 1–2 confirms the fact, if any doubt existed, that the group holds a major position in the U.S. economy. There is no telling exactly how much of the sales reported by the 187 took place inside the United States because the consolidated statements of these large corporations generally contain a considerable part of the sales of their overseas subsidiaries. Inasmuch as there is a higher proportion of sales by foreign subsidiaries among the 187 than among all U.S. enterprises, the 39 percent figure in the table no doubt overstates the relative importance of the 187 enterprises in the U.S. economy. Perhaps 32 or 33 percent would be close to the mark, which is formidable enough.

The dominant position of these enterprises, pronounced as it is in relation to the U.S. economy as a whole, is even more evident in transactions between the U.S. economy and foreign countries. The importance of the multinational enterprises in the U.S. export trade was already suggested by the analysis on which Tables 1–1 and 1–2 are based. According to that analysis, the 187 enterprises tended to produce items that were heavily export oriented; the affinity to exportable products was evident when compared with the other *Fortune*'s 500

TABLE 1-2

One Hundred Eighty-seven U.S.-controlled Multinational Enterprises Compared with All
U.S. Manufacturing Enterprises, by Industry, 1966[a]

| | 187 ENTERPRISES | | | ALL U.S. ENTERPRISES | | 187 ENTERPRISES AS PERCENT OF ALL ENTERPRISES | |
INDUSTRY (Standard Industrial Classification Number)	NUMBER OF ENTERPRISES	SALES	ASSETS	SALES	ASSETS	SALES	ASSETS
Motor vehicles and equipment (371)	11	$ 41.9	$ 26.9	$ 49.6	$ 31.2	84.5%	86.2%
Drugs (283)	15	5.5	4.3	7.2	5.8	76.5	74.2
Fabricated metal products (34)	10	5.0	3.7	6.6	4.4	75.9	84.1
Petroleum refining (29)	9	31.7	42.1	46.4	61.4	68.5	68.6
Chemicals (minus drugs) (other 28)	25	22.3	21.6	37.3	33.5	59.5	64.5
Rubber and miscellaneous plastic products (30)	5	7.7	5.9	13.5	9.1	57.1	64.8
Electrical machinery, equipment, and supplies (36)	19	24.5	20.9	49.2	32.7	49.8	64.0
Instruments and related products (38)	5	4.5	3.9	11.2	8.6	40.2	45.4
Nonelectrical machinery (35)	20	15.4	13.2	48.2	33.9	32.1	38.9
Food and kindred products (20)	29	24.5	12.1	77.6	34.0	31.5	35.6
Primary nonferrous metals (333)	7	4.6	5.4	15.8	14.5	28.1	24.8
Aircraft and parts (372)	4	5.4	2.3	19.2	12.6	28.1	18.3

ALL SALES AND ASSETS FIGURES ARE GIVEN IN BILLIONS OF DOLLARS.

TABLE 1-2 (continued)

INDUSTRY (Standard Industrial Classification Number)	187 ENTERPRISES			ALL U.S. ENTERPRISES		187 ENTERPRISES AS PERCENT OF ALL ENTERPRISES	
	NUMBER OF ENTERPRISES	SALES	ASSETS	SALES	ASSETS	SALES	ASSETS
Stone, clay, and glass (32)	7	3.7	3.4	14.1	12.7	26.2	26.8
Paper and allied products (26)	5	3.7	3.5	17.0	14.6	21.8	24.0
Other transportation equipment (other 37)	3	1.0	1.1	5.8	4.8	17.2	22.9
Leather products (31)	1	0.8	0.3	5.9	2.7	13.5	11.1
Miscellaneous manufacturing and ordnance (39)	2	0.8	0.9	8.1	5.4	9.8	16.7
Lumber and wood products, excluding furniture (24)	1	0.8	1.0	9.1	6.5	8.8	15.4
Furniture and fixtures (25)	2	0.6	0.4	6.8	3.2	8.8	12.5
Tobacco manufacturing (21)	1	0.5	0.5	6.5	4.5	7.7	11.1
Textile mill and apparel products (22 and 23)	4	2.2	1.8	37.6	18.8	5.9	9.6
Primary iron and steel (331)	1	1.2	1.3	26.2	23.6	4.6	5.2
Printing and publishing, excluding newspapers (27)	1	0.5	0.4	13.1	8.3	3.8	4.8
Total	187	208.8	176.9	532.0	386.8	39.2	45.7

ALL SALES AND ASSETS FIGURES ARE GIVEN IN BILLIONS OF DOLLARS.

aFor coverage of sales and assets figures, see p. 11.

Source: For data on 187 enterprises, see *Fortune*, July 1967, p. 196 et seq.; for data on all U.S. enterprise, see *FTC-SEC Quarterly Financial Report on Manufacturing*, 4th quarter, 1966.

companies and stronger still when compared with U.S. industry as a whole.*

But there was more direct evidence of this relationship. The results of a 1965 Department of Commerce survey, covering some 264 U.S. parents and their foreign subsidiaries, offer a strong clue to the importance of multinational enterprises in U.S. export trade.[6] Inasmuch as the 187 enterprises covered here probably make up the great bulk of the firms in the Department of Commerce survey, this survey offers some useful leads. The study indicates that the 264 U.S. parents and their foreign subsidiaries were responsible, whether as buyers or as sellers, for about half of all U.S. exports of manufactured goods. This huge total was about evenly divided between parent-to-subsidiary sales and sales involving a parent alone or a subsidiary alone. If one were also to include the exports of goods produced by U.S. parents that were shipped indirectly through middlemen, the relative importance of such enterprises would be even greater.

With multinational enterprises performing a dominant role in U.S. exports, U.S. policy-makers concerned with the balance-of-payment question quite understandably have been preoccupied with the factors that motivate these enterprises. One question is how fast U.S. parent firms are likely to act, when shifting the means of provisioning their overseas markets; more specifically, how far they will go in curtailing their exports to U.S. markets and using the output from their foreign subsidiaries to fill the overseas demand. Not that there has been much evidence of a relative weakening in net exports of the type of goods in which multinational enterprises specialized; the evidence, such as it is, runs rather to the contrary.† But with

* The statistical measures were calculated by making the same assumptions as those in Table 1–1, note f. On that basis, for 1963, the output of the 187 enterprises consisted of products in which 6.9 percent of the total was exported; this compares with 6.3 percent for the other *Fortune*'s 500 companies, and only 4.6 percent for U.S. manufacturing enterprises as a whole.

† The U.S. net export balances of the products listed by the 187 enterprises behaved quite "favorably" between 1959 to 1964, as compared with the rest of

manufacturing subsidiaries being set up overseas in large numbers, the question is natural enough.

Another kind of issue that has been raised by the large
interaffiliate trade of the multinational enterprises is the extent
to which the normal tools of national trade policy have lost
their relevance and effect. The implementation of trade policy
through such tools as tariffs is generally based on the assumption that transactions across national boundaries are conducted
at arm's length between independent buyers and sellers. The
question for official policymakers has been whether these governmental measures can be expected to evoke anything near
the desired response when the transactions are between parent
and subsidiary.

The balance-of-payments question has had added urgency
because of the importance of the capital-related transactions
of the multinational enterprises. During 1969, U.S. parents
were reported shipping $3,200 million of added capital and
reinvesting $2,200 million of overseas earnings in foreign sub-
sidiaries. Meanwhile, the subsidiaries were generating a return
flow to the United States of about $7,000 million annually in
interest, dividends, royalties, and management fees. If the figures could be gotten separately for the 187 U.S. enterprises
covered in this study, the indications are that the totals would
not be much smaller. These are enormous figures, larger than
most of the figures that purportedly represent the annual U.S.
balance-of-payments "deficit" itself.

In some respects, the importance of the foreign subsidiaries
of U.S. multinational enterprises is probably even greater than
the official U.S. balance-of-payments data suggest. As the regu-

---

the economy. As with similar statistical measures referred to earlier, the assumptions are found in Table 1-1, note f. "Products" in this context were SIC
five-digit categories. "Export balance" was the excess of exports over imports,
calculated as a percentage of U.S. shipments. For the products of the 187
enterprises, this ratio changed between 1959 and 1964 by—.61 percent on the
average; for the products of the rest of *Fortune*'s 500, by —1.07 percent; and
for U.S. manufacturing as a whole, by —1.00 percent.

lar statistics of the U.S. Department of Commerce portray the picture, the foreign direct investments of U.S. firms—that is, the book value of long-term equity and debt held in foreign subsidiaries by U.S. parents—are represented as amounting to $71 billion at the end of 1969. Though this figure is impressive, extrapolations based on the reports of a sample of large companies indicate that in 1967, when the Department of Commerce figure was only $59 billion, the U.S. parents were managing about $110 billion of overseas assets through their positions of control; that about $55 billion of the $110 billion were relatively liquid; and that these liquid assets exceeded the short-term liabilities of the subsidiaries by $20 billion or so. Most of these assets—perhaps as much as 80 percent—were in the hands of the 187 enterprises in the study. Hence, a relatively small number of U.S. enterprises were controlling a huge pool of liquid foreign assets whose management from year to year could greatly affect the seeming position of the U.S. dollar.

The Foreign Country Perspective

That the U.S.-controlled multinational enterprises are important for the U.S. economy is apparent. But how important are the overseas interests of these enterprises to the foreign economies in which they are located?

Table 1–3 provides the familiar figures of the U.S. Department of Commerce purporting to measure the foreign direct investments of U.S. enterprises by geographical areas. Though these figures include some investments that would not be thought of as elements of a U.S.-controlled multinational enterprise, they are a fairly reliable guide to the geographical distribution of the foreign interests of such enterprises. If the investments that were not a part of a multinational enterprise were excluded, such as the subsidiaries of U.S. parents that

TABLE 1-3

Foreign Direct Investments of U.S. Enterprises, by Industry and Area, 1969[a]
(millions of dollars)

AREA	MANUFAC- TURING	PETROLEUM	MINING AND SMELTING	OTHER	TOTAL
All foreign countries	$29,450	$18,277	$5,635	$14,339	$67,702
Canada	9,389	4,359	2,764	4,563	21,075
Latin America	4,347	3,722	1,922	3,821	13,811
Mexico	1,108	35	136	352	1,631
Argentina	789	b	b	455	1,244
Brazil	1,112	100	99	321	1,633
Europe	12,225	4,805	72	4,452	21,554
European Community	6,340	2,243	17	1,593	10,194
France	1,518	295	10	268	2,091
Germany	2,750	1,067	b	434	4,252
Italy	716	506	b	201	1,423
United Kingdom	4,555	1,563	2	1,037	7,158
Other Europe	1,329	998	52	1,822	4,202
Southern dominions[c]	2,029	836	479	510	3,854
Asia and other Africa	1,459	4,555	399	992	7,407
Japan	639	447	0	131	1,218
India	143	b	b	150	294
Other	677	b	b	5,218	5,895

[a]"Foreign direct investment" is defined as the book value of equity and long-term debt of U.S. enterprises in those foreign enterprises in which the U.S. enterprise holds 25 or more percent of the equity. Investment attributed to "international shipping" is excluded. All data are preliminary.

[b]Combined in "other" industries. As a result, subtotals in petroleum, mining and smelting, and "other" columns cannot be obtained by addition of constituent areas.

[c]Australia, New Zealand, and South Africa.

Source: Survey of Current Business, October 1970, p. 28.

had interests in fewer than six countries, the effect would probably be to reduce the emphasis on Canada a little. Moreover, the adjusted figures probably would not exhibit quite so much importance in investments in "other" industries, that is, in industries outside the manufacturing, petroleum, and mining categories.

Even after proper discounting, Canada emerges as an area of heavy U.S. involvement in every type of industry. The U.S. stake in the United Kingdom and Germany lags well behind. After that, the interests of the United States are well dispersed, with Mexico, Brazil, France, and Italy showing some prominence in the list.

The figures shown in Table 1–3, however, are not much of a guide to the perceptions of the foreign nations in which the subsidiaries of multinational enterprises are located. From the point of view of many host countries, the presence of a Du Pont subsidiary connotes the presence of Du Pont. When a consid erable number of the 187 U.S.-controlled enterprises are represented in an economy, the country concerned may think of itself as confronting the awesome collective might of the United States. This state of mind generates poetic hyperbole; accordingly, U.S. overseas investors are sometimes dubbed the "world's third greatest power."

In fact, there are only a few countries in the world where the subsidiaries of U.S. parents represent a dominant proportion of all enterprise in that country, whether dominance be measured by sales or assets or employment; but these few countries are hardly to be overlooked. Once again, Canada is the outstanding case. During the mid-1960s, U.S.-controlled companies that were engaged in manufacturing in Canada accounted for about 60 percent of total manufactures in that country.[7] In asset terms, the same companies accounted for 50 percent of the total for all entities engaged in manufacturing.[8] In important Canadian industries such as automobiles, chemicals, and electrical apparatus, U.S. dominance was even greater. Not all these U.S.-controlled manufacturing companies were elements of a multinational enterprise, as defined here; some were incidental adjuncts of U.S. enterprises whose interests were almost totally oriented to the U.S. domestic market. But the subsidiaries that were part of a U.S.-controlled multinational enterprise probably represented about two-thirds of the total, as best that proportion can be estimated. In Canada's raw material industries, approximately the same degree of U.S. involvement existed.

In Europe, where so much political ferment has been generated in recent years as a result of the increasing role of U.S.-controlled enterprises, the place of such enterprises in the national economies is generally quite small. If one lumps together the United Kingdom and Western Europe in a single aggregate, U.S.-controlled subsidiaries engaged in manufacturing accounted for less than 6 percent of the total sales of all manufacturing firms in that area.[9] Moreover, the 6 percent figure is not unrepresentative of individual countries in Europe; the United Kingdom is on the high side at about 10 percent, and Italy is on the low side with 3 percent. In short, measured on this gross and insensitive scale, the U.S.-controlled multinational enterprises are not especially prominent in the European manufacturing economy.

Still, there is tension. The tension is generated, in part, by the specter of the parent's power that is thought to lie behind the subsidiary. It is generated also by the propensity of the U.S.-controlled enterprises to concentrate in the "advanced" industries. The figures in Table 1–1 indicate that multinational enterprises tend to have certain characteristic attributes, at least as measured against the U.S. industry mix. In general, they tend to be concentrated in industries where large firms dominate, in industries that devote considerable resources to innovation and differentiation of product—all this, in relation to the general run of industries in the United States. As Table 1–4 demonstrates, the relatively strong position of U.S.-con-

TABLE 1-4

Sales of U.S.-controlled Foreign Manufacturing Subsidiaries in Relation to Sales of All Manufacturing Establishments, Canada, Latin America, and Europe, 1964

AREA INDUSTRY	SALES OF U.S.-CONTROLLED MANUFACTURING SUBSIDIARIES (MILLIONS OF DOLLARS)	TOTAL SALES OF MANUFACTURING ESTABLISHMENTS (MILLIONS OF DOLLARS)	SUBSIDIARIES' SALES AS % OF ALL SALES (PERCENT)
Canada			
Food products	$1,280	$6,157	21.8%
Paper and allied products	1,145	2,685	42.6
Chemicals	1,585	3,159	50.2
Rubber products	400	554	72.2
Primary and fabricated metals	1,330	5,308	25.1
Machinery, except electrical	1,030	1,030	100.0
Electrical machinery	1,060	1,547	68.5
Transport equipment	2,420	2,420	100.0
Other products	1,200	a	a
Latin America			
Food products	950	12,120	7.9
Paper and allied products	145	790	18.4
Chemicals	1,250	4,420	28.3
Rubber products	355	611	58.1
Basic metals and metal products[b]	1,840	9,104	20.2
Other products	560	2,484	22.5
United Kingdom and Europe			
Food products	1,450	46,246	3.1
Paper and allied products	130	10,976	1.2
Chemicals	2,250	36,289	6.2
Rubber products	540	4,237	12.7
Primary and fabricated metals	1,030	43,664	2.4
Machinery, except electrical	2,890	29,697	9.7
Electrical machinery	1,700	18,658	9.1

TABLE 1-4 (continued)

AREA INDUSTRY	SALES OF U.S.-CONTROLLED MANUFACTURING) SUBSIDIARIES (MILLIONS OF DOLLARS)	TOTAL SALES OF MANUFACTURING ESTABLISHMENTS (MILLIONS OF DOLLARS	SUBSIDIARIES' SALES AS % OF ALL SALES (PERCENT)
Transport equipment	$4,700	$36,656	12.8%
Other products	1,810	65,361	2.8

aNegligible total. Owing to estimating errors, the original sources suggested a negative figure in this category

bIncludes primary and fabricated metals, nonelectrical and electrical machinery, and transport equipment.

Source: Survey of Current Business, November 1965, p. 19; and G. C. Hufbauer and F. M. Adler, *Overseas Manufacturing Investment and the Balance of Payments* U.S. Treasury Department, (Washington, D.C.: 1968), pp. 37-38.

trolled multinational enterprises in industries with these characteristics applies not only to the U.S. economy but also to the other economies in which the subsidiaries of these enterprises are located.[10] In Canada, the chemicals and machinery industries exhibit an especially heavy participation by U.S.-controlled subsidiaries; the ratios fall away in other industries, following a pattern that corresponds roughly to the U.S. pattern. In Europe, the configuration is much the same.

Just why U.S. enterprises should be so strong in these particular types of industry in the advanced countries is a subject that will be explored at length in later chapters. The point to be emphasized here is that even though U.S.-controlled manufacturing subsidiaries in the aggregate account for about 6 percent of the total manufacturing sales in Europe, these subsidiaries loom much larger in some of the industries presented in Table 1-4. And the more narrowly one chooses to define an "industry," the more commonly one encounters extreme rates of U.S. participation. In Italy, during the 1960s, U.S. enterprises were reported as controlling 100 percent of the ballbearing industry and most of the heavy electric mechanical industry;[11] in Great Britain, more than 75 percent of the carbon black industry and 40 percent of the computer industry; in France, more than 90 percent of carbon black output, more than 40 percent of the telegraph and telephone equipment, and more than 35 percent of the tractor and agricultural machinery output.[12] Everywhere, national computer industries lay overwhelmingly in the hands of U.S.-controlled enterprises. Viewed through the eyes of the host countries, these were more vivid and more relevant data than the bland 6 percent average for industry as a whole.

The U.S. investments to which the Europeans have been most sensitive have been rather different in character from those that generated tension in Latin America. From a historical point of view, the best-known investments of U.S.-controlled raw material producers in Latin America are those in oil and minerals. During the late 1960s, the $5 billion of annual sales on the part of the Latin American subsidiaries of these enterprises constituted more than 5 percent of the gross domestic product of that area, and a very much larger percentage of the total oil and mineral output of the area. To the extent that the tension associated with foreign-controlled enterprise is a function of the dominance of the enterprise, it is fairly evident why such tension existed in Latin America.

As for manufacturing in Latin America, the figures presented in Table 1–4 also offer some indication of the place of U.S.-controlled subsidiaries. Taken over all, the sales of these subsidiaries seem to have run at about one sixth of the total manufacturing sales in Latin America, that is, nearly triple the relative level in Europe.[13] Once again, the impact of such investment is magnified by its propensity to concentrate in certain industries: in automobiles, in chemicals, and in machinery, for example. Even where the concentration is not very great in relation to local industry, as in food products, the most prominent trademarks and brands tend to be those of the U.S.-controlled enterprises.

The question of whether U.S.-controlled enterprises have generated tension in the countries in which they are located is not to be confused with the question of whether they contributed to the welfare of those countries, however "welfare" may be defined. Tension, it should hardly be necessary to point out, is just as commonly associated with constructive forces as with those that make a negative contribution. Later on, I shall return to an appraisal of the welfare issue, but not until after the operations of these multinational enterprises have been explored in much greater depth.

[2]

The Raw Material
Ventures

The operation of a multinational enterprise would have been hard to picture before the middle of the nineteenth century. Very soon thereafter, however, European and North American businessmen who were interested in raw materials, liberated by extraordinary advances in transportation and communication, were already building the foundations of organizations of this sort. From the first their problems and prospects bore a striking resemblance to those encountered today. The existence of seeming historical parallels provokes the usual question: Can something be learned from history about the problems and prospects of the multinational enterprise?

The conclusion of this chapter is that there are some consistent lessons in history. It is not wholly accidental that foreigners are no longer so prominent in the coffee, cocoa, and tropical fiber industries of the world as they were formerly, nor accidental that their participation in the sugar and tea industries is declining. The waxing and waning of the power of foreign-owned raw material enterprises, according to the evidence, has been a function of (1) the scale of undertaking required for effective performance; (2) the complexity of the technology associated with the activity; and (3) the importance of captive overseas markets as an outlet for the raw material. The cultivation and sale of coffee may have seemed a formidable undertaking to the Yucatecan farmer of 1900; the management of a sugar plantation may have appeared beyond the reach of the Cuban peon of 1950. But these pursuits eventually lost their occult quality. In short, the foreign enterprise whose successful establishment had rested on some superior capability or knowledge lost its security of position as time eroded the initial advantage.

The general proposition is more complex than it may appear. Enterprises have sometimes had their initial advantages restored as the technology of the industry grew more complex or as the optimum scale expanded. Others have retrieved their position by moving into new activities in the country where the raw materials were located—such activities as refining or fabricating. The shifts in strength and the strategic responses are nicely illustrated by the case of oil.

The Case of Oil

To many people, the phrase "multinational enterprise" immediately suggests the giants of the international oil industry— Jersey Standard, the Royal Dutch/Shell group, British Petroleum, and four or five others. As far as U.S. enterprise is concerned, there is a solid basis for this association. The U.S.-controlled oil industry has a larger commitment in overseas branches and subsidiaries than does any other U.S. industry; at the end of 1969 the foreign direct investments of U.S. oil companies amounted to more than $20 billion, most of it in raw material extraction and manufacturing. This sum accounted for more than one quarter of all U.S. foreign direct investment at the time. Though the men who managed these overseas oil ventures usually thought of their problems as unique, distinctive, set apart by size and character from those of any other industry, the similarities with other industries were at least as striking as the differences.

STRATEGY OF DEVELOPMENT

The forces that pushed U.S. oil companies toward a multinational basis of operations were forces to which many other U.S. industries would eventually be exposed. When the industry first came into existence in the United States during the 1850s it had many of the attributes of a highly competitive industry, with numerous small buyers and sellers. If it had remained in that state, the multinational side of its activities might never have developed. But this period was shortly followed by one of shakeout and consolidation, leading eventually to the creation of the giant Standard Oil Trust.[1] According to the usual historical accounts, part of the consolidation process was based on physical coercion and financial power; but part was based on scale economies that were rapidly being developed in transportation, refining, and marketing.[2]

By 1870 the U.S. oil industry had acquired two characteristics that seem to predispose enterprises toward overseas investment: The industry was selling about two thirds of its U.S. output to foreign markets, and firms in the industry had achieved a considerable degree of concentration and scale. What was still lacking, and what was nearly thirty years in coming, was a willingness to assume the costs and risks of oil production in foreign countries. The incentive to make such investment grew steadily after 1870. Dutch producers located in Sumatra began to challenge the American exporters in their Asian markets, while Russian and Rumanian producers stepped up the competition in Europe. Until 1900 or so, however, the response of the U.S. oil companies was to try to gain control over available marketing outlets in those areas in which they were facing international competition rather than to try for the control of nearby crude oil sources. Marketing had been a principal source of strength for the large companies in the United States, and it seemed natural to try to duplicate that strength abroad.

By the turn of the century, however, it was evident that the strategy of buying up marketing outlets in foreign countries simply would not work. Entry into the marketing end of the business was much too easy, and competitors could readily create new distribution facilities where existing ones had been preempted. If there was any strategy by which competition could be contained, it was by controlling the supply of crude oil. Accordingly, there was a fundamental shift in strategy. Thenceforth, most of the major oil companies would make their plans on the principle of internal balance or vertical integration, that is, on the principle of self-sufficiency within the enterprise for the production, processing, transportation, and marketing of petroleum.[3]

This commitment to a strategy of self-sufficiency is central to any explanation of the propensity of the oil companies to invest so heavily in crude oil and refining facilities throughout the world. The rationalization for the strategy has been elaborated thoroughly in other sources, however, and only a few words of recapitulation are needed here.[4]

As the oil companies see it, the exploitation, refining, and distribution of oil entail important economies of scale. Some of these economies are a consequence of the insurance principle; some, according to the companies, are a function of high fixed costs. With scale economies playing so large a role, an oligopolistic market structure is likely to develop. With oligopoly and declining costs, each oil supplier hesitates to use reductions in price as a means of stabilizing its production and sales, for such reductions can generate responses from the other participants that defeat the purpose of the reductions. To secure the necessary assurances regarding markets, therefore, each producer of crude oil tries to develop its own downstream refining and marketing facilities.[5] At the same time, refiners and marketers who lack their own sources of material supply are fearful because of their exposed position; the vertically integrated sellers, being few in number, are in a position to raise prices at the raw material stage and to wipe out the profit margin for refiners and marketers. The market-oriented operators, therefore, rapidly try to capture sources of crude oil in order to reduce their vulnerability.

So much for familiar argument. How does the argument relate to the oil companies' interest in discovering and producing oil in foreign areas? One possibility, of course, is that at the price level maintained by a market of oligopolistic sellers, practically any potential oil development seemed attractive. But other explanations will serve as well.

As long as the U.S. oil companies concentrated principally on marketing, the level of crude oil prices was not of vital concern; they were free to buy from the cheapest sources and to pass on the burden of price increases as they occurred. Once the U.S. oil companies had settled on a strategy of vertical integration, however, they had to worry that competitors might have access to cheaper sources of oil than those to which they themselves were tied. All at once, therefore, the oil companies were acutely concerned with any threat to the maintenance of the prices of crude oil in world markets. One way of reducing such a threat was to follow a policy of participating in the exploration of any new major areas in which present or prospective competitors were involved. It would be oversimplifying the situation to think of such an investment policy simply as an effort to maximize profits at the margin. In economic terms, the cost of development could better be attributed to the hedging of risk—the risk of losing control of the price structure in established markets. The expenditure could also be thought of, in part, as an investment—an investment in the acquisition of knowledge about production costs in new, untried areas.*

* An even more complex motivation for investment, akin to the idea of the effective deterrent in game theory, is found in the official Royal Dutch history: "Standard Oil had obtained a firm footing in the Netherlands Indies . . . . Being hard pressed by this keen competition, the Royal Dutch/Shell group made a successful attempt to extend its business to the American continent." See

After 1900, one began to see various applications of the new strategy. The case of Mexico was especially important. The existence in Mexico of a few uncontrolled American oil prospectors, along with an unaffiliated British enterprise, accelerated the interest of the main U.S. producers in Mexican oil and led to large investments in that area.

The early history of the major oil companies suggested another principle of a prudential sort. A well-diversified supply of resources, they rapidly discovered, was especially useful in dealing with supply blockages, whether threatened or actual. This lesson was borne home repeatedly over the decades: in the bitter negotiations with Mexico during the 1930s; in the battles with Mossadegh over Iran's oil during the early 1950s; in the various closings of the Suez Canal during the 1950s and 1960s; and in Bolivia's nationalization of Gulf Oil's holdings during 1969. In their search for stability, the major oil companies constantly felt the need not only to acquire well-diversified sources of oil but also to acquire them in areas that roughly matched the locations of their principal competitors. To that end, the Americans fought stubbornly—and, in the end, successfully—to break their way into the special oil preserves that the British and the French were maintaining for themselves in the Middle East. By the 1920s they had managed to achieve this objective.

The search for stability did not stop here, however. In 1928, in continued pursuit of that elusive goal, the big oil companies entered into a set of agreements that were destined to govern their competitive relations for the next twenty years. These agreements called for a division of world markets among them on an "as-is" basis, and they included a commitment that exploration for all new oil deposits in Saudi Arabia, Iraq, and certain other nearby areas would be done only on a partnership basis.

Koninklijke Nederlandsche Petroleum Maatschappij, N.V., *The Royal Dutch Petroleum Company 1890–1950* (The Hague, 1950), p. 18.

TABLE 2-1
Geographical Spread of Nine U.S.-controlled Multinational Enterprises in Petroleum, 1910-1967[a]

CRUDE OIL OPERATIONS	1910	1920	1930	1938	1957	1967
Number of enterprises engaged in such operations	1	5	7	7	9	9
Number of countries in which engaged	1	5	12	20	22	31
Number of country operations[b] in Canada	0	0	1	1	7	9
United Kingdom and Europe[c]	1	2	3	8	9	11
Southern dominions[c]	0	0	0	0	0	3
Latin America	0	6	15	18	18	28
Other	0	1	5	13	29	45
Total country operations	1	9	24	40	63	96

SUBSIDIARIES OF ALL TYPES	1913	1919	1929	1939	1957	1967
Number of subsidiaries by area						
Canada	1	16	22	40	135	220
United Kingdom and Europe[c]	59	70	137	202	333	626
Southern dominions[c]	2	2	4	10	32	68
Latin America	8	10	41	68	202	329
Other	3	4	8	31	84	199
Number of subsidiaries by principal function						
Extraction	3	7	20	27	33	60
Manufacturing	16	19	43	52	92	279
Sales	36	43	78	110	156	289
Other[d]	7	13	39	65	208	325
Unknown	11	20	32	97	297	489
Total subsidiaries	73	102	212	351	786	1,442

[a]The U.S. enterprises covered in the table are Cities Service, Continental, Gulf, Mobil, Phillips, Standard Oil of California, Standard Oil of Indiana, Standard Oil (N.J.), and Texaco. These comprise all the oil companies in the group of 187 enterprises introduced in Chapter 1.

TABLE 2-1 (footnotes continued)

ᵇCrude oil operations are commonly carried on through foreign branches of U.S. companies rather than subsidiaries. Each country operation in the table represents the presence of one of the enterprises in a country, whether by way of branches or subsidiaries. The figures are subject to larger error than those in the lower half of the table.

ᶜEurope includes Ireland and Turkey. The Southern dominions are Australia, New Zealand, Rhodesia, and South Africa.

ᵈIncludes holding, R & D, serving and entertaining, banking, transportation, and name protection.

Source: Harvard Multinational Enterprise Study. For background and methodology of study, see J. W. Vaupel and J. P. Curhan, *The Making of Multinational Enterprise* (Boston: Harvard Business School, 1969), pp. 1-8.

But Table 2–1 demonstrates that, in spite of the as-is commitment of 1928, the number of foreign installations of U.S. parent firms grew persistently until World War II. And once hostilities ended, the growth became positively explosive. The leapfrogging and expanding process by this time was being stimulated by forces too strong to hold in check: the enormous rise in the world demand for oil after the war; the discovery of rich new fields in the Middle East; and the desire of the various major companies to keep their internal structures in "balance." By 1948, the as-is agreement had been weakened beyond recognition, and the efforts to freeze the partnership pattern in the Middle East had been abandoned.

TWILIGHT OF STABILITY

Many new areas of oil production were opened up during the decade following World War II. As countries such as Libya and Nigeria discovered their blessings, they issued many invitations to the exploration sweepstakes, accepting those entrants that seemed capable of raising the funds, providing the technology, and marketing the product. With the costs of crude oil production at $.30 or $.40 per barrel and the sale price at $1.50 or $2.00, there were numerous takers. Among these takers were the big international companies. Even if they seemed already to have extensive reserves in the Middle East and elsewhere, the fundamental insurance principles of spreading the geographical risk and matching the competitor's locations continued to operate.

With the spread of the big international companies after World War II, the old geographical spheres of dominance associated with each company were badly eroded. Though there had always been a certain amount of market interpenetration among the big companies, the degree of such interpenetration increased. The large U.S. firms managed to acquire and extend their refining and distributing positions in European markets, with a resultant increase in the number of their subsidiaries in that part of the world. At the same time, the British and Dutch companies succeeded in expanding their foothold in North American markets. Indeed, market interpenetration was carried to new levels when in 1969 British Petroleum acquired a lien on the huge Sohio distribution system in the United States. Today, though each major company is still associated with an explicit national identity, the spheres of interest of these companies can no longer be defined on simple geographical or political lines.

The oil industry is a good example not only of how multinational enterprises have come into existence but also of the sources of vulnerability of that dominant position. While the nine big oil companies covered in Table 2–1 were spreading their overseas operations to foreign jurisdictions, the number of oil companies that seemed ready and able to deliver the necessary package of capital, technology, and markets for operations of this sort was increasing with great rapidity. In the years following World War II, several dozen U.S. petroleum enterprises that had previously been confined to domestic markets took the plunge into international markets. Adding slightly to the threat was the fact that a few large U.S. chemical companies, driven by the need for cheap sources of crude oil as a raw material, also moved into the business of oil exploration and production.

In addition to all the other new entrants, a number of companies operating with the political and financial backing of their governments entered the oil business on a large scale. To be sure, this kind of development was not new for a product as strategic as oil. The British Petroleum Company, for instance, traced its origins to the early twentieth century when the British government underwrote the expansion of the Anglo-Persian Oil Company in order to reduce Britain's dependence on American-owned oil. The Compagnie Française des Pétroles had been brought into existence in 1924 by the French government, sparked by similar preoccupations. Later still, the government-owned Italian enterprise, Ente Nazionale Idrocarburi (ENI), stumbled into the international oil business, pushed not so much by Italian government policies as by the personal ambitions of its appointed head. But this group of state-owned companies, though engaging in sporadic warfare with the Americans, had recognized the community of interest in the industry quickly enough to leave the international price-making and marketing structure of the industry relatively stable and secure.

The state-supported companies that have become active since World War II fall into a number of different patterns. Those that were set up by oil-importing countries, such as Argentina, India, and Thailand, have generally followed the strategy that the French pursued for several decades earlier. Using the bargaining power implicit in the government's control over domestic markets, these state-owned companies have generally tried to loosen the hold of the international companies over the importation and domestic distribution of the oil. Success in this effort has varied from one country to the next. On the whole, however, efforts of this sort have had only a marginal effect on the basic international structure of the industry.

The increased activities of the state-owned enterprises of oil exporting countries after World War II, such as the companies of Venezuela and Iran, have had a much greater potential as destabilizing forces in world oil markets. These enterprises were tangible evidence of the fact that some of the long-time barriers to entry into the industry at the exploitation and refining stage had at last been lowered. Enough of the basic technology had been standardized and disseminated in the decade after World War II so that exploring and drilling specialists could be had on hire. An analogous situation obtained for the refining stage. Most of the formidable patents that once dominated the refinery process had expired, allowing the technology to move into the public domain.[6] In fact, the petroleum industry began to lose its attributes as a technology-intensive industry; its personnel in research and development, which had risen from 4.3 percent of the labor force in 1927 to 10.2 percent in 1940, dropped to 5.3 percent in 1952 and 2.8 percent in 1957.[7]

Although the technology of exploitation and refining in the oil industry never stopped improving, independent producers of crude oil found it easier to overcome barriers to entry at those stages. At the same time, the marketing barrier also was weakening. Despite the fact that long-established firms never ceased in their efforts to secure and control the outlets for their production, the number of large buyers of oil continued to increase, not decrease. Even though an unintegrated marketer had to face high risks and thin profit margins, some new unintegrated enterprises, such as the Standard Oil Company of Ohio, the Migrol firm in Switzerland, the "white stations" in Germany, and ENI's distributing subsidiary in Italy, managed to beat their way to the top.

The fact that these competitive forces did not seem to reduce the price of crude oil in world markets can be attributed to several factors. First, during the 1950s the United States imposed restrictions on imports of petroleum, thus effectively separating the management of that key market from the rest of the world. Then the restrictive regulations of the Texas Railroad Commission were used to prop up the price of the licensed imports and of domestic production high inside the protected market. Outside the United States, it fell to the six or seven big international companies to manage international supplies. Their ability to achieve that result successfully stemmed in part from the long period in which they had been obliged to coexist. It derived also from the fact that the governments of oil-exporting countries were not the only nations eager for high prices; oil-importing countries also threw their weight in that direction. Many would have been disconcerted if prices had fallen, fearful of the competition that imports might generate for domestic energy sources such as coal and high-cost oil.

The maintenance of price stability on the part of the major oil companies demanded tight control over marketing. Accordingly, any new international seller of oil soon learned that the availability of markets was still a significant barrier to entry. The new state-owned enterprises of exporting countries soon learned that their aspirations to do their own international marketing would take some time to achieve.[8] One question hanging over the industry was whether the eagerness of such enterprises to overcome this barrier would accelerate the incipient competitive tendencies in the international oil markets, loosening the organizational links between production and distribution and driving crude oil prices down.

Multinational Copper and Aluminum

As every industry specialist will insist, no two industries are quite alike. And the juxtaposition of copper and aluminum alongside oil emphasizes this fact. Though the U.S. copper industry is second and the aluminum industry third in U.S. overseas investment in raw materials, neither has developed on a pattern that altogether parallels oil. Still, there have been marked similarities among these leading raw-material-based

TABLE 2-2

Geographical Spread of Nine U.S.-controlled Multinational Enterprises in Nonpetroleum Extractive Industries, 1910-1967[a]

NONPETROLEUM EXTRACTIVE OPERATIONS	1910	1920	1930	1938	1946	1957	1967
Number of enterprises engaged in such operations	3	6	6	6	6	9	9
Number of countries in which engaged	1	5	11	13	13	19	22
Number of country operations[b] in:							
Canada	0	2	1	1	1	5	6
United Kingdom and Europe	0	0	2	2	1	2	3
Southern dominions	0	0	1	1	2	5	8
Latin America	3	9	12	15	13	20	25
Other	0	0	1	1	2	2	3
Total country operations	3	11	17	20	19	34	45

TABLE 2-2 (continued)

SUBSIDIARIES OF ALL TYPES	1913	1919	1929	1939	1945	1957	1967
Number of subsidiaries by area							
Canada	1	3	7	9	9	30	55
United Kingdom and Europe	1	1	4	8	6	16	121
Southern dominions	0	0	1	5	5	17	52
Latin America	4	13	17	44	43	83	119
Other	0	0	3	3	3	29	70
Number of subsidiaries by principal function							
Extraction	3	9	13	32	31	71	67
Manufacturing	3	4	9	13	12	44	165
Sales	0	0	0	1	1	9	77
Other	0	3	6	15	14	32	65
Unknown	0	1	4	8	8	19	43
Total subsidiaries	6	17	32	69	66	175	417

[a]The U.S. enterprises covered in the table are Alcoa, American Metal Climax, American Smelting and Refining, Anaconda Copper, Engelhard Industries, Kaiser Industries Corporation, Kennecott, Phelps Dodge, and Reynolds Metal.

[b]For definitions of terms, see Table 2-1.

Source: Harvard Multinational Enterprise Study.

industries. Many of the forces that have created the multinational enterprises, as well as the factors that have contributed to their weaknesses and their strengths, are common to all the leading industries.

The international role of the U.S. copper and aluminum industries, like that of the oil industry, was built up in the first instance on the basis of a strong domestic market. This was followed by the emergence of a vigorous export trade and by a steady outward push. The rate and extent of that spread are indicated by the figures in Table 2–2, which covers all the large U.S. enterprises outside the petroleum industry with major overseas interests in the extraction of raw materials.* Though the figures in Table 2–2 cover all the extractive industries except petroleum, it is copper and aluminum that dominate the totals. If these two industries were shown separately, both would exhibit the same general tendencies of growth and spread. As a result of these tendencies, the interests of U.S. firms are now quite global in scope. At the same time, a few of the large firms of other nations seem intent on developing operations in North America. The fairly sharp geographical division of markets that was generally associated with the various international metal cartels before World War II no longer seems possible; instead, the commingling and overlap of markets among the large firms of the advanced nations seem to be growing more pronounced.[9] At the same time, however, the less-developed countries are becoming more persistent in their efforts to influence management decisions relating to their raw material exports. The inherent conflict between these tendencies seems strong.

Anyone who is familiar with the conditions of the copper and aluminum industries would, however, resist describing the tensions of both in similar terms. During the early 1970s the

* Seven of the nine companies in the table were included among the 187 enterprises introduced in Chapter 1. Two more, Anaconda Copper and Kennecott, were added in order to include all of the companies in *Fortune's* 500 with major foreign raw material interests.

aluminum industry was still giving off an aura of invulnerability in its relations with less-developed countries, whereas the copper industry seemed to be losing ground rapidly to the governments it confronted.

Negotiations between foreign governments and the multinational copper enterprises were nothing new of course; indeed, they had been almost continuous and uninterrupted from the 1920s on. But during the 1960s and early 1970s, the negotiating issues changed from the familiar questions of taxes and other such benefits to the more vital issues of ownership and the prerogatives of management. In Chile, the government first took a majority interest in its copper mining industry, then nationalized the industry altogether.* In Zambia, the evolution of relationships in the copper industry was very much the same; by 1969 that country had taken a 51 percent position in the erstwhile foreign-owned copper companies. In Mexico, what remained of U.S. copper interests had already been "Mexicanized," that is, diluted by the forced imposition of local Mexican partners in a majority role. In Peru, it was beginning to appear that the government would not long delay a series of moves in the same direction. Inasmuch as the production of copper ore in Chile, Mexico, and Zambia alone made up about one third of the production in the noncommunist world—indeed, about 45 percent if the United States is excluded—a basic restructuring of the industry was clearly in progress.

The difference between the seeming invulnerability of the aluminum industry from attacks by host governments and the apparent vulnerability of the copper industry can be explained in terms of relative bargaining positions in the two industries. In the first place, nature has distributed copper ore and bauxite, which is the principal ore of aluminum, rather differently on the face of the earth. Bauxite of a quantity and

---

* Some observers claim, however, that the Chilean government struck a poor bargain when taking the first of its two bites, giving up a great deal to the companies and getting very little. Keith Griffith, *Underdevelopment in Spanish America* (London: Allen & Unwin, 1969), pp. 162–166.

quality appropriate for metallic production can be found in many places, copper in only a few; accordingly, the aluminum companies could afford to pick and choose between the safe and the unsafe areas, while the copper companies had rather less latitude in their choice of countries. But this is only one of the important differences. The other differences have already been suggested by the generalizations with which this chapter began. One critical difference is in the tie between ore production and marketing. In the use of copper, the leading companies had been slow to integrate their activities downward into the fabricating stages, much slower than in the case of aluminum or oil. This difference in behavior may have been owing to the fact that until about 1939, security and stability seemed possible for the major copper producers even in the absence of vertical integration. Until that time, the producers were relying on a series of international cartel agreements aimed at restricting output and at keeping prices high and stable. Because high-grade copper was to be found in only a few locations, such agreements had a chance of succeeding. Though the copper agreements gave way a number of times during the depression years of the 1930s, they served the industry's need for stability reasonably well.[10]

When the cartel approach to stability became infeasible after World War II, the leading companies began to turn to vertical integration as a second-best means for reducing their risks. During the 1950s and 1960s, as the industry moved into a period of sharp changes in demand, the advantages of a vertically integrated structure became obvious to the companies. During those unstable years, the control over transfer prices that went with vertical integration proved of great help to the companies. When the demand for copper sagged, as it did briefly during the period, the companies could avoid the displeasure of the countries in which their ore was located by limiting reductions in the price of the ore while shrinking their fabricating margins. When the demand for copper increased and the U.S. government put pressure on the companies to hold down the price of copper ore as an antiinflationary step, the companies could also oblige, making up some of the lost profits by widening their margins at the fabricating stage. Of course, because the copper companies controlled only a portion of the world's ore supply and the world's fabricating facilities, the manipulation of transfer prices meant that a two-price system was bound to develop—one set of prices being maintained by the copper companies for their transactions with affiliates and favored buyers, another set being maintained for "free" transactions. Despite the visible discrimination, the system could be sustained for considerable periods of time.[11]

Notwithstanding these efforts, the copper companies gave ground to the countries in which the ore was located. The vulnerability of the copper companies can be traced back to the usual root cause: Measured in terms of their control over technology, capital, and markets the copper companies were in a more dispensable position than the aluminum companies. The technology of copper refining was already well established and widely available by the end of World War I; the main innovation after that date was a continuation of the shift from selective to nonselective methods for the mining and concentration stages of the copper fabricating process.[12] As for markets, the general shortage in world copper resources, referred to earlier, weakened the copper companies' position still further in relation to their host governments.

The situation in the aluminum industry developed quite differently. During the half century in which the bargaining strength of the copper and oil companies appeared to reach a peak and then recede, the aluminum companies appeared to be maintaining their grip serenely on the bargaining situation with countries in which their facilities were located.[13] The need for cheap power might have increased their vulnerability in the course of time. But until the early 1970s, unutilized power sources could still be found in many countries. And the possibility of nuclear power on the horizon looked as if it might free them even from that location restraint.[14] It was the huge economies of scale associated with the refining process that provided the companies with their trump card. Because refining costs in aluminum amounted to about 60 percent of total production costs, such economies were critically important. In sharp contrast, the comparable figure in the case of oil was only about 6 or 7 percent, and in the case of copper about 15 percent.[15] Therefore, if a country could not scrape together the tens of millions of dollars for the construction of an optimum-sized aluminum refinery, as most could not, it was handicapped in its negotiations with the foreign aluminum producers.*

The aluminum industry's strength was fortified by one more fact—the existence of many partnerships among the leading enterprises in the extraction of bauxite and the production of alumina, from which aluminum is made. Partnerships of this sort occurred occasionally in copper mining as well, as illustrated by the case of the Southern Peru Copper Company; they also occurred in the exploitation of crude oil, as illustrated by ARAMCO in Saudi Arabia, by the Iraq Petroleum Company, by the Kuwait Oil Company, and so on. But in operations that involved the mining of bauxite and its refinement into alumina, such partnerships were even more common than in copper or oil. Agreements linking Kaiser with Reynolds, Pechiney with Kaiser, Alusuisse with Pechiney, and other such pairings, characterized the structure of the aluminum industry.

The motivations that led to partnerships in the aluminum industry no doubt had much in common with those that created the partnerships in oil and copper. Only the weights

* The high capital intensity and high concentration of the aluminum refiners, as compared with the copper and oil refiners, can be seen in a rough and ready way in value-added-per-establishment and horsepower-per-establishment data from the U.S. Census of Manufactures, and in the industry concentration measures compiled by the Bureau of the Census from such data. An analysis of the financial statements of major firms in the three industries adds further confirmation, albeit at a low level of statistical rigor.

given to the various considerations may have varied a little among the industries. One of these motivations, especially important in bauxite mining, was to share the high and lumpy risks of exploitation operations; it takes a certain courage to commit large quantities of hard cash to the building of ports, roads, railroads, and urban infrastructure in remote places, especially when these places are bristling with political and physical risks. This is particularly true for enterprises that have been in existence long enough to develop a corporate memory, enterprises that can recall the bleached bones of Ford's twenty-year fiasco in rubber raising in the Amazon[16] or the frustrations of International Mineral's five years of fruitless negotiation over a phosphate project in the Spanish Sahara. Perhaps another objective in these complex pairings of major enterprises was to create a common set of global interests among the major companies, thereby increasing the probability of a common industry view on issues that might arise in the future; as a cautionary measure, such a step would make good sense in an oligopoly, even if the issues themselves could not be identified.

Still, one cannot say that the glacial placidity of the industry was altogether complete. Guyana, fortunate in possessing a rare type of bauxite that was needed by the refractory industry and that required no expensive processing, nationalized its bauxite mines in 1971. Jamaica, less advantageously placed for bargaining because its ores were of the more conventional metallic type, was still looking for some measure of control over the exportation of its bauxite. There was the usual jockeying for position among the key firms in the industries. Firms that did not control their own facilities for the further fabrication of the aluminum they produced felt some need to acquire such facilities as a cautionary measure.[17] That very tendency, however, further strengthened the position of the aluminum industry in relation to the countries from which they drew bauxite and other raw materials.

The Pressures from Government

While various forces have been shaping the strategy of the foreign-owned multinational enterprises in the raw material industries, there have also been some major forces at work that have operated on the side of governments. These forces, too, seem to have had certain elements of regularity and predictability.

THE OBSOLESCING BARGAIN

There may have been a time in international affairs when foreign producers of raw materials anticipated that a bargain with a government, once made, would not come unstuck. Today the opposite is generally assumed. And the assumption derives in part from an increasing appreciation of the process that leads governments repeatedly—almost predictably—to re-open the issues involved in the exploitation of raw materials.

When a foreign investor in raw materials takes the plunge into the dark and chilly waters of a less-developed country, the event is generally celebrated by the signing of some sort of contract between the investor and the government. In practically all cases, the bargain is quite formal in character, and includes a series of commitments on the part of both parties.[18]

The foreign investor generally undertakes to engage in certain stated programs of exploration and exploitation, according to a schedule of greater or lesser rigor and specificity, and he usually is committed to the payment of certain taxes. The investor may also undertake to provide his local labor force with housing and social services, to train and upgrade local personnel in the local management hierarchy, to use local suppliers for specified goods and services, to supply the needs of local industry out of his prospective output, and so on. On the government side, the undertakings generally consist of a series of self-denying commitments: not to tax the foreign-owned enterprise beyond certain levels; not to prevent the import of needed machinery and supplies; not to interfere with the use of essential expatriate help; not to restrict the enterprise in remitting profits abroad; and similar provisions. Both parties, foreign investor and national government, approach these agreements with a long-term perspective. The duration of such agreements is usually quite extended; thirty years is common, and even longer periods are often found. Yet, almost from the moment that the signatures have dried on the document, powerful forces go to work that quickly render the agreements obsolete in the eyes of the government.

Consider first the inevitable change in perspective that time brings to any bargain between a government and the foreign enterprise. When a developing country acquires its first inkling that it may have been blessed with some raw material, the discovery is seen as a windfall, but a windfall whose exploitation is thought to be totally beyond the capability of the host country. The processes of production and marketing appear overwhelmingly complex and the financial risks of development seem forbidding. As a matter of fact, there are good reasons for this reaction, though less so in exploration and production than in marketing and finance. Exploration and production skills can be secured on a for hire basis except where the physical conditions are very unusual. But marketing is another matter; the development of a network of reliable buyers is generally a difficult, costly, time-consuming affair. As for finance, the host governments are in a poorer position than the foreign investor for various reasons: first, because the investor is generally entitled in his home country to write off failures as a tax loss; second, because the investor can average out his gains and losses over a number of independent explorations in various parts of the world. An attractive short-term strategy for most countries, therefore, is to invite as many foreign companies as possible to bid for the putative resources and to turn the job of exploration and exploitation over to the highest bidder.

A pronounced change in outlook can be expected to occur, however, after the initial exploration has been completed. The projects that fail drop out of sight, their cost borne partly by the foreign investor and partly by his tax authorities at home. The projects that succeed take the limelight; what was once a wistful hope becomes a tangible bonanza. The level of risk associated with the enterprise, as perceived by the parties, drops precipitately.

If the raw material operation is located in an advanced country, that change in perception generally makes no great difference to the relation between governments and raw material enterprises. As a rule, the enterprises have been brought into the country under the provisions of general law, without extraordinary concessions of an extensive sort, and they are expected to continue on that basis. In the less-developed countries, however, where special provisions generally surround the foreign operations, the change in perceived risk has a more marked effect. The returns to the foreign company no longer seem appropriate to the risk, and the government feels justified in demanding more out of the project.[19]

Apart from this shift in the perception of the less-developed country, however, there are also changes in the objective conditions surrounding these raw material investments. The efficient exploitation of raw materials such as oil and minerals usually requires the foreigner to take physical possession of extensive tracts of land. The tracts are commonly situated in remote places, far beyond the administrative reach of the local government. As a result, governments often elect to require the foreigner to provide many of the services that would ordinarily be expected of government, such as education, health, and the provision of public utilities; the foreigner, doubtful of the ability of the government to perform the necessary services, is generally willing to oblige.

Arrangements of this sort are a familiar aspect of the operations of large-scale enterprises in remote places: ARAMCO in Saudi Arabia, Southern Peru Copper in Peru, the LAMCO iron-ore operations in Liberia, and scores of others. Sometimes arrangements of this sort have grown up simply as a matter of joint convenience. At other times, however, they have been provided for by explicit agreement or sanctioned by special law. As long as these foreign enclaves were isolated enough not to have contact with the economy surrounding them and as long as the local government did not aspire to extend its jurisdiction inside these areas, the existence of such regimes probably was not a source of political friction. But contrary to the hypotheses associated with such well-known development economists as Hans W. Singer, Raul Prebisch, and Gunnar Myrdal, enclaves of this sort have rarely remained isolated for many decades. Unless they were established in altogether desolate and inaccessible territory, they attracted underemployed people from the surrounding countryside, who generally developed an economy outside the cyclone fence.[20] In some cases, men who had been trained as employees inside the fence eventually joined those outside to continue their trade as independent contractors.

The rate and process by which the enclaves that were producing raw materials made contact with the surrounding economy varied considerably according to the geography and the culture of the local environment. In relatively advanced nations, such as Chile and Mexico, the isolation was less complete and less enduring than in relatively backward countries such as Ecuador, and in well-inhabited Sumatra or Turkey the isolation was less complete and less sustained than in the Andean *altiplano*. Law and administration also played a part in determining the rate and nature of the contacts. In the excolonies of Britain, extreme forms of isolation were rarely allowed to develop in the first place, simply because the colonial administration was set up to provide effective government in all parts of the colony.[21] In a country with rudimentary internal administrative capabilities such as Liberia, on the other hand, the initial isolation and self-dependence of the foreign enterprise could be total, and the speed of its breakdown comparatively slow.

Whatever the starting conditions of the foreign enclave, contacts with the local economy generally developed. When they did, they usually created new difficulties. Foreign-owned enclaves in isolated areas that had begun their existence on a self-sufficient basis, importing their machinery and supplies, soon found that their self-sufficiency was the object of bitter resentment. In time, the surrounding economy was eager to provide a certain portion of what the foreigners needed: not bulldozers, perhaps, but fresh fruits and vegetables; not engineering services, but small-scale construction. At the same time, the economy stirring around the enclave began to see some advantages in having access to the power plant, the railroad line, or the hospital that the foreign enterprise had installed for its use. The foreigners, bent singlemindedly on overcoming the difficulties of mining their ore or extracting their oil, often resisted the idea of shifting their procurement to untried local sources and of sharing their facilities on a public utility basis. At times, the struggle toward some new kind of relationship proved bitter and painful.

These were not the only difficult aspects of the integrative process. As governments achieved the administrative capacity for enforcing the law, providing education, and maintaining the roads in distant corners under their jurisdiction, they encountered the self-contained systems the foreigners had created in response to an earlier situation. And when they tried to integrate the systems, the foreigners sometimes resisted. In some cases, the foreigners were unwilling to give up the heady right to be masters in their own domain. Sometimes they resisted out of a well-founded fear that the services which the government proposed to provide would be poorer in quality and higher in cost; in such cases, they often found allies in local labor unions, which were also concerned that the cost and quality of local services might deteriorate if the government were responsible for providing them. There were times, however, when the shoe was on the other foot and it was the foreigner who forced the integrating pace, eager to divest himself of the distasteful and sensitive role of company town manager.

Forces operating to shift the perspective of host governments have come from other directions as well. In most countries and in most periods, the party in power occasionally finds it useful to make a show of independence from the foreign investor. The obvious way for a political group in power to respond to the opposition charge of being a lackey of the foreigner, for instance, is to open up existing arrangements for renegotiation. At one time in the late 1960s, President Eduardo Frei in Chile, President Kenneth Kaunda in Zambia, and President José Velasco in Peru were all being pushed by this political imperative.[22] By 1970, Frei's party had lost its control of the government to a coalition on the left, headed by Salvador Allende, who promptly nationalized the foreign-owned mines. Meanwhile, Kaunda and Velasco were taking the necessary measures against the foreigners to avoid the likelihood of a similar political disaster.

The stimulus to tighten the terms of the bargain with foreigners has often come not only from politics but also from the exigencies of budget balancing. When governments increase their revenue from new raw material operations, their problems of budget balancing do not decline. It is a near-invariant law of public finance that an increase in the supply of funds creates its own long-term demand. As the level of recurrent expenditures rises, the risk that revenues may one day fall off becomes intolerable. Governments feel constantly threatened by the fact that the flow of money seems to depend on the sustained willingness of foreign investors to continue their operations. The size of this putative threat ought not to be overstated. For Latin America as a whole, for instance, the taxes derived from U.S.-controlled oil and mining operations come to only 6 or 7 percent of government revenue.[23] In some countries with extensive raw material operations, however, the proportion of governmental revenue derived from foreign enterprises has occupied an overwhelming position in national budgetary planning. Oil reportedly accounts for 85 percent of Saudi Arabia's revenues, 94 percent of Kuwait's, 80 percent of Iraq's, and 55 percent of Iran's.[24] Less recent data for the Venezuelan government, covering the year 1964, indicate that it obtained about 60 or 70 percent of its gross revenue from taxes paid by foreign petroleum and iron-ore operations.[25]

There are, of course, other measures that mirror the sense of heavy dependence of the less-developed countries on the raw material operations controlled by foreigners—measures, for instance, of the contribution of such operations to the country's gross domestic product. In Saudi Arabia, Libya, and Kuwait, the oil produced and marketed by foreigners at the beginning of the 1970s came to more than half of all the goods and services produced in the country; in Iraq, to about one quarter; in Venezuela, Algeria, Nigeria, and Indonesia, to smaller proportions, but proportions too large for comfort.[26] All these gauges point in the same general direction: As foreign raw material operations become more and more integrated in the economic life of host countries—through increasing payments to government and the increasing use of local labor, materials, and resources—the vulnerability of the economy to changes in these operations inevitably seems to increase. The psychic sense of dependence on foreign interests generated by this situation has produced occasional eruptions. The obscure questions of law, the complex issues of fact, and the generous outpourings of ideology that have been injected into the disputes on these occasions have not masked the prime fact— that the sense of dependence that host governments experienced was at times beyond bearing.

The factors just enumerated would be sufficient to explain the sources of tension and unhappiness on the part of host governments. Yet there is still another factor that operates in the same direction. National ideologies are ephemeral commodities; as governments come and go, one set of national tenets displaces another. In countries where the characteristic transition is by way of revolutionary coups, the changes can be especially dramatic. Accordingly, foreign investors must resign themselves to the fact that the national goals and preferences to which they were responsive at the time they entered any country are likely to undergo periodic metamorphoses. As the case of Libya demonstrates, even when the original agreement between foreign investors and the government is modern and well balanced, this fact adds only marginally to the security of the investor. In the Libyan case, the basic agreements, originally drafted with the help of independent experts recruited by the Libyan government, had been a model in the protection of national interests. But when the new plebeian government threw out the ancient monarchy in 1968, the need for setting a new tone of strength and independence transcended all other political needs. Imperatives of this sort have determined the pace and quality of the pressures on foreign investors in the past; no doubt they will continue to play that role in the future.

OUTCOME OF THE PRESSURES

On the one hand, governments are under constant pressure to raise their demands on the foreign investor. On the other, investors are increasingly committed to a project by the sinking of commitments and by the sweet smell of success. The outcome in such a situation is predictable. As illustrated by the data in Table 2–3, governments over the years have managed to elevate their share of the profits substantially. Though the data are subject to various statistical weaknesses, as any share-of-profit figure is bound to be, they serve well enough to indicate the trend. The figures in Table 2–3 are even more

TABLE 2-3

*Host Country Share of Pretax Profits of
Foreign Investors in Raw Material Enterprises*

	VENEZUELA (OIL) %	CHILE (COPPER) %
1930	n.a.	16
1940	58[a]	28
1950	51	58
1955	52	69
1960	68	65
1965	66	69[b]

[a]In 1943.
[b]In 1964.

Source: G. G. Edwards, "Foreign Petroleum Companies and the State in Venezuela," and Markos Mamalakis, "The American Copper Companies and the Chilean Government, 1920-1967," in R. F. Mikesell, ed., *Foreign Investment in the Petroleum and Mineral Industries: Case Studies on Investor-Host Relations* (1970), chaps. 5 and 16.

impressive if one recalls that in the decade preceding 1930, host countries' shares of profits could not as a rule have exceeded 10 or 15 percent. Moreover, in the early 1970s, they seemed headed for a level in excess of 80 percent as a result of further concessions squeezed out of the oil companies.[27]

Governmental efforts to gain control over their foreign-owned raw material projects, that is, to reduce their sense of passive dependence on such projects, have also made considerable progress. By the 1950s, foreign raw material enterprises in most countries seemed to be accepting the desirability—or, at any rate, the inevitability—of maintaining close ties with the surrounding economies: of hiring and upgrading local labor; of buying and using local supplies and services; of using national power and transport where they were available, and of sharing the enterprises' facilities with the local economy in other cases.

The provisions on these points written into concession contracts grew progressively more explicit and more demanding.

The results were to be seen in the management practices of the producers of raw material. In the field of labor recruitment, for instance, the upgrading of local talent into posts entailing management responsibility has been especially noticeable. Between 1959 and 1964, the Venezuelan subsidiary of the Standard Oil Company of New Jersey raised the Venezuelan component of its senior staff from 48 percent to 68 percent. ARAMCO in Saudi Arabia raised the Saudi Arabian component of supervisory jobs from an imperceptible fraction during the late 1940s to about 56 percent by 1967. Caltex in Indonesia, starting at close to zero during the late 1950s, brought the comparable ratio to about 80 percent by 1969.[28]

In retrospect, however, it seems clear that the success of the oil-exporting less-developed countries on these various fronts provided no long-run answer to their sense of excessive dependence and lack of control. On the contrary: Each increase in the revenues derived from the foreign-owned enterprise, each enlargement in the role of the enterprise as a buyer of local goods and services or as an employer of local talent, simply increased the apparent vulnerability of the local economy to the foreign enterprise.

One response to the galling sense of dependence in the less-developed countries has been the creation of the state-owned companies in raw materials, referred to earlier. The hope of such countries as Iran, Iraq, Venezuela, Zambia, and Chile is that the state-owned companies they have created will eventually assume full control not only over the production of raw materials in their territories but also over the fabricating and marketing facilities at home and abroad. There is some distance yet to go, however, before the hope is realized. Still, enough experience has been accumulated so that one can begin to make some tentative judgments regarding their ability to perform.

A few state-owned companies, such as Pemex in Mexico, have not done badly. In other cases, however, state-owned companies have failed to measure up to national expectations. Argentina's President Peron, for instance, felt obliged in 1953 to ease the terms for foreign oil company concessions in his country in order to offset the lagging performance of the state-owned oil company, Yacimientos Petrolíferos Argentinos (YPF).[29] In fact, even for the oil that YPF actually produced, the social return to the Argentina economy seems to have been lower than the social return generated for a like volume of production by the foreign oil companies in Argentina.[30]

State-owned companies have also at times been disappointing in their lack of success in shifting from imported to indigenous inputs of goods. The state-owned National Iranian Oil Company has been indistinguishable from the foreign companies in Iran in terms of its use of indigenous supplies. Like the foreigners, NIOC appears to have drawn only about 10 percent of its purchases from local sources.[31] Still, some national companies such as Mexican-owned Pemex have performed adequately in the exploration and production of crude oil, and others may eventually be expected to do so. Adequate performance may become progressively easier as specialized production functions, such as oil field exploration and offshore drilling, become increasingly available for hire in the open market.

The state-owned companies' failure to perform has been most pronounced in international marketing. The inadequacy has been more apparent in oil than in copper. So far, the state-owned oil companies of the exporting countries have arranged a few government-to-government deals and have supplied a few independent distributors. Corners of the Japanese, Pakistani, Turkish, and Indian markets have been opened up to these companies by means of various bulk-purchase arrangements. So far, however, the total quantities moved by the state-owned companies in international trade have been small. The worries of the major oil companies that the state-owned companies may shake the price structure of the world oil market relate more to the future than to the past.

Though the less-developed exporting countries have not yet succeeded in using their state-owned companies as a vehicle for displacing the foreign-controlled enterprises in international markets, they have nonetheless gone some distance in obtaining a voice in the management decisions of the foreign companies. In both copper and oil, the question of levels of production has become a central issue in the negotiations between the foreign producers and their host governments. Iran has managed to extract some commitments on this sensitive point from the oil companies; Zambia, Chile, and Peru have obtained parallel commitments from the copper companies. The same situation holds with regard to the prices; these can no longer be freely fixed by the foreigners in response to an international strategy. Before foreigners can export Venezuelan iron ore or Chilean or Zambian copper, or crude oil from any source, their prices are passed through a screen of governmental surveillance. Sometimes the screen is fairly coarse, sometimes very fine. But the direction of the monitoring trend is clear.

Pressures from host governments to share somehow in the downstream profits related to processing, distribution, and marketing are bound to grow. To advance the objective, governments will maintain their efforts to shift the source of the crude materials and to vest some of the ownership in local hands. In the case of oil, the fact that more pressure has not been exerted in this direction is probably owing to the realization that the oil companies assign very little profit to the refining phase, preferring to take the lion's share of their income at the crude oil production stage. And that is just where the host governments would like to see the profit taken as well.

But simple refining is not the only use to which crude oil can be put. There is also the possibility of processing the oil for complex petrochemicals, fertilizers, detergents and other oil-based products. NIOC in Iran has made especially determined moves in this direction, generally in joint ventures with U.S.-controlled enterprises; NIOC provides the raw material while the U.S. enterprises provide the technology and the markets. This may be an indication of the future strategy of other state enterprises.

It has been evident for some time, however, that no single raw material exporting country has the power to draw added revenue from foreign-owned enterprises and foreign consumers unless the bargaining demands of the countries move in step with each other. This is easier said than done: The history of international commodity agreements is rich with incidents in which individual exporting countries upset such agreements in order to steal a march on competing suppliers.

Still, the raw material exporting countries have moved doggedly ahead to create effective international mechanisms by which to concert their strategies. The Organization of Petroleum Exporting Countries (OPEC), created in 1960, has had considerable success in maintaining a thread of common strategy in the negotiations of its members with the foreign firms. OPEC has given a great deal of thought to ways of maintaining world oil prices, so that some new mechanisms could be rapidly substituted whenever the pricing system developed by the international oil majors fails to produce a suitably elevated price. The spectacular success of a group of OPEC members in concerting their strategy at Teheran in 1971 speaks well for the strength of that group.

But that performance was achieved in a period when all the parties anticipated a prolonged shortage in oil supplies. The real test would not come until there were expectations of surplus. Because of the number of state-owned companies involved, the disparity of interests among them, and the critical needs that each feels for added revenue, disinterested outsiders doubt that OPEC alone will be able to maintain a common strategy on prices. According to this view, the control of the multinational oil companies would be indispensable for that purpose.[32] But judgments of this sort, as history occasionally demonstrates, are sometimes belied by events.

Strong initiatives on the part of the governments of less-developed countries to control the key factors in the exploitation of their raw materials are likely to continue. And as they do, the capacity of host governments to participate in management will increase. It is another question, however, whether the host countries will feel that their "dependence" on the outside world has declined simply because their management role has increased. As long as the product requires marketing in foreign countries, "dependence" will presumably continue in some form.

[**3**]

The Manufacturing Industries

To turn from the raw material activities to the manufacturing activities of U.S. enterprises in foreign countries requires no great shift of direction. The enterprises that began their existence as raw material producers often became manufacturers in the end; crude oil enterprises became petrochemicals producers, copper miners became metal fabricators, and so on. At the same time, enterprises that had originally concentrated on manufacturing activities sometimes found themselves propelled into the production of raw materials.

The ties between overseas investments in raw materials and in manufacturing go further, however. Striking parallels are to be perceived in both the timing and the motivations of the investing enterprises, suggesting the existence of an underlying process that could be described in very similar terms.

Orders of Magnitude

It is often forgotten that by 1870 or 1880, large U.S. manufacturing enterprises were already engaged in a rather considerable amount of foreign direct investment.[1] Toward the end of the nineteenth century, while the United States was importing large quantities of European capital for railroad and land speculation, two or three dozen large U.S. manufacturing enterprises set up major producing facilities in foreign countries, mainly in Canada and Great Britain. By the beginning of the twentieth century, there were perhaps seventy-five to 100 establishments manufacturing outside the United States under the control of U.S. parents.

The data in Table 3–1 show the geographical spread of these establishments. Being based on a count of subsidiaries, the figures do not give proper weight to the fact that many of the Canadian undertakings were set up as branches of the U.S. parent rather than as separate corporations. In other respects, the figures adequately reflect the geographical preferences of U.S. businessmen in that era when establishing foreign manufacturing facilities—a preference for Great Britain, followed in order by Germany and France.

Once the process of overseas subsidiaries began to take hold, nothing could stop it. Though pervasive international cartel arrangements existed in world markets prior to World War II,

TABLE 3-1

Number of Foreign Subsidiaries of 187 U.S.-controlled Multinational Enterprises, by Area and Function, 1900

AREA	PRIMARILY IN MANUFACTURING	PRIMARILY IN OTHER[a]	TOTAL
Canada	6	3	9
United Kingdom	13	10	23
France	8	4	12
Germany	10	8	18
Other Europe	6	24	30
Latin America	3	9	12
Other	1	2	3
All areas	47	60	107

[a]This column includes thirteen subsidiaries whose function is unknown.

Source: J. W. Vaupel and J. P. Curhan, *The Making of Multinational Enterprise* (Boston: Harvard Business School, 1969), chap. 3.

these were insufficient to suppress the expansionist tendencies of U.S.-controlled enterprises. As Table 3–2 indicates, the number of foreign manufacturing subsidiaries generated by U.S. parents in the group of 187 rose rapidly during the twentieth century. To some extent, the growth came from the appearance of new U.S. parents and, to some extent, from new subsidiaries of enterprises already in existence. Canada and Europe figured prominently in both the degree of U.S. involvement and the rate of growth prior to 1929. After that time, however, the fastest rates of growth appeared in the Southern dominions and in Latin America. By 1950, even more remote locations—mostly in Asia and Africa—were beginning to be attractive to U.S. enterprise. By 1960, these remote areas were leading in the growth in number of manufacturing subsidiaries. One had the general impression, in short, of a gradual widening of the horizons of involvement on the part of U.S.-controlled enterprise, a gradual fanning out from

TABLE 3-2

Number of Foreign Manufacturing Subsidiaries of 187 U.S.-controlled Multinational Enterprises, by Area, Selected Years 1901-1967

AREA	1901	1913	1919	1929	1939	1950	1959	1967
Canada	6	30	61	137	169	225	330	443
Europe and								
United Kingdom	37	72	84	226	335	363	677	1,438
France	8	12	12	36	52	54	98	223
Germany	10	15	18	43	50	47	97	211
United Kingdom	13	23	28	78	128	146	221	356
Other Europe	6	22	26	69	105	116	261	648
Southern dominions	1	3	8	25	69	99	184	361
Latin America	3	10	20	56	114	259	572	950
Other	0	1	7	23	28	42	128	454
Total	47	116	180	467	715	988	1,891	3,646

Source: J. W. Vaupel and J. P. Curhan, *The Making of Multinational Enterprise* (Boston: Harvard Business School, 1969), chap. 3.

the geographically and culturally familiar to the geographically and culturally remote areas of the world.

The regularities exhibited by Table 3–2 are illuminated a little further by the data in Table 3–3. Here, a simple count of manufacturing subsidiaries is replaced by another kind of measure—one based on the number of product lines established by each subsidiary. To develop this count, manufactured products were classified into forty-eight groups; a subsidiary manufacturing in any country in two such groups was counted twice. The figures indicate that the spread of manufacturing subsidiaries in all areas of the globe took place hand in hand with a rapid spread in the production of "skill-oriented" products— products, that is, in which the emphasis on development and innovation in the United States was relatively strong.* The timing of that spread was somewhat different from one area to the next. According to the table, Latin America only began to be attractive to such industries during the 1930s, after the rate of spread had passed its peak in Europe. Unlike the situation in Europe, the number of new skill-oriented products established in Latin America was much higher during the 1930s and the war decade of 1940–1950 than it had been earlier. But after 1950, the proliferation of subsidiaries and products was very rapid everywhere.

These developments generated the very heavy investments by U.S. parents in overseas manufacturing subsidiaries that are reflected in the familiar U.S. Department of Commerce series. The salient figures, reproduced in Table 3–4, are unsatisfactory from various technical points of view, probably rather substantially understating the size of the U.S. commitment abroad. But the main trends are unmistakable. From their prewar and wartime base, commitments grew rapidly in all areas of the world, but the rate of growth, on the whole, was

---

* The products were chosen on the basis of U.S. industry characteristics of the sort used in Chapter 1: R & D expenditure as a percent of sales; and scientists and engineers as a percent of the work force.

TABLE 3-3

Number of Product Lines Introduced by Foreign Manufacturing Subsidiaries of 187 U.S.-controlled Multinational Enterprises, by Area and by Product Class, 1901-1967[a]

PRODUCTS AND AREAS	PERIODS OF INTRODUCTION					
	1901-1919	1920-1929	1930-1939	1940-1950	1951-1959	1960-1967
Food and kindred products						
Canada, Europe and						
United Kingdom	13	50	56	21	72	208
Southern dominions	5	7	6	7	12	42
Latin America	10	7	18	23	42	146
Japan	0	0	0	0	5	7
Other	0	4	5	0	11	23
All areas	28	68	85	51	142	426
Skill-oriented products						
Canada, Europe, and						
United Kingdom	107	160	153	144	427	1,008
Southern dominions	7	14	38	26	98	156
Latin America	14	26	44	107	274	397
Japan	3	0	4	3	22	86
Other	1	6	6	14	53	163
All areas	132	206	245	294	874	1,810
Other products						
Canada, Europe, and						
United Kingdom	29	66	62	44	167	365
Southern dominions	1	6	13	11	23	98
Latin America	5	10	29	65	119	132
Japan	0	3	0	0	3	31
Other	5	6	4	8	17	59
All areas	40	91	108	128	329	685
All products						
Canada, Europe, and						
United Kingdom	149	276	271	209	666	1,581
Southern dominions	13	27	57	44	133	296
Latin America	29	43	91	195	435	675
Japan	3	3	4	3	30	124
Other	6	16	15	22	81	245
All areas	200	365	438	473	1,345	2,921

[a]The products manufactured by each subsidiary were classified according to a forty-eight category classification, corresponding to a two-and-a-half digit SIC breakdown. Each such product category in a subsidiary is counted as one observation. There were eight food and kindred product categories, twenty-seven skill-oriented product categories, and thirteen other product categories. Skill-oriented products were selected on the basis of high R & D expenditure as a percent of sales, as well as large numbers of scientists and engineers as a percent of the industry work force, as reported in U.S. industry data.

Source: J. W. Vaupel and J. P. Curhan, *The Making of Multinational Enterprise* (Boston: Harvard Business School 1969), chap. 3.

especially rapid in the "new areas" of the world where strong forces were at work pushing U.S. enterprises outward into unfamiliar territory.

The Product Cycle Model

It is a good deal easier to describe the investment behavior of U.S.-controlled enterprises in the census-taker's terms than to determine the stimulus for that behavior. Still, the motivation and response of U.S. enterprises during the century or so in which they set up and operated their overseas subsidiaries have had such persistent regularities that there is a certain efficiency in looking at the process in terms of a behavioral model. Such a model, like any observed generalization, constitutes a deliberate simplification of reality. Apart from simplifying the economic aspects of the process, the model makes no pretense

TABLE 3-4

Foreign Direct Investment of U.S. Enterprises
in Manufacturing Subsidiaries, by Areas, 1929-1969
(book value in millions of dollars)

YEAR	ALL AREAS	CANADA	LATIN AMERICA	EUROPE AND UNITED KINGDOM	ALL OTHER AREAS
1929	$ 1,813	$ 819	$ 231	$ 629	$ 133
1936	1,710	799	192	611	108
1940	1,926	943	210	639	133
1950	3,831	1,897	781	932	222
1957	8,009	3,924	1,280	2,195	610
1964	16,861	6,191	2,507	6,547	1,616
1969	29,450	9,389	4,347	12,225	3,489

Source: U.S. Department of Commerce, *U.S. Business Investments in Foreign Countries* (Washington, D.C.: Government Printing Office, 1960), p. 96; and *Survey of Current Business,* various issues.

at capturing the even more complex sociological, political, and idiosyncratic factors.

Still, there is a basis for picturing the development of overseas manufacturing facilities in the following terms: To begin with, U.S.-controlled enterprises generate new products and processes in response to the high per capita income and the relative availability of productive factors in the United States; they introduce these new products or processes abroad through exports; when their export position is threatened they establish overseas subsidiaries to exploit what remains of their advantage; they retain their oligopolistic advantage for a period of time, then lose it as the basis for the original lead is completely eroded.

The first stage in the sequence involves a unique stimulus and a unique response. During most of the past century, businessmen in the United States were exposed to such a stimulus because they confronted a set of problems and opportunities distinctly different from those facing the business interests of the other main industrial powers.[2] None could compare with the United States in terms of accessibility and cheapness of water and fossil power, forest products, and arable land. But labor in the United States has always been scarce, especially labor skilled in production techniques. In terms of comparative advantage, labor has been scarcer and more costly in the United States in relation to the country's other endowments than it was in other advanced countries in relation to their other endowments.

Despite the limited capabilities of U.S. labor as measured by their production skills, incomes in the United States have been high. A rich supply of raw materials in the early part of the period and ample supplies of capital in the later part, coupled with a high level of general literacy and education, more than made up for the lack of production skills. High productivity went hand in hand with high per capita income, and high per capita incomes generated a high level of internal demand. To satisfy this demand, U.S. entrepreneurs had to find a way of producing the wanted goods by means that used little skilled labor.* Sewing machines sharply increased the productivity of scarce seamstresses during the 1850s. Drip-dry shirts reduced the need for services of scarce laundresses during the 1950s.

But why was it U.S. producers that responded to these special U.S. needs? Why not European producers? In the open and frictionless world of classical economic theory, of course, there would be no special reason to assume that the demand for new products in the United States would be met in the first instance by U.S. producers; European producers, sensing the opportunity for profit, might have been expected to respond, especially if their production costs were lower.

Experience suggests that in the early stages of introducing a new product, producers have usually been confronted with a number of critical, albeit transitory, conditions that deeply affect the choice of a production site. If the first use of a product was for the U.S. military, as it sometimes was, a U.S. location was often indispensable. When producing for nonmilitary buyers in the United States, however, there were also reasons to produce at home. First, there was no particular incentive during the early stages for a producer to look outside the consumer country for a location where production costs were low. Because of the demand conditions that producers confronted at those stages, they were less concerned with costs

---

* These are treacherous concepts, to be handled with care. An invention need not substitute one factor for another; on the contrary, it can be saving of both labor and capital at the same time. See W. E. G. Salter, *Productivity and Technical Change* (Cambridge: Cambridge University Press, 1960), pp. 43–44. Under classical conditions, this fact undermines the justification for assuming the existence of any particular factor bias in cost-saving innovations. But if innovation is thought of as a scarce factor that commands a monopoly rent and if the innovating activity is thought of as involving a lumpy commitment with resulting economies of scale, then the probability that there will be factor-saving bias in innovation is once more rendered plausible. For more on this issue, see Nathan Rosenberg, "The Directions of Technological Change: Inducement Mechanisms and Focusing Devices," *Economic Development and Cultural Change* 18, 1, pt. 1 (October 1969): 1–24.

than they were likely to be later on. (The pioneer radio fan of the early 1920s, for instance, was much less sensitive to the price of his product than was the suburban family of the 1970s.) This phenomenon, well-explored among marketing specialists, seems to stem from the high degree of product differentiation or the existence of monopoly in the early stages.* Second, there was an especially urgent need at this early stage for swift and effective communication inside the enterprise, and with customers, suppliers, and even competitors outside the enterprise. Producers have been uncertain regarding the ultimate dimensions of the market, the efforts of rivals to preempt that market, the specifications of the inputs needed for production, and the specifications of the products likely to be most successful in the effort.[3] These considerations have tended to argue for a location in which communication between the market and the executives directly concerned with the new product was swift and easy. In the choice of location, flexibility and swift response were given more weight than capital and labor cost.[4]

By specializing in the development of labor-saving innovations and high-income products, U.S. businessmen found themselves with product lines that had real promise in foreign markets. After 1879 or so, the rest of the world found itself tracking over an economic terrain that U.S. businessmen had already traversed. During the latter half of the nineteenth century, the price of labor in Western Europe was rising rapidly relative to the price of other factors and per capita incomes were moving parallel with the price of labor.[5] Thus, in Great Britian from 1850 to 1910, money wages rose by about two-thirds

---

* Some products inherently lend themselves to standardization less than others. See G. C. Hufbauer, "The Impact of National Characteristics and Technology on the Commodity Composition of Trade in Manufactured Goods," in Raymond Vernon, ed., *The Technology Factor in International Trade* (New York: Columbia University Press, 1970), pp. 145–231. The statement in the text is therefore to be thought of as an intertemporal statement for a given product, not one to be applied in comparing different products.

while prices were generally stagnant. After World War II, money wages continued to outrun prices all over Europe.

According to the product cycle concept, innovation has provided a basis for the export of manufactured goods from the United States. The utility of the product cycle concept as an explanatory device can be tested, therefore, in the patterns of trade of the United States and other countries. Here, the evidence in support of the view that some such phenomenon has existed is fairly impressive.

Various studies indicate that the United States has tended to specialize in the export of products from industries that employ a relatively high proportion of scientists and engineers in their labor force and that spend relatively large proportions of their income on research and development. This point, of course, was already stressed in Chapter 1. These analyses, however, push beyond the message of Chapter 1 in one important respect: They show that U.S. export concentration on products of this sort has systematically been greater than the export concentration of other countries in such products.[6] As added confirmation of the distinctive character of U.S. exports, other analyses suggest that the price elasticity of demand for U.S. exports has tended to be considerably lower than for U.S. imports or for the exports of other countries.[7]

Though the cumulative persuasiveness of these studies is considerable, one has to recognize that the underlying data in such analyses tend to be fairly aggregative, perhaps too much so to provide the kind of sure footing that is needed to test the product cycle concept. Besides, inasmuch as most analyses are based on cross-sectional data reflecting a single point in time, they suffer from the vulnerabilities usually involved in testing a dynamic concept with static evidence. It is reassuring, therefore, to find that confirmation for the existence of the sequence appears in a number of studies that do not suffer from these particular disabilities, analyses that trace the experiences of specific narrowly defined products over periods of time.

To begin with, studies of individual products in the U.S. market confirm the assumption that products commonly go through a cycle of initiation, exponential growth, slowdown, and decline—a sequence that corresponds to the process of introduction, spread, maturation, and senescence suggested earlier.[8] Moreover, there has been some systematic testing of export patterns for individual products, One analysis, for instance, measures the change in U.S. exports of twenty well-established consumer durable products between the early 1950s and the early 1960s. The anticipation, based on the product cycle concept, was that the U.S. export position during those years would be best sustained in products whose ownership was associated with high income and whose introduction to the market was comparatively recent. Thus, the United States was seen as having a less vulnerable export position in vacuum cleaners or electric mixers—products that are comparatively new and associated with high incomes—than in radios or gas cookers. The data confirm these expectations very nicely.[9]

Still another analysis has traced the experience of the United States and other countries in the production and exportation of nine major petrochemical products from their genesis to the year 1966. Here, too, the data confirmed the existence of a pattern which began with innovation in the United States, moved on for a time to growth of U.S. exports to other markets, and finally displayed a visible braking or actual reversal of such export growth.[10]

Innovation and export, according to the product cycle hypothesis, have eventually induced many U.S. enterprises to produce abroad and to serve their markets from a foreign location. How has that decision been reached? For the period after World War II, the foreign investment decision is a much-studied field.[11] It has at times been probed by investigators who were looking at the phenomenon from the viewpoint of the capital-exporting country, at other times from the viewpoint of the capital-importing areas, at still other times from the viewpoint of the decision-making firms. Some of the studies have used the extensive survey approach, some the intensive in-depth analysis of individual cases.

Studies that were based on the extensive survey approach have generally not been designed to test a hypothesis as elaborate as the product cycle sequence. Still, they are helpful. Superficially, studies of this sort generally report that the overseas subsidiaries of manufacturing enterprises were set up primarily to increase sales, serve an expanding market, meet local competition, overcome an import barrier, increase profits, and so on. It is only when these replies are interpreted in light of some of the more intensive analyses of individual cases that they begin to take on meaning in terms of the product cycle sequence.[12]

As noted earlier, the decision to set up manufacturing facilities abroad has commonly been triggered by the perception of a threat to an established export market. The exact form of the galvanizing threat has differed from one case to the next. Over time, however, there has been a remarkable similarity in some of the patterns. Table 3–5 presents a summary of the motivations of ten major U.S. parents that by 1900 had already established a major presence overseas. Their motivations in doing so do not appear to have been very different from those of the producers who would follow them fifty or sixty years later. In the case of the nine petrochemicals cited earlier, for example, the original producers did not set up a plant outside their domestic market without first being threatened by the appearance abroad of some uncontrolled competitor. More generally, unlicensed imitators or parallel innovators have commonly provided the immediate threat that has led to the initial overseas investment.

The decision of U.S. businessmen to invest abroad has often been made easier by the fact that by the time the step was taken, the technology of production had settled down sufficiently to be transferable to a foreign facility without considerable cost

TABLE 3-5

Characteristics of Foreign Manufacturing Plants Established before 1900 by Specified U.S. Parents

U.S. PARENT	PRINCIPAL PRODUCTS	LOCATION OF FOREIGN PLANTS	SUBSTANTIAL U.S. EXPORTS PRIOR TO FOREIGN INVESTMENT?	ASSERTED REASONS FOR FOREIGN INVESTMENT[a]
Colt	Firearms	Great Britain	Yes	Local competitive threat
Singer	Sewing machines	Great Britain/ Austria/Canada	Yes	Local competitive threat, lower costs
ITT	Communications	Great Britain/ Belgium/Germany/ Austria/France/ Italy/Russia/Japan	Yes	Local competitive threat, lower costs
General Electric and its predecessors	Electrical products and equipment	Great Britain/France/ Germany/Canada	Yes	Local competitive threat, lower costs, national pressures
Westinghouse Air Brake	Air brakes and signal equipment	Great Britain/France/ Germany/Russia	Yes	Local competitive threat, lower costs, national pressures
Westinghouse Electric	Electrical products and equipment	Great Britain/ France/Russia	Yes	Local competitive threat, lower costs

TABLE 3-5 (continued)

U.S. PARENT	PRINCIPAL PRODUCTS	LOCATION OF FOREIGN PLANTS	SUBSTANTIAL U.S. EXPORTS PRIOR TO FOREIGN INVESTMENT?	ASSERTED REASONS FOR FOREIGN INVESTMENT[a]
Eastman Kodak	Photographic goods	Great Britain	Yes	Local competitive threat, lower costs
United Shoe Machinery	Shoe machinery	Great Britain/ France/Germany/ Switzerland	Yes	Not determined
Parke, Davis	Pharmaceuticals	Canada	Yes	Lower costs
American Radiator and Standard Sanitary's predecessor	Radiators	France	Yes	Lower costs, larger demand

[a]The asserted reasons given in this column are inescapably a matter of interpretation to some extent, subject to the usual biases that go with such a process.

Sources: Principally Mira Wilkins, *Emergence of Multinational Enterprise* (Cambridge: Harvard University Press, 1970), and company annual reports.

and inconvenience to the U.S. enterprise, especially if the transfer was being made to a fairly advanced country. It is true that at times, especially after World War II, some backward areas have offered special governmental inducements to the U.S. investor. Much more important, however, has been simple growth in national demand. That growth opened up the possibility that the average delivered cost for an overseas production facility would no longer be disadvantageous by comparison with the marginal cost of output from the United States. Big markets, therefore, tended to be attractive sooner than small.

The readiness of multinational enterprises to cross the threshold from exports to direct investment may well have been enhanced by the realization that once the production process was free of its dependence on the specialized inputs of the U.S. economy—once the conventional costs of capital and labor came to dominate the calculation—foreign locations might be more attractive than U.S. production sites. As far as the financial costs of capital are concerned, these are often presumed to be uniform by multinational enterprises, irrespective of where a facility might be located. Even when the national capital costs are allowed to vary by location or when local borrowing at different interest rates is contemplated, the effect of capital cost differences on total costs of production is not generally significant enough to be crucial for the locational decision. Therefore, labor has often proved the source of the real difference between costs in the United States and those abroad.[13] Once the question of costs has become important, that consideration has tended to draw industry away from a U.S. location.

The readiness of U.S. enterprises to search out a lower cost location abroad at some point in the development of their products has probably been enhanced as well by the fact that the profit margins associated with the manufacture of fabricated industrial products commonly decline as the early monopoly stage begins drawing to a close.[14] The reasons for the decline stem partly from change on the supply side: As products mature, the average costs of production tend to drop, and as the oligopolistic structure of the industry weakens, the decline in cost is reflected in the price. Price declines have also been induced by change in the structure of demand: As the markets for new products widen, the added buyers generally tend to be more price responsive than the pioneer buyers. These changes make the original producers increasingly sensitive to the question of production costs.

Once a U.S. producer has decided to place his production facilities closer to a foreign market in order to reduce his costs, this decision seems to provide a stimulus for parallel behavior among the producer's oligopoly partners.[15] Such a response is strongly reminiscent of the responses of the raw material producers described in Chapter 2. To reestablish the equilibrium of the oligopoly market, leading enterprises have sometimes felt compelled to take a position that matched the advances of a rival firm.

The decision of innovators to try to prolong their hold on overseas markets by direct investment has induced not only their rivals but also their suppliers to take similar action. Here again, threat has vied with promise as the stimulus for action. Whenever a U.S. supplier of industrial materials has been invited by a major customer to set up a supplying facility in some foreign location, the danger in rejecting the invitation has generally not been missed by the supplier. As a result, automobile component suppliers in the United States have been drawn abroad by the major automobile companies, chemical producers by the processors of petrochemicals and plastics, packaging material producers by the food companies.

One added variant on the familiar product cycle sequence bears mentioning, a variant that has repeatedly been observed in the history of U.S. foreign direct investment. In many cases, the first competitive edge that a U.S. businessman thought of himself as possessing was one that could not be tested by export. Food-processing companies, for instance, have commonly thought of themselves as having a special capacity for mobilizing, financing, and directing the activities of independent farmers; for standardizing and controlling quality in the mass production of complex organic materials; and for controlling the distribution of perishable products in ways that reduced the threat of deterioration. The bulky character of the final product, however, has generally prevented the producing firms from testing and developing large foreign markets by way of exports from the United States.* In these cases, because no prior market test was available through exports, the U.S. businessman's decision to use his apparent advantage as a basis for setting up an enterprise in a foreign country has sometimes involved special risks.

The sequence sketched out in the last few pages carries the product cycle to the threshold of its final stage. The enterprise, having lost its oligopoly advantage, finds that it can no longer claim any cost or other advantage over its imitators, local and foreign; even its overseas subsidiaries, operating in an economic environment no different from their competitors, begin to feel the pressure. At this stage, diseconomies associated with large size and an elaborate organizational apparatus threaten to outweigh the economies. Confronted with a loss of market, U.S.-controlled enterprises have been observed responding in a number of different ways.

One such response has been to slough off the product as no longer of much interest, as a commodity in the pejorative parlance of the food and chemical trades. A second has been to try to create new oligopoly advantages by making changes in the product or in the services associated with it. A third,

---

* These cases are not confined to food products. A recent decision by Armco Steel to manufacture preengineered steel building systems in Germany, despite the fact that a market for such systems had not yet appeared in Europe, is illustrative of the same phenomenon. "U.S. Industry Ties Keep German Producer Independent," *The New York Times*, December 26, 1969, p. 49. It is doubtful if the market for such a product, which notably conserves skilled labor, could be developed by exports from the United States.

barely distinguishable from the second, has been to try to create the illusion of such advantages through stepped-up advertising. Finally, there have been efforts to find a very much lower-cost production site for the product where competitors could not easily pursue, a site whose costs would be low enough to offset the disadvantages of scale of the large organization.

All these reactions, separately and in combination, have appeared in the responses of multinational enterprises. The first three reactions, involving such stratagems as the trivial manipulation of drug molecules and the repackaging of food products, have not entailed new locational decisions on the part of the multinational enterprise. But when the reaction of the enterprise has been to look for lower-cost production sites, the location issue has been raised again. In part, it is this process that accounts for the spread of multinational enterprises beyond locations in advanced countries into less-developed areas and for the rise in international cross-hauling among their constituent units.

Model in Operation: The Advanced Countries

The strength of a model such as the one we have just described is in its simplicity; its weakness is in the telescoping of time and place, and in the suppression of many details that enhance an understanding of the process. Some of these details are especially illuminating, even indispensable, in understanding the current reactions of advanced countries to the presence of U.S.-owned subsidiaries.

THE EARLY STAGES, 1850–1900

Looking back a century or more, one is struck by the suddenness with which Europe came to recognize the existence of the United States as a potential industrial power. By the middle of the nineteenth century, Great Britain, Germany, and France already had a long industrial tradition.[16] It was, however, a tradition based in considerable part on the expansion of individual artisan shops and on the "putting out" tradition in manufactures; though large plants were not unknown, they often consisted of the assembly of many artisans under a single roof. The United States came late to the industrializing process.

When the process finally began in the United States, it was conditioned by the fact that men skilled in the working of materials and metals were hard to find. In their efforts to respond to this challenge, the U.S. businessmen of that era had no scientific community, no government-financed research programs to support them. On the other hand, the design of new machines at that time lay in the province of the inspired tinkerer, not that of the scientist; Jefferson and da Vinci, for instance, would have done very well in this era.[17] One answer to conserving artisan labor lay in subdividing the complex skills of the artisan into many smaller tasks, and of using semi-skilled production workers to perform the tasks on a repetitive, routine basis. The product turned out by such methods generally lacked style and finish—and certainly individuality. But it served its purpose: It demanded less skilled labor in the making.* If the idea was to commit each worker to a limited task, it was no great extension of the idea to commit him to a single machine, and no great leap from there to build each machine to a highly specialized purpose. By the 1850s, U.S. woodworking machines had become specialized for sawing, planing, mortising, tenoning, and boring to a degree unmatched

* The classic much-cited illustration was, of course, the manufacture of rifles. The "American method" was so clearly superior to that of Britain as to lead in 1855 to the establishment of Enfield Arsenal in Britain, based on the American techniques. There are numerous other illustrations of the same point; see, for instance, A. L. Levine, *Industrial Retardation in Britain 1880–1914* (New York: Basic Books, 1967), pp. 44–49.

anywhere in the world. Metalworking machines, such as the turret lathe, had taken on the same specialized characteristics. Such machines were, as a rule, wasteful of raw materials, but they conserved skilled labor, and this was the main objective.

The innovative drive of U.S. businessmen is not to be confused with any outstanding capacity to invent. The function of U.S. businessmen in many instances was simply that of accepting the risks and costs associated with developing the invention and introducing it in the U.S. market. Many inventions first conceived in Europe were developed and introduced in the United States. The British were responsible for the key ideas that lay behind the development of the Northrop loom, shoe-making machinery, the interlocking block signaling system, and the screw-making machine; the French and Germans for the electrical dynamo; the Belgians and Hungarians for the electric transformer. In fact, one compilation covering significant inventions from 1880 to 1899 shows Europe accounting for 63 percent of the total.[18] But the United States was responsible for the actual introduction of many of the products involved.

While U.S. industry was introducing products that responded to the labor-saving and high-income needs of the U.S. economy, European businessmen were busy responding to the special needs of their national environments. As a rule, European innovators developed and introduced machines that were more general and more versatile in purpose than the American machines. Such machines tended to require more labor skill and to use less material than the special purpose machine, an emphasis of the sort we would expect. Europe's stress on material conservation was also reflected in her leadership in the introduction of innovations in the steel industry, a leadership that carried well into the twentieth century.[19] The outstanding material-saving innovation during the nineteenth century, the Thomas converter, was developed and applied extensively in Europe before it came to the United States. Another European-based innovation, the Siemens-Martin furnace, was adopted much more quickly by U.S. producers, but it was directed mainly to the improvement of quality rather than to the conservation of materials.

Still another illustration of European leadership was the development of the German chemical industry. Great Britain and France probably contributed as much to the origins of modern chemistry as did Germany. Germany's interest in the artificial dyestuffs sector of the chemicals industry developed with the Napoleonic continental blockade of the early nineteenth century, when her military establishment was cut off from this vital raw material.[20] Her lead in synthetic fertilizers can be attributed to a similar kind of stimulus. Once the importance of fertilizer was recognized among the land-hungry countries of Europe, Britain was in a position to satisfy some of her needs from the natural guano deposits off the Peruvian coast. Germany, however, was much more wary about using distant resources for so critical a need.

Germany's early leadership in pharmaceuticals offers a variant on the theme that the conditions of the national market determine the direction of the nation's innovations.* Germany was a leader in compulsory health insurance, introducing her first general law on the subject in 1889. The introduction of that law is said to have created a major market for drugs.

There were cases, therefore, in which Europeans developed and introduced products with a future, such as synthetic fertilizers and drugs. On the whole, however, nineteenth-century U.S. innovators were pushed and prodded by their environment to produce advances with an even more assured future. Innovation in response to the high cost of labor proved a more

---

* The nineteenth-century dominance of Germany in the medical sciences is a striking fact whose explanation is not immediately apparent. Of 747 medical discoveries in the nineteenth century, 296 were made in Germany and only seventy-seven in the United States; see Joseph Ben-David, *Fundamental Research and the Universities* (Paris: OECD, 1968).

rewarding path than innovation in response to the high cost of materials.

THE CARTEL ERA, 1900 TO WORLD WAR II

By 1900, the American industrialists had already made themselves felt as aggressive and indefatigable rivals throughout Western Europe. Much of the American presence was manifested through the export of manufactured goods from the United States, but part of Europe's awareness of American industry came about by way of the manufacturing subsidiaries that had been established in her midst. As an illustrious economic historian has stated:

> The European press . . . from the 1880's on, resounded with complaints against the "American menace," or the "American invasion," and with proposals for concerted action to deal with it . . . In 1897, Count Goluchowski, the Austrian foreign minister, in a circular letter to other European countries, proposed that the countries of Europe combine to take concerted action directed against American commercial competition.[21]

The process of invasion was not all one way, to be sure. A few European firms, but only a few, managed to establish their manufacturing subsidiaries in the United States. The German enterprises of Bayer and Merck, leaders in the dyestuffs and pharmaceutical fields, had already set up manufacturing facilities in the United States during the nineteenth century. Courtaulds, relying on its impressive technical lead in rayon-spinning technology, developed through a decade of experience in Europe, established its first U.S. subsidiary in Pennsylvania in 1910.[22] In these cases, the sequence from innovation to export to foreign investment offered striking parallels to the typical U.S. case. True, the dyestuffs and rayon were material-saving innovations, reflecting the bias that the conditions of a European market had generated. Once developed, however, these products sparked sufficient demand in the United States to create a flow of exports. And in the case of Courtaulds, at any rate, the record is clear that a threat to that export position, in the form of a sharp rise in U.S. tariffs, had precipitated the decision to set up a U.S. subsidiary.

Most European firms, however, stayed at home. If they ventured abroad, they showed a strong preference for the sheltered markets of the colonies. Their first contacts with the expanding U.S. enterprises therefore probably occurred in areas the Europeans regarded as their own preserves. For some European firms, the experience of confronting new competition from little-known rivals within their own reserved markets must have been close to traumatic. As long as the Europeans were selling against the competition of their own nationals, the degree of predictability of the business environment was fairly high; in such cases, the rivals they confronted came from a similar technical background and operated under the constraints of a similar cost structure. Besides, if a national industry consisted principally of a few large firms, the likelihood was high that some sort of explicit or implicit truce had developed. Competition from foreign sources was, however, quite another story. Here one confronted producers whose managerial habits and technological capabilities were not well known. Moreover, as the Europeans must have been aware, the new entrants in an oligopolistically structured market had a good deal less to lose from a temporary breakdown in market stability than did the leading local firms already in control. All this added up to an imperative need, as Europeans saw it, to reachieve equilibrium among competitors by some kind of explicit agreement.

As a result, between 1900 and 1940, international cartel agreements were developed in practically every important processed metal, in most important chemical products, in key pharmaceuticals, and in a variety of miscellaneous manufactures running the alphabetical gamut from alkalis to zinc.[23] The object of these agreements was generally the same as that of similar agreements in the raw materials industries: to take the uncertainties out of the market. Practically all such agreements included some provision for the geographical division of markets among the participants. If the product was standardized and price sensitive, as in the case of alkalis and steel, some arrangements were also made for the fixing of prices; if the product was technologically difficult and relatively insensitive to price differences, as in the case of advanced chemicals and machinery, there were measures to prevent any participant from stealing a technological march on the others. As a result of arrangements of this sort, U.S. participants generally found their freedom of action curtailed in Europe, Africa, and the British Commonwealth; at the same time, U.S. firms usually gained some relief from competition in North America and Latin America.

Despite these cartel agreements, however, U.S.-controlled manufacturing enterprises expanded their foothold in Europe. As Tables 3–2 and 3–3 demonstrate, the breadth and depth of U.S. involvement grew rapidly throughout the 1920s. The motives that persuaded U.S. manufacturing enterprises to take the plunge into foreign operations during the first half of the twentieth century were not very different from those prevailing in the preceding half century. Overseas markets originally served by exports from the United States eventually were threatened by local production. In Canada and the southern dominions, the threat was heightened by tariff increases during the 1920s and by the extension of the Imperial Preference system during the 1930s.

During the first few decades of this century, the demand in Europe for U.S.-generated products and processes was being stimulated by a new element, namely, a relative decline in the supply of artisans.[24] Cause and consequence are intermingled in this development. But the continuous shift in Europe from small shops to large plants was changing the mix of skills in the national economies, substituting semiskilled operatives for artisan workers. Once that decline was apparent, U.S. products generated in response to the special conditions of the U.S. market became even more appropriate to the European market.

The new U.S. industries at the forefront of this wave of expansion, however, were rather different from those in evidence before 1900. Though a good deal of creative energy continued to go into industrial machinery, new industrial frontiers were being established at the same time in chemicals, electronics, automobiles, and aircraft. As a result, the electrical and non-electrical machinery industries, already well-established in foreign markets by 1900, showed a steady rate of continued expansion abroad. The motor vehicle industries, more recently arrived, achieved their highest rate of spread in the 1920–1929 period, then continued their spread at a more sedate rate. But the industries that showed real acceleration in rate of spread were chemicals and drugs. Though these U.S. industries had begun the half-century epoch without any clear claim to technical leadership, they finished the period as the most expansive in the group.

The new industries of this era differed from those of earlier periods, however, in more than name. Innovation in the new industries was no longer based on the work of the inspired tinkerers. Now industrial advances depended more substantially and more proximately on achievements of a fundamental scientific character. The major advances of the chemical and drug industries during this period depended critically on an improved understanding of molecular structure and on advances in the study of bacterial behavior, those of the aircraft and electronics industries on progress in the study of aerodynamics and radio waves.

It is likely, therefore, that the U.S. lead in these new industries was not unrelated to its increased national capabilities in scientific fields. There were numerous indications of these increased capabilities. The number of students enrolled in science in the United States, for instance, increased from about

30,000 in the years 1911 to 1915 to 100,000 in the years 1951 to 1953; in Germany, to the extent that comparable figures can be found, they seem to show only a small rise, from about 10,000 to 16,000, during the same general period. By the 1920s, the United States at last began to earn Nobel prizes in the sciences, closing the science gap with Europe. At the same time, U.S. dominance in the field of industrial inventions became much more evident. One careful compilation indicates that the U.S. share of the world's "inventions and discoveries," which had amounted to 37 percent during the last two decades of the nineteenth century, rose to 54 percent during the 1930s and to 88 percent during the 1940s.[25]

While the United States was securing a commanding international lead in some of the technologically oriented industries, she was also establishing an international lead in some industries on the basis of other factors, notably on the basis of an ability for producing standardized products on a mass basis and of promoting a related trade name. The successful overseas expansion of such companies as Corn Products, General Foods, and Coca-Cola during the 1920s and 1930s drives home the point that this kind of success depended on the development of some oligopolistic advantage, whatever the nature of that advantage might be. These industries, like those associated with industrial innovations, were dominated by large firms and were highly concentrated in structure. In those manufacturing industries where large firms and high industry concentration had not emerged—lumber and wood, apparel, printing and publishing, leather products, furniture products, stone, clay and glass products—one encountered few foreign subsidiaries.

It has to be emphasized, however, that oligopoly was a necessary, not a sufficient, condition for overseas expansion. In the steel, aircraft, and tobacco industries, where oligopoly prevailed, there was no strong tendency for the establishment of overseas manufacturing facilities. In the case of steel, the oligopoly structure of the industry was not of the sort that could have launched subsidiaries safely in foreign markets. After the 1920s, the U.S. steel industry lost what pretensions it may have had to world leadership; there was no oligopoly basis either in differentiated product or marketing skill on which it could hope to penetrate foreign markets successfully.[26] As for the tobacco and the aircraft companies, one has to look for some other kind of explanation. No doubt, the major U.S. firms in these industries did regard themselves as world leaders in their respective lines—the tobacco firms in marketing skills, the aircraft firms in technology. Indeed, early in the century, the U.S. tobacco companies had extensive manufacturing facilities abroad. It may be, however, that in both instances governmental pressures have determined the distribution of the facilities; many foreign governments discouraged the U.S. tobacco companies from establishing producing facilities in their local markets, whereas the U.S. government discouraged the aircraft companies from establishing overseas facilities. If government pressures were involved, as they probably were, their effectiveness was enhanced by the fact that shipping costs in these industries have not been important in determining international trade movements.[27] The business costs of acquiescing to governmental pressures may not have been prohibitive, therefore, for the industries concerned.

THE POSTWAR PERIOD

By the end of World War II, the phenomenon of U.S. parents with extensive overseas manufacturing interests was solidly established. Much of what happened in the succeeding decades was simply an extension of earlier history. But some of the developments were new in character or in magnitude.

World War II left Europe in an economic daze, concentrating on the repair of the war's destruction. The American economy, tuned up to a wartime pitch of production, was looking about with trepidation for ways of managing the transition to a peacetime economy. U.S. enterprises had had six or seven years of war-induced bonanza markets, during which these enterprises had developed, tested, and introduced all sorts of new products and processes. All that was needed to trigger overseas investment was the perception of a market opportunity that could not be satisfied by exports, or the detection of a threat to existing markets that could be reduced by a direct investment.

The Marshall Plan improved the outlook for markets in Europe by generating a flow of $17 billion of foreign aid to Europe from 1948 to 1952. In the decade or two following, Europe's per capita income rose dramatically. As it did, the European consumer began to acquire products in a sequence that the U.S. consumer had already experienced a few years earlier. High per capita incomes in Europe also brought higher labor costs; not perhaps so high as those in the United States, but high enough to make some established U.S. labor-saving innovations relevant to European conditions. If market opportunity was required as a condition for U.S. investment, it was clear that the opportunity existed.

Some analyses of postwar U.S. policy in Europe flirt with the idea that the Marshall Plan may have been principally a political vehicle by which expansionist U.S. businessmen were helped by the U.S. government to gain a footing in the weakened European economy. Later on, I shall discuss some of the social and political implications of the growth of U.S.-controlled multinational enterprise. At this point, however, it may be enough to observe that U.S. policies in the Marshall Plan period seem too complex to conform to any simple Marxist interpretation of that sort. For instance, during the Marshall Plan years the United States made strenuous official and private efforts to reinvigorate European industry; all sorts of channels were used to transmit not only goods but also technology to European industry, even though it was clear that industry would eventually represent a threat to U.S. exporters.

As it developed, the technology transfer was not all that difficult. "Best practice" in Europe and Japan was commonly not much behind "best practice" in the United States; indeed, in some notable cases, it was not behind at all. But the extent of diffusion of best practice in foreign countries was usually very much more limited than in the United States. Many European and Japanese businessmen who were aware of the latest technology were slow to apply it.[28] The difference between U.S. industry and the industry of Europe and Japan, therefore, lay not so much in the state of industrial knowledge as in the development and application of that knowledge. This difference, noted repeatedly during the nineteenth and twentieth centuries, is consistent with the view that businessmen's expectations—especially their market expectations—greatly influenced the timing of the introduction of industrial innovations in different economies.

After a few years, the chemical, electronic, transport, and machinery industries of Europe and Japan began to revive rapidly. Operating behind a certain amount of tariff protection, using well-established technologies, exploiting relatively low-cost labor, catering to markets large enough to sustain economies of scale, the new producers represented strong competition. If a threat was needed to stimulate U.S. investment in Europe and Japan, the threat was rapidly becoming visible.[29]

There were, however, differences between prewar and postwar conditions, many of which increased the interest of U.S. businessmen in the markets of the advanced overseas countries. For one thing, the elaborate network of cartel agreements that had grown up between the wars had been largely dismantled. Fragile at best, these agreements could not survive the U.S. antitrust prosecutions of the 1940s and the changes brought on by the war.[30] In addition, there was a sharp decline in the time costs involved in exploring distant markets. When air transport replaced the ocean steamer and the rail car as the businessman's medium for overseas exploration and discovery, it cut the European working visit for U.S. executives from, say, six weeks to perhaps two. Improvements in transoceanic telephone and cable connections had a reinforcing effect.

There were other stimuli to the formation of U.S. subsidiaries abroad, among them the creation of the European Economic Community (EEC). One of the familiar lessons of economic history has been that any new wave of discrimination against imports of manufactured goods tends to encourage the establishment of foreign-owned subsidiaries inside the protected market. When the EEC was created in 1959, it was not surrounded by very high tariff walls. The producers inside the walls could, however, count on having duty-free access to an internal market comparable in size to that of the United States. The existence of this market probably had powerful effects on the locational decisions of U.S.-controlled enterprises that were establishing subsidiaries in Europe. On the whole, the development encouraged greater plant specialization by such firms and greater cross-hauling across the boundaries of EEC countries.

The EEC may have led to somewhat higher levels of investments by U.S.-controlled enterprises. But investment of this sort would have increased rapidly in the EEC countries in any case, whether or not the EEC itself had come into existence.[31] The more important effect was probably on the functions of the plants established by U.S. enterprises in the EEC, which might otherwise have been less specialized and less extensively linked across the borders of Europe.

Apart from the special effects of the EEC, however, one could discern other new elements in the postwar situation, elements suggesting the possibility that U.S.-controlled subsidiaries might come rapidly and irreversibly to dominate some key lines of production in other advanced countries. One of these elements was the heightened importance of technological change in many branches of industry.

THE TECHNOLOGY ISSUE

One new force that was widely thought to have altered the postwar balance between the United States and Europe was the existence of extensive research and development programs sponsored and financed by various agencies of the U.S. government According to this view, the stimulus provided by military-based research widened the development lead of U.S. enterprises well beyond anything previously encountered in modern industrial history.

The fact that the United States developed a dominant position in world science after World War II is, of course, indisputable. From 1951 to 1969, for instance, the United States took twenty-one of the thirty-eight Nobel prizes in physics, nine of the twenty-seven prizes in chemistry, and twenty-three of the forty prizes in medicine and physiology. Nothing approaching this sort of U.S. lead had existed in the prewar period. Furthermore, U.S. dominance was found not only in science but also in technology and industrial development. U.S. gross expenditure on research and development during the middle 1960s was approximately fifteen times that of Germany, ten times that of the United Kingdom, and three times that of all Western Europe combined. Moreover, a large part of that research and development effort—about two-thirds in expenditure terms—was financed by public money.[32] Even if the productivity of a dollar of U.S. research expenditure was only a fraction of the productivity of European expenditure, the bulk of the world's research and development effort outside the Communist countries would still be represented by government-induced expenditures in the United States. And if research and development output was an index of a nation's industrial lead, the noncommunist world's industrial leadership would lie in U.S. hands, as a consequence of U.S. official policy. Finally, if an industrial lead is sufficient for the successful establishment of overseas subsidiaries, then it is the official

U.S. research and development program that has generated U.S. overseas dominance.

The weak link in the argument, as is widely realized in Europe and elsewhere, is the assumption that nations engaged in industrial innovation need depend exclusively or even primarily on scientific advances developed in their own country. Most of the scientific discoveries that have laid the basis for twentieth-century industrial innovations have come from the university rather than from industry or the government. One extraordinary study, covering the origins of five major U.S. innovations during the 1950s, shows that the universities accounted for three-quarters of the scientific events that laid the basis for industrial innovations and that half of these events occurred outside the United States.[33] As a rule, the scientific advances were freely available to any prospective user, foreign or domestic, provided he had the receptor apparatus for understanding them. The scientific community in the Western world is generally recognized as being an extraordinarily open society, in which news and discoveries travel fast. Because there is a characteristic lapse of a decade or more between any major industrial innovation and the scientific advances on which it depends,[34] enterprises with a capability for understanding the output of the scientific world have ample opportunity to scan that output for potential leads.

But the contention that something new was being added in the postwar period by the U.S. public research and development program is generally based not only on the effects these programs have had on the level of the scientific activity, but also on the promise of new markets which the programs have offered to U.S. enterprises. If the earlier analysis is valid, the promise of new markets predisposes enterprises to commit themselves to the processes of scanning, digesting, adapting, and testing that are involved in industrial innovation—in short, to the development activities that make up the largest part of U.S. research and development. What is stressed, therefore, is that the advantages of the U.S. market that had historically given U.S. enterprise a lead in certain categories of innovation had been extended to provide an even larger lead.[35]

The argument goes further, however. During the nineteenth century, an inspired tinkerer working by himself could occasionally generate a new marketable product of major importance: witness Eli Whitney, Samuel Morse, and Thomas Edison. By the early twentieth century, that possibility was already disappearing fast. And by the 1940s and 1950s, most major industrial innovations had become even less amenable to the one-man approach. A single major innovation often required the assembly of ideas from many different branches of science. In the airframe industry, the scientific principles of aerodynamics and metallurgy converged; in the internal combustion and gas turbine engines, numerous aspects of chemistry and physics were involved; in the machine tool industry, the computer sciences and metallurgy were brought together.

As a result of the increasing complexity of industrial innovation, the process came to be associated with the existence of large and complex organizations, with commitments of considerable sums of money, and with programs extending over long periods of time. Du Pont's costs in the postinvention development of nylon, excluding costs in the construction of the first commercial plant, were reported at $2 million in 1935 dollars; for orlon, at $5 million in 1940 dollars.[36] For the postinvention phase in each of eight major advances in petroleum refining, the principal oil companies spent between $200,000 and $30 million in 1920–1950 dollars.[37] IBM is said to have spent several billion dollars in developing the third-generation computer (though it is not altogether clear just what estimates of this sort cover). The development of the Concorde airframe, according to some seemingly careful estimates, also cost in the neighborhood of $2 billion; and even the less innovative job of developing an engine for the Tristar air bus cost Rolls-Royce about $400 million.[38]

The scale problem is not only a problem of money but also of time. Enterprises that commit themselves to the postinvention development of a major product or process generally take on a task that stretches over many years. One compilation, covering the postinvention development periods for twelve innovations, all beginning after 1928, recorded an average period of seven and a half years.[39] Another study in depth, exploring the origins of the video tape recorder, oral contraceptives, and the electron microscope, all post-World War II innovations, yields estimates of the same order of magnitude.[40] Long-term commitments of the sort suggested by these prolonged periods of development are generally taken on more easily by large firms than by small; with the outcome of any individual gamble uncertain, the importance of being able to average out risk over a larger number of cases can loom very large.[41]

It is true that there were some changes in the nature of industrial innovation which may have been operating in the opposite direction, reducing the advantages of scale and improving the position of small firms. One of these, according to informed accounts, was the increasing predictability of the outcome of innovational effort. As long as industrial advances had been the product of chance and inspiration it was hard to predict where the lightning would strike. But as the innovational process became the subject of systematic reason and experiment, the predictability of innovational output for any given level of effort tended to rise.[42] As a result, the threat of being wiped out by an unsuccessful gamble, always a bigger problem for the smaller firm, was reduced.

On balance, however, growing economies of scale were probably tipping the advantage in favor of the large firm. In this context, of course, "scale" refers to the processes of industrial innovation rather than to the antecedent processes of scientific invention. As various studies have demonstrated, the connection between firm size and firm inventiveness remains obscure;

many inventions continue to originate in small rather than in large producing firms.[43] Moreover, various studies continue to suggest that small producing firms in a given industry may not differ very much from the large in their propensity to use resources on research and that their use of such resources may be no less efficient.[44]

The relevant question in analyzing the growth of U.S. enterprise in the postwar era, however, was not whether firms of a given size were more efficient in the production of innovative ideas. The question was whether there were economies of scale in the full multistage process that consists of generating an innovation, developing it, and marketing the embodied output. The spectacular successes and equally spectacular failures in the evolution of the computer industry, for instance, suggested that major economies of scale might well exist in connection with the full development process. IBM's success could hardly be attributed to outstanding scientific skill; yet its special blending of capabilities—including a sensitivity to scientific advances, an appreciation of market needs, and a capacity for the production of dependable hardware—did seem a function of size.[45] Besides, there was other more systematic evidence to suggest that success in the development process was not independent of the firm's size. Not surprisingly, large firms tended to apply new techniques more rapidly than small.[46] And it also appeared that the amount of sales per unit of research effort was greater for large firms than for small.[47]

It would be difficult to assert conclusively that the growth of European enterprises was insufficient to keep pace with the growth in firm size needed for an effective industrial innovation effort. There are no historical series by which to test whether the amount of resources demanded by the average industrial innovation has grown faster than the resources that can be provided by the average industrial enterprise. Still, the conclusion that the demands of innovation have outstripped the growth of enterprises outside the United States may well be accurate.

Apart from the possibility that scale economies in the innovation process may be growing, there is also the possibility that scale economies of a more traditional sort, such as economies in the fields of production and marketing, are also growing. Sometimes this growth is accompanied by real technological change. Even if there were no change in the technology of an industry, however, the optimum scale of production would rise if international transport costs and trade barriers were falling relative to production costs; there is not much doubt that after World War II such a relative decline took place. For various reasons, therefore, the optimum scale for doing business rose in many industries. The optimum size polymer plant, for instance, is said to have been fifteen times greater in 1965 than in 1945.[48]

If scale economies of various sorts were growing rapidly, then the European tendency to worry about the irreversible industrial dominance of the large U.S. enterprise is easy to understand. One of the more meticulous studies of the relative size of the enterprises of different countries establishes unequivocally the relative bigness of the U.S. firm.[49] The leading U.S. enterprises are roughly twice as large as those of other countries, whether measured by assets or by sales. Though there are a few industries, such as chemicals, in which leading European enterprises match leading U.S. enterprises in size, a very large discrepancy exists in such leading sectors as aircraft, automobiles, and electrical machinery.

Even more comprehensible is the European worry that the ability of the U.S. government to mobilize the public and private resources for some innovational effort hopelessly outdistances the potential of any European nation. Nor is the consortium approach any answer to the development problem from the European viewpoint. In projects of that sort so far, the inherent difficulties of national cooperation have emerged rapidly, flushed up by pressures associated with the expenditures of large sums of money and by anxieties associated with national security and national prestige.[50] Euratom, one of Europe's early hopes in the atomic energy field, was brought near collapse by the national jealousies of its six member countries, especially of France; the European Launcher Development Organization, conceived in 1964 as a response to the U.S. and Russian lead in space, has failed miserably to realize its founders' hopes. Occasionally, a project produced results approximating its aspirations; but, as the Concorde project suggests, most of these were remembered for their difficulties, their high costs, and their disappointing payout.[51]

If the various links in the causal sequence are valid, then the sharp increase in the reach and involvement of U.S.-controlled multinational enterprise in the postwar period is partly a consequence of U.S. official policy and U.S. public power. The forebodings of many Europeans that U.S.-controlled enterprises are bound to maintain their technological lead without serious challenge from Europe is easy to understand.

LIMITS ON GROWTH

There is another popular assumption in Europe, however, that seems much less solidly based: the assumption that U.S.-controlled enterprises are moving steadily toward the domination of all branches of European industry. With the apparent speed-up in the generation of scientific knowledge, it is sometimes assumed that the spread of U.S. dominance, branch by branch, is only a matter of time.

There are at least two different questions of trend involved in understanding the likely future role of U.S.-controlled multinational enterprise. The first is whether the periods of post-invention industrial innovation—the period between the businessman's first recognition of the feasibility of a product or process and its commercial introduction—have grown shorter. The second is whether the period required for successful imitation by others has also declined.

There is some evidence to suggest the existence of a real speed-up during the postinvention period.[52] The evidence is not spectacular, nothing like the lay impressions in the popular press, but it is persuasive enough. This speed-up opens the possibility that U.S.-controlled multinational enterprises will be able to respond even more swiftly to major new market opportunities—in five years, say, instead of ten. And if their propensity to innovate continues to exceed that of their competitors, then the speed-up could strengthen their dominance in world markets.

That kind of projection, however, assumes that nothing has happened in the meantime to the length of the period it takes competitors to imitate or parallel a U.S.-generated innovation. Here the evidence of acceleration is less direct. All one can say with assurance is that new products and processes, once introduced, tend to be adopted faster than was once the case—roughly twice as rapidly after World War II as in the interwar years.[53] The period in which an innovator can hope to exploit his lead in comparative peace has shortened. Evidently, imitators are quicker to master the technology and introduce the related changes inside their organizations. When multiple sources of a technology are in existence, of course, the likelihood that a multinational enterprise can dominate the market on the basis of its technological lead declines.*

* In a study of the history of nine petrochemicals, cited earlier, there was striking evidence of the fact that imitators could successfully stay clear of the ownership and control of the innovators. In these nine petrochemicals, 100 percent of the "initial" plants were those of multinational enterprises—four of them being U.S. enterprises and five German. In the first following stage—a stage of rapid growth in demand—only 59 percent of the additional plants established were those of multinational enterprises; in the second following stage, a period of slower growth, the comparable figure was 47 percent; and in the third following stage, one of still slower growth, the figure was 36 percent. See R. B. Stobaugh, "The Product Life Cycle, U.S. Exports, and International Investment," unpublished D.B.A. thesis, Harvard Business School, June 1968, app. c.

Once the increased rate of diffusion is brought into the predictive model, it generates an indeterminate result regarding the future relative importance of U.S.-controlled innovating enterprises in world markets. New products and processes may be introduced in greater profusion, but the oligopolistic edge may not last so long.

Model in Operation: The Less-Developed Areas

The figures in Tables 3–2 and 3–3 have already indicated that the interests of U.S.-controlled manufacturing enterprises have been growing as rapidly in the less-developed areas as in the advanced countries, relative to historical norms. The growth in the less-developed areas began somewhat later as a rule, but it has in recent decades kept pace with the early starters.

The factors responsible for the spread of U.S. manufacturing interests into the less-developed areas were not very different from those that explained their spread to the advanced areas. Threat was intermingled with promise, as U.S. exporters worried about losing access to nascent large markets or about being elbowed out of established small ones. Besides, there were the advantages of drawing on lower cost labor or power or materials, advantages that became more tangible and credible as distances shrank and communication improved. But some distinctive elements in the less-developed countries generated the U.S. investments as well. One of these was the coercive power of the state.

Aspirations toward industrialization are nothing new in the less-developed parts of the world. The history of Brazil, Mexico, and India, among others, records numerous abortive efforts in that direction before the twentieth century. Tangible steps toward creation of a modern manufacturing sector began to appear sixty or seventy years ago in some of the larger countries. More advances were made during the two world wars as a result of the fact that needed supplies from the advanced countries were hard to get. All told, however, progress was limited up to the end of World War II. By that time, there were some facilities in the less-developed areas devoted to the fabrication of local raw materials, such as the foreign-owned meat plants of Argentina and the foreign-owned copper smelters of Chile; some foreign-owned plants that produced labor-intensive products for the markets of the colonial powers, such as the textile plants of India; and some that had been set up to reduce the transportation costs involved in shipping products from the advanced countries for local use, such as the automobile assembly plants of Latin America.

During World War II, import substitution in Latin America and Asia was a necessity; after World War II, it was turned into a virtue. And as Africa during the 1950s emerged from her period of colonialism, her countries were quick to adopt similar policies. As a result, most countries in the less-developed group systematically scanned their lists of imports, searching for products that might be manufactured locally. Most instituted procedures by which local businessmen could bring such opportunities to the attention of the appropriate ministries. Practically all the less-developed countries were prepared to prohibit the importation of a product as soon as the obstacles to local production no longer seemed utterly insurmountable.

As a rule, the decision in less-developed countries as to whether a product should be locally produced has had little to do directly with its cost; the decision has depended more on the existence of a domestic market coupled with the availability of local inputs. The first products generally proved to be consumer goods—indeed, the last stages in the chain of fabrication of consumer goods. These stages characteristically demanded relatively little in the way of labor skills or capital and could be undertaken on a comparatively small scale.

Assembly operations for radios, refrigerators, and automobiles were, therefore, the first industries offered protection and the first in which the foreigners were forced to consider investing.

The widespread impression in the less-developed countries is that foreign investors have never moved much beyond the assembling and packaging of materials shipped from outside. The facts themselves, however, tell a somewhat different story. Table 3–6 indicates that as early as 1957, U.S.-controlled subsidiaries were buying a large proportion of their total inputs from local sources. The figures represent, of course, "local payments"; and in the case of materials, a local payment is not the same thing as a payment for locally produced materials. But on any reasonable guess, the first is a high proportion of the second. Between 1957 and 1966, there was an even further deepening of the ties between U.S.-controlled subsidiaries and local suppliers, especially in automobiles and electronics. The fact that the local payments as a proportion of total sales fail to show much change during this period suggests that some of the newer foreign arrivals were repeating the cycle of the older investors, that is, beginning at the assembly and packaging end, eventually to become more deeply integrated in the economy.*

Because the investment process in the less-developed countries has been so greatly influenced by the use of heavy local protection, there have been some aspects of the investors' responses that differed from their situation in the advanced countries. Engineering standards of efficiency have had much less to do with investment decisions in the less-developed areas than in the advanced countries. Once imports were prohibited and local prices left free to rise, investors could plan on coming out whole from their investments even if the anticipated

---

* For a perceptive account of the process, involving Nestlé in the Dominican Republic, see W. J. Bilkey, *Industrial Stimulation* (Lexington, Mass.: Heath Lexington Books, 1970) p. 113. Though Nestlé is technically a Swiss-owned enterprise, the account is characteristic of U.S.-owned enterprises.

TABLE 3-6

Operations of U.S.-controlled Manufacturing Subsidiaries
in Latin America, 1957 and 1966

	1957		1966	
	AMOUNTS (MILLIONS OF DOLLARS)	PERCENT OF TOTAL SALES	AMOUNTS (MILLIONS OF DOLLARS)	PERCENT OF TOTAL SALES
Total sales	$2,286	100.0%	$6,548	100.0%
Local	2,203	96.4	5,880	89.8
Foreign: to affiliates	83[a]	3.6[a]	347	5.3
to others			321	4.9
Local payments[b]	1,868	81.7	5,369	82.0
Materials, supplies, services	1,212	53.0	3,274[c]	50.0
Wages and salaries	354	15.5	1,147[d]	17.5
Income taxes	149	6.5	464	7.1
Other local payments	153	6.7	484	7.4
Foreign payments[b]	308	13.5	813	12.4
Materials and services	246	10.8	666[c]	10.2
Remitted profits	62	2.7	147	2.2

[a]Breakdown not available.

[b]The sum of local payments and foreign payments is less than total sales because of the exclusion of retained earnings and depreciation from payments.

[c]Estimated total payments for material, supplies and services are reported at $1,458 and $3,940 million respectively for 1957 and 1966. For 1957, imported materials, supplies and services were reported at $246 million; for 1966, the same proportion would produce a figure of $666 million.

[d]Approximately 3,000 U.S. nationals were employed by these enterprises, suggesting annual payments in the neighborhood of $60 million. If half of this sum was remitted to the United States, then $30 million might be subtracted from local payments and added to foreign payments.

Source: Council for Latin America, *The Effects of United States and Other Foreign Investment in Latin America* (New York: January 1970); U.S. Department of Commerce, *U.S. Business Investments in Foreign Countries* (Washington, D.C.: Government Printing Office, 1960).

volume of local sales was only a fraction of the amount needed to achieve the lowest possible production costs. Accordingly, enterprises have tried to crowd their way in, even when existing production capacities were excessive. And governments—even governments with formal screening devices for foreign investment—have tended to let the crowding develop.[54] At times the crowding was simply the result of the government's inability or unwillingness to find a basis for discriminating among the applicants; at other times, it has been the result of the government's desire to avoid a monopoly of the local market by one big producer.

Despite the high costs and inefficiencies that were typical of the less-developed countries, many manufacturing subsidiaries of U.S.-controlled multinational enterprises found it expedient to export some of their output from those areas. For one reason or another, the exports of manufactured goods from the less-developed countries by U.S.-controlled multinational enterprises have grown very rapidly.

The extent of the growth is indicated by the striking data presented in Figure 3–1. The figure demonstrates that U.S.-controlled manufacturing subsidiaries, wherever located abroad, have rapidly expanded their exports from the host country. The exports from subsidiaries located in Latin America have begun to represent a considerable total. By 1968, the exports of manufactured goods by U.S.-owned subsidiaries in Latin America had passed $750 million, more than 40 percent of all Latin American exports of manufactured goods in that year;[55] and they had come to include large quantities of chemicals, machinery, and automobile parts.

The tendency for U.S.-controlled multinational enterprises to designate subsidiaries in less-developed countries as points of export has not been confined to subsidiaries in Latin America. The trends in the bottom-most portion of Figure 3–1, portraying the "Elsewhere . . ." area, are mainly determined by

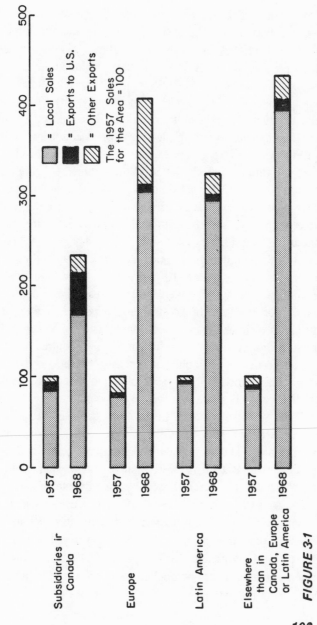

FIGURE 3-1

Sales of Foreign Manufacturing Subsidiaries of U.S. Enterprises, by Market Destination, 1957 and 1968.
Source: U.S. Department of Commerce.

the record of U.S.-owned manufacturing subsidiaries in the less-developed areas of Asia. Exports of manufactured goods from subsidiaries in these areas have also been growing rapidly. The products involved have included items of some sophistication, such as office machines, telecommunications equipment, and motorcycles. Increasingly, the destinations of the products have been the markets of advanced countries.[56]

The capacity to use the less-developed countries as areas of production for export appears to have been intimately related to the multinational character of the exporters. Without multinational links, the subsidiaries probably would not have increased their exports on anything like the same scale. Illustrative of that tie is the fact that although U.S.-controlled manufacturing subsidiaries accounted for 41 percent of Latin America's manufactured goods exports in 1966, they were responsible for less than 10 percent of Latin America's gross manufacturing value added in that year. Even more to the point was the type of goods being exported. These were the products of industries in which barriers to entry were relatively high and in which successful marketing required a relatively advanced degree of sophistication and control. As a result, the marketing process itself generally required the services of affiliates as well as the supervision of the parent.[57]

The use of subsidiaries in the less-developed areas as points of export has had its difficulties of course, organizational inefficiencies and government regulations being common impediments.[58] But there were many instances in which these drawbacks were overshadowed by the advantages of low labor costs. And even when the low labor costs proved illusory, as they often did, the decision to export from a country such as India or Mexico sometimes carried with it the right to sell in a highly protected local market. In that case, the profits to be gained in the internal market could be applied as an offset to the high costs of producing the exports.

The Manufacturing Industries

Multinational enterprises have also in a few cases discovered that rare types of labor, such as skilled artisans, could be found in the less-developed countries at a cost and in a quantity not available in the United States. This discovery has led a few automobile and aircraft companies to assign fairly difficult manufacturing tasks, such as the making of jigs and forms and the hand-finishing of complex engine parts, to their subsidiaries in less-developed countries.

Some economies have been more attractive than others as export points. In economies with overvalued exchange rates and high internal costs, foreign-owned enterprises have hesitated to export unless forced by government pressures. In Mexico, for instance, where internal production quotas have been fixed for each foreign-owned automobile subsidiary, the government has been obliged to manipulate the quota as a way of compelling the subsidiaries to export. India has laid down similar conditions.[59] Both have emulated patterns that the more advanced countries were already using, albeit on a more restrained basis.[60] But it is pretty clear that the propensity of U.S.-controlled subsidiaries to export their manufactured products from less-developed areas would eventually have occurred in the absence of governmental pressures, even if at a slower pace.

In general, the pressure that governments of the less-developed countries have applied to foreign-owned subsidiaries engaged in manufacturing has been less intense than that applied to subsidiaries engaged in raw materials extraction, such as those in copper mining and oil production. To be sure, countries such as India, Mexico, and Nigeria, possessing relatively large internal markets, have laid down numerous conditions on the entry of manufacturing subsidiaries, relying for their bargaining power on the foreigners' eagerness to get into the market. However, in practically all less-developed countries, after the entry of the foreign-owned manufacturing subsidiaries, the pressures have rarely been so draconian as to force the foreigners to withdraw.

There have been various reasons for this relatively benign approach. One of these is the ability of manufacturing subsidiaries to blend into the local environment more effectively than the giant oil and mining operations so that governments have felt less political pressure to "do something" about the foreigners. But another set of factors also seems to have operated, a set first encountered in the earlier discussion of the differences between the invulnerable position of the aluminum producers and the vulnerability of the copper producers.

On entering the local economy, foreign-owned manufacturing subsidiaries have usually appeared to be offering some resource—capital, technology, or market access—that was scarce or unique. As their distinctive starting position in the local economy has been eroded by time, they have moved on to other activities: from simple manufacturing processes and products toward complex ones; from easy marketing in the local economy to difficult marketing abroad. Like the aluminum producers, many of the manufacturing subsidiaries have constantly renewed the elements that gave them invulnerability, relying on the esoteric character of their new activities to offset the erosion of time. Unlike the raw material producers these subsidiaries were in many cases no more vulnerable to local pressures during the early 1970s than they had been fifteen or twenty years earlier. True, the pressures persisted: pressures from local governments to reduce what was left of their imports; pressures from local competitors to relinquish what they had of local markets; pressures from local capitalists to sell off a portion of their equity interests at bargain rates. But whether the foreigners' ability to resist these pressures was declining, or whether it was becoming more formidable, was not very clear.

Toward Another Model

The product cycle sequence may have seemed an efficient concept by which to describe the activities of U.S.-controlled multinational enterprises during most of the decades of their existence. But by 1970, the concept was frequently exhibiting procrustean tendencies—that is, tendencies to discard or distort information in order to have the facts conform rather more nicely to the theory. For instance, the product cycle sequence relies heavily on the assumption that the special conditions of the U.S. environment—especially factor costs and consumer tastes in the United States—will set in train a sequence that leads step by step to international investment. Though this may be an efficient way to look at enterprises in the U.S. economy that are on the threshold of developing a foreign business, the model is losing some of its relevance for those enterprises that have long since acquired a global scanning capacity and a global habit of mind.

By the late 1960s there were plenty of illustrations that U.S. manufacturing enterprises were already capable of a considerable degree of global scanning. U.S. parents were better equipped than they had ever been to evaluate foreign opportunities and assess foreign threats, and to respond to these opportunities and threats by developing complex logistical networks among their affiliates. IBM was producing integrated circuits in France, and mounting materials for the circuits in Germany; it was concentrating one type of computer assembly in its French plant, another in its German; and it was producing hybrid circuits for both at still a third location.[61] Bendix was using the cheap labor of Taiwan to assemble automobile radios for world markets. Ford was making fender steel in Holland for car production in the rest of Europe and tractor components in Germany and motors for compact models in Britain to be used in U.S. assembly plants.[62] Singer was cross-hauling its many makes and models of sewing machines between Scotland, Canada, Japan, and the United States, concentrating the production of different types where markets and factor costs suggested. More generally, the networks established by U.S.-controlled multinational enterprises, by the late 1960s, were handling an international trade in manufactured goods of impressive proportions: about $9,000 million annually in exports from the United States; $12,000 million from Europe and Canada; and $1,400 million from the less-developed parts of the world.

By 1970, the product cycle model was beginning in some respects to be inadequate as a way of looking at the U.S.-controlled multinational enterprise. The assumption of the product cycle model—that innovations were generally transmitted from the U.S. market for production and marketing in overseas areas—was beginning to be challenged by illustrations that did not fit the pattern. The new pattern that these illustrations suggested was one in which stimulation to the system could come from the exposure of any element in the system to its local environment, and response could come from any part of the system that was appropriate for the purpose.

Of course, before an organization could be thought of as global in outlook, one would expect it to have shed any non-rational preferences for U.S. money, personnel, or markets. It would be an exaggeration to say that this has yet happened to any great extent. But it is no exaggeration to note the palpable existence of that tendency. With large sums of long-term money being raised in foreign markets, with key personnel being hired in foreign countries, and with major fixed assets being established in foreign jurisdictions, the trend could hardly be avoided.

Despite the tendency toward a global outlook, it is safe to assume that U.S.-controlled multinational enterprises will generally think of themselves as American companies for a long time to come, long after the concept has lost some of its meaning in day-to-day operational terms. That, of course, is understandable. To accept some measure of confusion about one's national identity is not an easy thing for anyone raised in a system of nation states. But the American identification will not prevent U.S.-controlled enterprises from ranging widely through the globe in search of inspiration, capital, labor, materials, and markets.[63]

If U.S.-controlled enterprises prove able to evolve from a parochial national orientation to an Olympian view of their threats and opportunities, one may well ask whether the Europeans and the Japanese cannot eventually develop something like the same view. Presumably they could; indeed, some already have. But if my argument is valid, the economic grounds for such an expectation are not so great as they have been for U.S. enterprise.

According to my argument, the special conditions of the U.S. market—high per capita income, scarce artisan labor, costly labor in general, large internal markets including military purchases—generated innovations that later would be wanted abroad. The special conditions of the European market, on the other hand, encouraged innovations with a less certain international future. Whereas a global secular growth in the demand for high-income and labor-saving products was reasonably sure, one could not be nearly so sanguine about the growth in demand for material-saving and capital-conserving products.

Still, new products could be envisaged, generated under the stimulus of European conditions, so distinct in quality from available U.S. products as to create their own demand. Such innovations might have application in third countries where conditions more closely approximate those of Europe than those of the United States. They might even have application in the United States itself. Material-saving or capital-saving innovations urgently needed in the European setting could be applied anywhere, including the United States, if they had cost-lowering effects. An oligopoly edge based on such innovaticns could lead to an increase in European-controlled or Japanese-controlled subsidiaries in the United States.

But this is only armchair speculation. The actual record until a few years ago showed no significant movement of European-owned subsidiaries to the United States, based on the strength of European innovations.[64] Some of the European-owned enterprises that were found in the United States seem to have been propelled there by some idiosyncratic twist of events, obscure in character. Others—especially those with Canadian sources of raw materials—were pushed into the United States in order to climb over the U.S. tariff wall or to process Canadian raw materials closer to their market. A few —but only a few—had set up U.S. subsidiaries in order to exploit or protect an oligopolistic advantage. The establishment of a Courtaulds subsidiary in the U.S. market during the early twentieth century, based on a unique rayon viscose technology, had of course been such a case; so had the early entry of the German and Swiss fertilizer, dyestuffs, and drug companies.

There were however other instances in which the establishment by Europeans of manufacturing subsidiaries in the U.S. market seemed to be based on motivations familiar in terms of the previous analysis. Royal Dutch/Shell had, for instance, established its refineries and distribution facilities in the U.S. market in 1912 as part of an oligopolist's strategy for countering the appearance of Standard Oil in Asia.[65] According to press speculation, Pechiney was moved by similar motives when in 1962 it acquired aluminum-producing properties in the United States; in this case, the penetration of U.S. firms into European markets was said to have been a stimulus to the Pechiney acquisition.[66] In a response that also has its historical parallels, British Petroleum took a position in the U.S. market in 1969 through its acquisition of Sohio partly because of its oligopolistic need to integrate vertically and, more specifically, its need to find a captive outlet for a huge surplus of crude oil.[67] But when all these cases are added up, they do not offer much support for the expectation of transatlantic symmetry.

The semblance of symmetry could occur if European-controlled multinational enterprises were prepared to take the deliberate gamble of leaping to a global logistical structure that would match the U.S.-controlled enterprises. History has turned up a few cases that seem to fall in this category. Unilever's acquisition of a U.S. interest in 1897, says the company historian, came about because "Lever himself had been fascinated by the American scene. Many of his ideas on technology and marketing—more especially advertising—were the by-product of his observations on his American journeyings."[68] In the years that followed, the existence of the U.S. subsidiary helped Unilever to test some products at a stage when their cost made them prohibitive for anywhere except the U.S. market.[69] Such products as dishwashing detergent and synthetic soap were market-tested in the United States, then adapted and refined in close collaboration between the company's scientists and its marketing men. Once that experience was behind it, the Unilever system was in possession of a new asset, the lessons of experience and experiment in the U.S. market. At that point, the internal network of Unilever communications could spread the results to other markets, such as the United Kingdom and Germany.[70]

Olivetti's decision to buy the moribund Underwood company in the United States seems to have been sparked in part by a similar strategic concept, though the public rhetoric accompanying the step was too diffuse to establish the motive with certainty. But the Olivetti case illustrated something else as well, namely, that efforts by Europeans to establish their producing facilities in the United States, unaccompanied by any obvious technological advantage that could lubricate the transfer, are exceedingly hazardous. Olivetti's losses during the early years of its U.S. venture represented one of the highest tuition fees in history. At one time, Volkswagen too almost committed itself to a production facility in the United States, but saved itself in time by recognizing that much of the firm's competitive advantage lay in the labor supply conditions of the German market.[71]

Will the European penetration of the U.S. economy pick up in tempo as Europeans see more opportunities to press their existing oligopolistic advantages in the U.S. market? There are some signs of the beginning of such a trend, but these are still weak and wavering. In 1969, for instance, a German steel company announced its intention to set up a steel manufacturing subsidiary in the United States, relying on cost-reducing electric furnace technology first applied in Germany.[72] But it is too early to assume that many European enterprises are prepared to take the risks associated with such a step.

While there are not many signs that the Europeans plan to match the U.S. penetration of Europe by moving in force into the U.S. economy, there are plenty of indications that European enterprises are expanding their manufacturing facilities into other European economies and into the less-developed countries. That sort of move is paralleled by a large-scale expansion of Japanese direct investment in Asia and Africa, especially in light import-substituting industries. Some elements of the U.S. multinational pattern, therefore, are being emulated. In some areas and some industries, the multinational spread of U.S. enterprises is even being outmatched. But the phenomenon is seriously lacking in symmetry as long as the Europeans and the Japanese do not strongly challenge Americans on their home ground. In the future, as in decades past, therefore, the world may have to view the multinational enterprise as an asymmetrical phenomenon in which the American version is thought of as distinctive in scope and in strength.

[4   ]

Personality of the Multinational Enterprise

To determine where the U.S.-controlled multinational enterprise may be headed, observations from close in are needed, close enough to generate an understanding of the motivations and the processes that shape the activities of these large complex structures. Observations at close range have their dangers: Basic propositions can be obscured by a mass of trivial detail. Still, the risk is worth taking in order to gain added understanding on a few key points.

Objectives and Organizations

THE OBJECTIVES

Can the objectives of the multinational enterprise be explicitly defined? The multinational enterprises covered in this study are, as it turns out, nearly identical with the largest U.S. corporations, and the goals of large U.S. corporations have been a popular subject for analysis by numerous contemporary observers.[1] Many of the conclusions of my colleagues and myself regarding these goals are consistent with the conventional wisdom generated by others. Those who think of profits as a dominant force in the behavior of large U.S. enterprises will find little in this analysis to challenge that view. Those who believe that such enterprises place a heavy emphasis on their share of the market and on reducing the unpredictable elements in their business environments will find plenty of supporting evidence for their position. And if there is insistence from some quarter, as there generally is, that these goals are all compatible and even mutually reinforcing under the conditions of modern industry, this view, too, is quite consistent with the findings of this study.[2]

There is a related question, however, that may strike more sparks: Granting that all generalizations on the subject of corporate behavior represent a heroic simplification of reality, what is the most efficient simplification from which to begin? Can one begin with the pure classical model of economic theory, "a system consisting of an indefinite number of utilitarian men, completely informed, trading in individually owned commodities in a world with no indivisibilities, no externalities, no government, no taxation, and no money in frictionless instantaneous markets?"[3] Or is it better to begin with Galbraith's key assumptions: that the U.S. economy is so affluent that new demands for private goods have to be fabricated by the corporate world through the application of artificial stimuli; that U.S. corporations have captured their market environment to such an extent as to make the concepts of competitive market behavior irrelevant; and further, that the technocratic managers of the corporation have captured the corporation so completely as to alter the meaning of profit as a motivating force. Are there other generalizations, falling between these extremes, that provide a more efficient platform from which to view and understand the behavior of large U.S. corporations?

The choice unfortunately has ideological implications in the eyes of many commentators. Those who think of a decentralized competitive society as a "good thing," for instance, are sometimes reluctant to accept the view that the good thing might be remote from reality. At the same time, many who think of oligopoly or monopoly as exploitative are reluctant to believe that any substantial measure of competition may exist among the large corporations.

In the course of this study, tne simplifying model of the behavior of large U.S. corporations that has proved most useful is one quite far removed from the classical model. The usual setting encountered in these analyses has been one in which each enterprise readily identified its principal competitors and in which each action had to be weighed with due regard for the response it was likely to evoke. This part of the model, therefore, treads the familiar ground of E. H. Chamberlin and Joan Robinson.

A second feature of the corporate environment encountered in these studies was the pervasive presence of ignorance and uncertainty in the decision-making process. The justification for many major actions could only be explained as a hedge against the murky future or as a commitment to a learning process. Here, one is applying familiar ideas as well, ideas associated with such economists as F. H. Knight and K. J. Arrow.

This is not to say that rational textbook decision-making, based on the certainties of discounted cash flows, linear programs, and all the rest, is not employed by the large corporations that were the object of the study. But it is a good generalization that formal decision criteria of that sort were much more influential in the small decisions than in the large. On reflection, that is not a very surprising conclusion. Small questions, such as the question whether to substitute a set of machines for a set of men, generally involve familiar variables that are thought to be predictable within relatively narrow ranges; large decisions, such as whether to establish a subsidiary in Brazil, generally push the decision-maker into areas that he recognizes as terra incognita.

Still another set of characteristics emerged, to play a major part in explaining the observed behavior of large U.S. corporations. The sheer size and diversity of these entities have had considerable impact on their behavior. The decisions of a large corporation are not simply the sum of the decisions of many small corporations; they are different in nature. From close up, large U.S. corporations often give the impression of a group of cooperating forces joined together in one organization but managing to retain distinguishably different goals within it. In large organizations, the need to find some workable criteria to gauge the performance of each of the constituent parts tends to contribute to that result. "Workable criteria," at best, generally prove to be gross and imperfect surrogates for the contribution that each unit makes to the well-being of the enterprise.

The imperfect nature of measures of performance in large organizations is generated by various factors. Measures of profit are often shaped by the need for compliance with accounting conventions, the need for arbitrary decisions in the assignment of joint costs, and the desire to minimize taxes. Other measures, though not subject to the weaknesses of the conventional profit accounts, often have weaknesses of their own as gauges of the contribution to the well-being of the enterprise. The performance of marketing entities, for instance, is generally monitored by the increase in their gross sales or in their "share of market"; but some increases, as it turns out, are achieved at far greater cost than others and might better have been avoided in the interests of the enterprise as a whole. Production entities are often judged by cost per unit of output; but some of the costs, in practice, are arbitrarily assigned values that have little to do with their real cost to the firm. Yet each unit of the enterprise, aware of the standards by which it is being judged, tends to be responsive to those standards more than to any other, even if the total profits of the enterprise are not greatly helped by such responsiveness.[4]

The size and diversity of multinational enterprises are not always handicaps for the large enterprise. A multiproduct enterprise such as General Electric will usually be able to relate the various branches of its business in some kind of integrating strategy. Such a firm can, for instance, generally siphon off enough cash and creative personnel from the mature, large-volume, slow-growing lines of the enterprise, such as consumer durables, to finance and equip some of the newer, developing, as yet unprofitable products such as gas turbines. But from the viewpoint of a profit-maximizing entity, the shift in resources is achieved with many internal compromises and second-best solutions. In a similar vein, the enterprise whose operations are dispersed among many geographical areas may be able to reduce its commitment in the less promising areas and expand in those areas that seem more profitable, but not so rapidly or so simply as the Darwinian approach to the firm might suggest.

Because so many of the problems of large corporations are those entailed in adaptation and change, other emphases tend to appear that are not consistent with the usual profit-maximizing yield-on-investment model. Among other things, the management of the enterprise will generally regard its fixed assets as less unique and less difficult to reproduce than the people and practices and collective memory that comprise its organization; if there is an economic rent to be captured in the enterprise, therefore, it will be perceived as coming principally from the "investment" in the making of a functioning organization. On this assumption, the management is concerned with maintaining loyalty, incentive, and initiative over the long run and, if necessary, is usually prepared to modify the classic return-on-investment calculations to keep the principal members of the team in play.

THE ORGANIZATIONS

What most Americans know about the organization of large U.S. corporations is what they have been able to glean from *The Man in the Gray Flannel Suit, Up the Organization,* and

How to Succeed in Business Without Really Trying. In sources of this sort, large corporations are portrayed as structures ruled by iron conformity and false charisma, that somehow manage to survive and grow.

Like any other type of organization, from the Communist International to the U.S. Army, large U.S. enterprises generally try to create some sense of identity and style.[5] "Let's do it the company way, the company way is the way okay," is more than a ditty in a musical comedy. In years past, the objective was promoted by the existence of leaders with a touch of charisma, such as the elder Henry Ford and Thomas J. Watson, Sr.[6] Nor is charisma altogether lacking in the current crop of big business leaders. More often, however, the style and objectives of the organization are imparted by more matter-of-fact means. The object of the process, as always, is to ensure that the organization's various parts will respond to their problems in a way that is consistent with the organization's collective goals.

The first challenge for enterprises grown large has generally been to find a structure that allows the various elements of its management to specialize, so that the advantages and efficiencies of specialization, celebrated long ago by Adam Smith, can be realized. The first response of such enterprises has been to designate specialists according to certain functional fields, and to rely on their specialized contributions to inform the key decision-maker at the top of the pyramid. The president looked to vice presidents of production, marketing, and finance to make their respective contributions, augmented in some cases by men of equal rank concerned with personnel or control or research. When this organizational step had been accomplished, the organization was said by some organizational theorists to have moved out of a primitive, undifferentiated "stage 1" organization to "stage 2."

As long as the decisions of the large organization were relatively repetitive in character or relatively few in number, this kind of organization could work well enough. A large organization concerned with the production and sale of crude steel or pig aluminum, for instance, could execute its relatively simple strategies by means of a stage 2 organization, without feeling any strong sense of inadequacy. If the markets changed little and the technology moved slowly, it was perfectly feasible for the key functional men in the organization to gather around the president's conference table and make the major decisions. That, indeed, is the basic structure by which a few very large enterprises in the United States—but a very few—still do their business today.

More commonly, as the cross-functional decisions inside an organization have grown in number, the practice of generating these decisions at the top of the pyramid has become untenable. At this stage the president and his vice presidents become bottlenecks in the decision-making process, and the organization is obliged to adapt in various ways. Subordinating the functional breakdown to differentiations of other kinds, they have moved from stage 2 to stage 3. In stage 3, the primary organizational division was no longer based on function. Instead, it was based on some other distinction, such as a distinction among products or among markets. So common was the movement out of the functional structure that out of a group of 170 multinational enterprises which had once been organized on stage 2 lines, only eight retained this type of organization in 1968, the rest having moved on to stage 3.*

But stage 3 organizations have appeared in a number of different subtypes. Any organizational structure with differentiated functions searches for a breakdown into such units that the maximum amount of the needed coordination and support can take place inside the units. The constraint, of course,

* The analysis generating those data, conducted by J. M. Stopford, covered only 170 of the 187 enterprises. The difference is accounted for by Stopford's exclusion of a few enterprises that were added to the rest of the study at a relatively late date.

is that the units should remain sufficiently small to avoid running into the offsetting diseconomies that are associated with excessive size, such as inadequate supervision or "noise" in the communication that takes place within the units.

For some enterprises, these principles have led to a breakdown primarily by product groups, for others to a breakdown primarily by geographical areas. These breakdowns have rarely appeared in pure and unqualified form. Some functions, such as the financial function, generally remained firmly attached to the top executive's office and were rarely lodged in the main divisions without some strong central tie. Moreover, an organization that was set up primarily on a geographical breakdown is commonly found harboring some production or research activities outside the geographical structure. Still, the primary pattern was usually clear—clear enough to allow for a crude classification of organizations on lines suggested by the discussion so far. According to this classification, the product division was the most common stage 3 form, followed in number by complex combinations of product and area organizations, with fairly pure area breakdowns the least frequent of all.

In weighing the effects of U.S.-controlled enterprises in foreign countries, does it matter what structures they have adopted for management of their assets? A case can be made that the connection is tenuous; that strategies determine structure, not the other way around. No doubt, structures are determined partly by the strategies that enterprises have adopted. But once a structure is in place, its existence influences the way in which the enterprise defines its risk and identifies its opportunities. A given structure, therefore, predisposes to a given strategy. To determine the implications of that conclusion for the management of overseas subsidiaries, however, it is necessary first to take a closer look at the foreign side of the U.S.-controlled enterprises.

The Foreign Side of the Enterprise

ITS SCOPE

Though the U.S. market no doubt still dominates in the minds of the managers of U.S. enterprises, foreign markets have begun to make considerable impact. That fact is well illustrated by data derived from one of the more painstaking surveys of the foreign business of U.S. enterprises,[7] a survey that covered 140 of the 187 multinational enterprises in this study. The figures extracted from the survey and shown in Table 4–1 are riddled with definitional problems. Still, they show that as early as 1964, the foreign business of most of the enterprises was a substantial part of their total activity. The asset figures are particularly telling; of 101 reporting firms, fifty-five showed 20 percent or more of their assets as foreign.

From the viewpoint of the managers of U.S.-controlled multinational enterprises, their foreign commitments were not only large, they were also very widespread. As far as the group of 187 multinational enterprises is concerned, farflung operations are the general rule. For instance, 106 of the 187 enterprises had subsidiaries in five of the main geographical areas shown in Table 4–2; 62 had subsidiaries in four of those five areas; only 19 were more confined in geographical spread.*

The appearance of size and diversity that these figures project with regard to the foreign interests of the 187 enterprises can be supplemented by one more major impression: that of durability and depth of commitment. Table 4–3 indicates that the 187 enterprises had nearly 8,000 foreign subsidiaries in

---

* If the criteria for the identification of multinational enterprises had permitted the inclusion of comparatively small enterprises, some rather different patterns of geographical distribution would probably have emerged. Since the 187 enterprises account for 80 percent or so of total U.S. foreign investment in manufacturing and raw material extraction, however, it can be said that most of the foreign activities of U.S. parents is conducted in enterprises with wide geographical spread.

TABLE 4-1

*One Hundred Forty U.S.-controlled Multinational Enterprises,
Classified by Foreign Content of Operations, 1964*

PERCENT OF FOREIGN CONTENT	FIRMS CLASSIFIED BY FOREIGN CONTENT[a] OF			
	SALES	EARNINGS	ASSETS	EMPLOY-MENT
0-9%	11	14	16	2
10-19	25	25	30	10
20-29	22	17	27	14
30-39	19	9	17	7
40-49	10	6	5	4
50-59	4	5	4	7
60-69	1	3	2	6
70-79	0	1	0	5
80-89	0	1	0	1
90-100	1	0	0	0
Not recorded[b]	47	59	39	84
Total firms	140	140	140	140

[a]The definition of "foreign content" is not consistent among the 140 firms with respect to any of the four measures used. Inconsistencies are especially marked with respect to sales figures; in some cases, for instance, exports from the United States are included as foreign; in other cases, not.

[b]The identity of the firms not recorded differs from one column to the next. All the 140 firms were recorded for at least one of the four measures in the table; but the firms not recorded differed from measure to measure.
Source: N. K. Bruck and F. A. Lees, "Foreign Content of U.S. Corporate Activities," *Financial Analysts Journal,* Sept. Oct. 1966, pp. 1-6.

operation in 1967. Though sales subsidiaries, holding companies, and extractive operations made up much of the total count, manufacturing subsidiaries* constituted the largest

* The figures in Table 4–3 have to be interpreted cautiously with respect to the foreign extractive activities of U.S. enterprises, partly because of the basis of selection of the 187 enterprises and partly because of the preference of U.S. enterprises for the use of branches as a vehicle for foreign extractive activities. Figures separately compiled on the geographical distribution of these extractive activities indicate, however, that the data in the table are not misleading as to the relative importance of the various areas, even though the number of operations is substantially understated.

TABLE 4-2

One Hundred Eighty-seven U.S.-controlled Multinational Enterprises, Classified by Existence of Subsidiaries in Specified Foreign Areas, 1967

AREA	NUMBER OF ENTERPRISES HAVING AT LEAST ONE SUBSIDIARY IN A SPECIFIED AREA ENGAGED PRINCIPALLY IN[a]			
	MANUFAC-TURING	SALES	EXTRAC-TION	TOTAL ENTER-PRISES
All foreign areas	185[b]	162	45	186[b]
Canada	161	59	17	174
Latin America	171	100	28	182
Mexico	138	28	10	162
Argentina	80	17	3	99
Brazil	92	21	2	111
Europe and United Kingdom	183	136	10	185
European Community	171	112	5	179
France	122	52	3	151
Germany	113	59	1	149
Italy	106	36	1	132
EFTA	161	98	4	181
United Kingdom	145	59	4	167
Southern dominions	135	64	11	154
Asia and other Africa	134	79	18	158
Japan	90	37	0	117
India	53	8	0	64
Black Africa	27	20	12	62

[a]The sum of the three categories for any area is unrelated to the total enterprises figure for that area, partly because an enterprise may be represented in more than one of the three categories of subsidiaries and partly because some minor categories of subsidiaries have been omitted.

[b]The list of 187 enterprises was based on their status in 1963 and 1964; by 1967, however, a number of mergers and divestitures had occurred.

group. In fact, manufacturing subsidiaries dominated everywhere, even in less-developed areas such as Latin America and Black Africa.

But these counts, taken by themselves, say little about motivations and means. For clarification on these critical issues, one has to turn to a closer examination of the organizational changes that have accompanied the growth in the foreign side of the multinational enterprises.

TABLE 4-3

Number of Foreign Subsidiaries of 187 U.S.-controlled Multinational Enterprises in Specified Areas, Classified by Principal Activity, 1967

AREA	MANUFAC- TURING	SALES	EXTRAC- TION[a]	OTHER	UNKNOWN	TOTAL SUBSIDI- ARIES
All foreign areas	3,646	1,358	172	1,247	1,504	7,927
Canada	443	128	36	185	256	1,048
Latin America	950	233	56	338	347	1,924
Mexico	255	31	14	56	56	412
Argentina	108	20	4	23	32	187
Brazil	149	25	2	42	49	267
Europe and United Kingdom	1,438	722	15	529	697	3,401
European Community	759	327	7	245	337	1,675
France	223	81	3	95	91	493
Germany	211	91	1	53	100	456
Italy	161	44	1	29	75	310
EFTA	494	336	5	250	320	1,405
United Kingdom	356	112	5	131	196	800
Other Europe	185	59	3	34	40	321
Southern dominions	361	101	26	78	82	648
Asia and other Africa	454	174	39	117	122	906
Japan	144	40	0	24	25	233
India	62	8	0	4	12	86
Black Africa	43	37	20	36	30	166

[a]The data deal only with subsidiaries; branches are not included. This omission is particularly important in extraction industries, in which branches represent a fairly important form of foreign operations.

Source: J. W. Vaupel and J. P. Curhan, *The Making of Multinational Enterprise* (Boston: Harvard Business School, 1969), chap. 3.

Personality of the Multinational Enterprise

ITS MANAGEMENT

Recall that many U.S. companies acquired their first over-seas markets almost absentmindedly, as a result of a spontaneous and growing foreign demand for products that had originally been developed for the U.S. market. Up to the 1950s, the typical organizational response of large enterprises to the growth of their foreign sales was to designate some medium-level official as export manager, while leaving undisturbed the basic structure of the firm.[8]

The export-manager pattern served well enough, just as long as export volumes were relatively small and overseas production was not an important part of his activity. As the overseas demand for U.S.-originated products grew, however, neither of these conditions continued. According to the product cycle hypothesis, the established export markets of some U.S.-based producers began to be threatened; prospective producers in these markets began to find ways of appropriating the technology, of imitating or improving on the product, and of producing at costs that challenged the product delivered from U.S. sources. Other U.S. producers, meanwhile, woke up to discover that the brand names they had managed to establish in foreign markets by way of exports might be more fully exploited if the product were manufactured and distributed locally; or else that some rival brand was preempting the market and imperiling the U.S. producer's longer-run strategy of eventually introducing his own brand in the market. At such critical junctures, many U.S. innovators felt the need to fortify their export positions by setting up producing facilities in overseas markets. Production on the spot, it was thought, could serve the local market better and perhaps more cheaply than production by way of exports.

U.S. enterprises commonly accompanied developments of this sort with the creation at headquarters of an international division, more or less equal in status to the other main divisions of the enterprise. This step, according to the study referred to earlier, was taken at some point in the evolution of seventy-two of 170 enterprises surveyed. The international division was generally charged with establishing and operating the overseas producing subsidiaries of the enterprise and with keeping an eye on exports to foreign markets. The usual assumption was that foreign business, wherever it took place, had some common elements, thereby justifying its own corps of specialists. By segregating the problems of foreign business from the main body of corporate decisions and elevating them in status, the multinational enterprise could increase its operating efficiency. This step had already been taken prior to World War II by some of the more experienced U.S. parent companies such as General Motors and National Cash Register, and it was widely imitated in the decade following World War II.

Once an international vice president charged with overseeing the foreign domain had been created, a new vested interest existed inside the enterprise, an interest devoted to the expansion of offshore operations. New capabilities for scanning and responding were at work inside the firm, and new sensitivities to market opportunity and market threat generally appeared. If the firm had previously thought of itself as a member of an oligopoly centered largely in North America and Latin America and if it had thought of its other interests as ancillary, this perception tended to change. The rivals rapidly came to include those in the markets of Europe and the Far East.

However, the international division generally proved to be a transitional form of organization; fifty-seven of the seventy-two enterprises that adopted it at some point in their development had given it up by 1968. Why the international division came to be obsolete is not a trivial technical question: By inference, it reveals a great deal about the changing internal perspective of U.S.-controlled multinational systems as their foreign business continued to grow.

The very growth of the international division was a force

that tended to reduce its life span. As long as such a division was not outsized by comparison with the others in the enterprise, its constant needs for communication and coordination with the others could be tolerated and accommodated in the organization's picture. The endless problems of product design, pricing policy, quality control, research support, and so on could be dealt with as part of the ordinary process of interdivisional communication. Once those problems attained a sufficient volume, however, the process of interdivisional communication and coordination became difficult. Besides, the rapid growth of the international divisions has sometimes been seen as a threat by the other parts of the enterprise.

Difficulties of this sort were compounded by others. As the international division grew, problems of internal supervision arose. The simplistic notion that foreign business problems were more or less alike, wherever they arose, gave way to a much more realistic recognition of their heterogeneity. In many cases, recognition of that heterogeneity led to the creation of strong geographical units within the international division. More often, however, as the data indicate, reorganization went further; the international divisions were dismembered and their parts distributed.

Out of this metamorphosis, the various main organizational forms emerged. Some were based mainly on a geographical breakdown, some mainly on a product basis, and others on a mixture in which neither clearly predominated. The choice of alternative structures by the multinational enterprises was sensitive to many considerations, no doubt. But the characteristic of the enterprise that goes furthest to explain the choice of organizations was the width of its product line. Table 4–4 presents an analysis of 162 companies—the 170 mentioned earlier, less eight oil companies—showing the relationship of the diversity of the product line in the enterprise to the type of organization of the enterprise in 1968. Enterprises with comparatively few products seem content to remain with the inter-

TABLE 4-4

*One Hundred Sixty-two U.S.-controlled
Multinational Enterprises, Classified According to
Product Diversity and Organizational Structure, 1968*

ORGANIZATION	NUMBER OF ENTERPRISES, BY DEGREE OF PRODUCT DIVERSITY[a]			
	ONE PRODUCT	FEW PRODUCTS	MANY PRODUCTS	TOTAL
Stage 2	7	1	0	8
Stage 3				
With international division	10	47	25	82
Without international division				
Area divisions	9	6	2	17
Product divisions	0	4	26	30
Mixed structure[b]	0	7	18	25
Total	19	64	71	154
Stages 2 and 3	26	65	71	162

[a]The product classification was based on a two-and-a-half-digit SIC breakdown. The measure used for distinguishing few products from many products was an index calculated by multiplying the number of products by the proportion of sales accounted for by other than the leading product.

[b]This category included three enterprises organized on the principle that every operating unit would report both to a product division and to an area division simultaneously, and twenty-two enterprises organized partially on a product division and partially on an area division breakdown.

Source: J. M. Stopford and L. T. Wells, Harvard Multinational Enterprise Study.

national division or, if they abandon that structure, to organize themselves on a relatively simple area principle. But those with a comparatively large number of products seem drawn to more complex structures, containing a major element of product coordination.

The association exhibited by the figures in Table 4–4 indicates the intimacy of the tie between business strategy and business structure. Multinational enterprises may have at least two kinds of coordinating problems: those that relate to coordination between products and those that relate to coordination between areas. Whereas the number of products can proliferate without end, the number of areas tends to approach a certain limit. When enterprises have held down their line of products to a fairly modest number, as such companies as Timken and Caterpillar Tractor have done, their product-coordinating problems have remained within manageable proportions; they have, therefore, tended to build their organizations on the basis of a geographical breakdown, anticipating that the problems of product coordination among the regions could be handled by the interdivisional communication network. However, enterprises with more extensive product lines, such as Olin Chemical and FMC, have had to find some way of managing the exponential increase in problems of coordination across product lines. These have, therefore, gravitated toward product divisions, grouping the products in such a way as to internalize most of the problems of coordination within the divisions.

It bears repeating that none of these organizational adaptations was pure in form. There were various patchquilt improvisations aimed at achieving the best of all possible combinations of coordination. There were also measures to accommodate the existence of strong managers, even if the accommodation meant some ad hoc cutting and pasting in the organizational design. Still, the elements of regularity were in plain evidence.

One major implication of the adoption of the product-centered or area-centered type of organization will be immediately apparent. When problems are organized along product or regional terms, the identity of the subsidiary in which the problem arises loses some significance as the problem is perceived. If a large diversified chemicals enterprise encounters a problem in its French paint and varnish business, it may be more efficient to think of the problem as one relating to the European strategy or to the paint and varnish strategy of the multinational enterprise than as one relating to the strategy of the French subsidiary. The strategist may at times be obliged to take cognizance of the fact that national law requires the enterprise to build its structure with certain legally constituted building blocks: a U.S. company, a French company, a German company, and so on. The formal structure may even prove consistent at times with the needs of strategy. But for the strategist, the critical units of organization are those of the enterprise's creation, not those imposed by the state. The result is suggested by Figure 4–1. Behind the differences in perception implied by the figure lies another source of tension between the multinational enterprise and the state.

OPERATIONAL CHANGES

When an organization moves from a parochial view to a more global view of its operating arena, the relations between

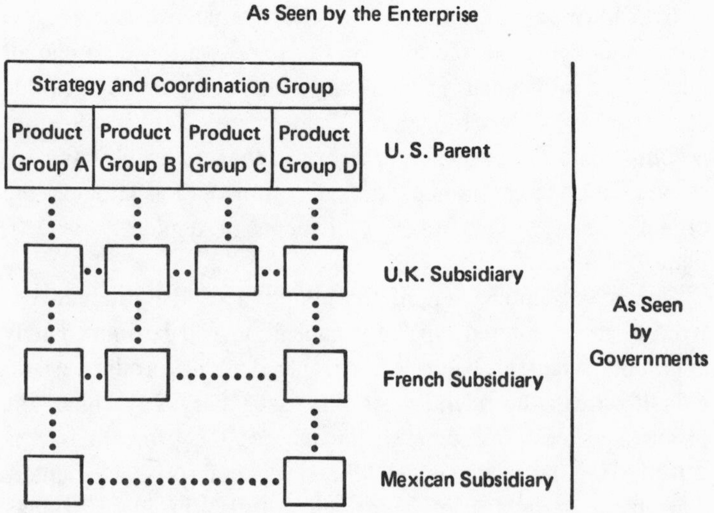

As Seen by the Enterprise

FIGURE 4-1
Alternatives Perceptions of a Product-centered U.S.-controlled Multinational Enterprise.

the center and the periphery of the organization are bound to undergo profound changes. But these changes are subtle and complex.

One major determinant of the direction of change in the exercise of authority is the starting condition of the parent and the subsidiary. Experienced parents with ongoing systems for the direction and control of their subsidiaries follow one pattern; inexperienced parents, uncertain and insecure concerning their ability to direct a foreign subsidiary, follow another. Subsidiaries that are being built anew from the ground up are exposed to changes of one sort; those that are being acquired as going businesses, to changes of another. Distinctions of a similar sort can be drawn between subsidiaries that are to be integrated tightly into a well-articulated global strategy and those that are expected to lead a semi-independent life.

Other books in this series will be exploring these distinctions in some detail. In the present context, the need is simply to get some sense of the general direction of these complex changes. One way of imparting that sense is to focus on the alteration in operating methods that appears to have occurred in one critical function, namely, finance.[9] The nature of this change has been sufficiently systematic to provide strong insights into the ways in which enterprises cope with other problems that accompany the multinationalizing process.

Upon setting up their first overseas subsidiaries, U.S. parent companies have generally been slow to respond to the fact that a new dimension was being added to their financial problems. Perhaps such enterprises have failed to recognize the fact that exchange-rate risks, interest-rate differences, and price-trend diversities among different countries would thenceforth offer both new threats and new opportunities. On the other hand, there may have been good reason for a slow and deliberate response: a recognition of the fact that a period of institutional learning would be useful before the appropriate organizational response became clear; or a realistic appraisal of the fact that, in view of the small starting scale of foreign operations, the cost of maintaining an adequate financial staff at headquarters to specialize in foreign problems would exceed any savings they were likely to generate.

In any event, newcomers to the multinational field have generally dealt with the problems of international financial policy on an ad hoc basis, often by default relegating them to the subsidiaries in the field. In such cases, for instance, the subsidiaries have decided how to raise short-term money and whether to hedge against foreign-exchange risk. To the extent that headquarters exerted control over the subsidiaries' financial activities, control was mainly exercised by screening and approving capital projects.

If this decentralized form of organization was adopted at first, the evidence suggests that it was eventually superseded by another stage in which much tighter controls from the center were the common rule. Of course, there usually had to be enough foreign business to justify setting up and maintaining a central financial staff. Moreover, some traumatic event was often needed to trigger the development, for example, the write-down of an investment, generated by a devaluation.[10] Trauma or not, a central staff concerned with international financial problems was generally created at some point. And the first disposition of such a staff was to hold a tight rein over the financial activities of the subsidiaries. At this stage, the headquarters staff was quite prepared to manage the cash flows of the entire multinational system: to decide when hedges against exchange rate changes were to be made, where borrowing and lending were to be done, when dividends were to be declared, and how idle cash was to be put to work.

A third phase has eventually appeared, however, as the foreign interests of the enterprise have continued to grow. In a seeming return to decentralized operations, the authority for many decisions has been delegated back to the subsidiaries or distributed to regional headquarters located in such centers as

Brussels, Bangkok, or Mexico City. Large capital expenditures might still be reserved for central decision, but for the rest, there was much more delegation of authority to the field.

The relatively relaxed rein that large, mature multinational enterprises seem to apply in their handling of the financial function stems from various factors. There appears to be some realization, growing out of experience, that the function can be overmanaged, generating more cost than benefit to the enterprise. This conclusion is suggested by a study of the hedging measures taken by twenty-five U.S.-controlled multinational enterprises with respect to their British subsidiaries during the 1967 sterling crisis. The study indicates that, as a rule, the mature and experienced firms took very limited and restrained action to protect their sterling positions against devaluation. Their asserted reasons for that restraint were various. One was a desire not to add to Great Britain's difficulties and to their own public relations problems by conspicuously burdening the British currency with their hedges. But another was the view that even the best of guesses regarding prospects of a currency devaluation was prone to major error and was therefore not worth the internal organizational effort.[11]

This vignette of the evolution of the finance function throws some new light on the evidence that has been collected in host countries regarding the style of the supervision by U.S. parents. One finding, reported by researchers in Britain, Canada, and New Zealand, is that the degree of U.S.-parent supervision tends to decline over time as the subsidiary gains experience.[12] The data are not without their ambiguities, but the underlying tendency does seem to exist.[13]

The evidence should not be interpreted to mean, however, that the subsidiaries of U.S. enterprises are free to conduct their own business strategies. All that it indicates is that in mature enterprises a seasoned financial corps comes into place, trained within the system of the enterprise and stationed at various key points in the field and at headquarters. This corps has generally been made up of men attuned to the signals and conditioned to the rules of thumb that the system has devised. The conditioning of the corps is fortified by internal manuals, the financial bibles of the organization, indicating the responses to be applied in various situations. Accordingly, U.S. parents tend more and more to supervise their subsidiaries according to the rule of Saint Augustine: Love God; then do what you like.[14] Enough conditioning, it is assumed, will breed the necessary conformity while allowing for local initiative and local adaptation. Supervision may be tightened up from time to time, especially if some gross error slips through the system's structure. But as a rule, discipline and coordination are maintained much more by common training and conditioning than by a stream of commands from the center. This style of control reduces the need for continuous consultation with the center and thus puts off the day when diseconomies of scale may drag the system down.

Home Country versus Host Country

What governments profess to be concerned about, however, is not the outlook of the management of multinational enterprises so much as the results that follow from that outlook. In assessing results, three kinds of questions repeatedly emerge: (1) How does the multinational enterprise distribute its functions geographically—especially such functions as production, exportation, and research? (2) How does the multinational enterprise distribute rewards between its subsidiaries, especially rewards that affect the level of local taxes? (3) How does the enterprise respond to governmental measurees aimed at increasing local benefits, such as requirements that the ownership of the subsidiary should be shared with local interests on a joint venture basis?

DISTRIBUTION OF FUNCTIONS

As the enterprise sees these issues, the distribution of functions among its subsidiaries depends more than anything else on the general strategy it is pursuing; highly integrated structures assign functions to the subsidiaries on one pattern, loosely structured enterprises, on another. Irrespective of the general strategy, however, there is a strong tendency for U.S. parents to surround their foreign subsidiaries with numerous formal restrictions, ostensibly confining their legal right to do business to specified geographical areas. An Australian study, referred to earlier, indicates that only 19 of 79 U.S.-controlled subsidiaries covered in its survey had freedom to export to any market, and a New Zealand study reports that only 57 out of the 115 foreign-owned subsidiaries with exportable product were actually free to export everywhere.[15]

The question of formal restrictions, however, is not to be confused with the question of how the subsidiary is actually used. When a parent expects to control its subsidiary effectively, formal restrictions are redundant; where they exist, the motivation is partly or wholly to ensure against the possibility that the parent may one day lose control of the subsidiary, through expropriation or otherwise. As long as control is secure, however, a rational parent will not hesitate to use the wholly owned subsidiary for any purpose—consistent or not consistent with the restrictions—provided that the use contributes to the strategy of the system as a whole.

This does not mean that a rational parent would be expected to make its decisions on a basis consistent with the achievement of the largest social gain for each host country. This, of course, would be impossible, if only because the social gain to one country may be the social loss to another. It does not even mean that the decisions of the parent will approximate those that would be taken according to globally conceived criteria of social gain; the gap between private gain and social gain can be fairly large, especially when an enterprise is prepared to go to some lengths to reduce its total tax burden.

How in fact have U.S.-controlled multinational enterprises made their decisions regarding the location of production facilities? The answer to that question has already been suggested in earlier chapters. Though the facts about the logistical use of subsidiaries by U.S.-controlled multinational enterprises are far from adequate, those that exist do suggest certain general tendencies. Early in the life of most manufacturing subsidiaries, both the parent and the host country typically envisage the main function of foreign-owned manufacturing subsidiaries as that of provisioning the local market. As a rule, the possibility of some wider use only occurs later, after the subsidiary has completed a period of learning and some measure of production scale has been attained. The possibility of wider use is more likely for enterprises whose strategy is consistent with the concept of international production and cross-hauling than for enterprises whose policies are built on national marketing and national product differentiation. For the latter, the differences in product characteristics, prices, and distribution channels between one national market and the next constitute a barrier to specialization and cross-hauling.[16] However, the likelihood of developing and exploiting opportunities for national specialization and cross-hauling has also depended partly on the alertness of the multinational enterprise to its opportunities, an alertness that has sometimes been stimulated by the pressures and threats of the host government.

The emphasis on the geographical neutrality of U.S.-controlled multinational enterprises can be exaggerated, of course. The fact that the leaders of these enterprises live in the United States unavoidably generates various geographical biases of a subtle sort. In complex locational decisions, the criteria are rarely very simple; but some reported decisions are consistent with the hypothesis that exciting work is kept close to home, where it can be more closely watched and managed. IBM's president has, for instance, been reported as having stopped the development of a small advanced scientific computer conceived by the company's London laboratory in favor of a model developed in the United States.[17] To be sure, a compact accounting system generated in the laboratories of IBM Deutschland was widely adopted by the company for European and overseas markets; but the Deutschland development was a cheap and efficient horse-and-buggy device with mundane applications, not a contribution to the growing edge of computer science.[18]

One illustration—a complex one at that—hardly makes a case. If corporate officials can be taken at their word, as they probably can, there has been a growing disposition on the part of the management of U.S.-controlled enterprise to move toward a state of geographical neutrality. As long as the headquarters of the enterprise is maintained in the United States, however, subtle locational influences of the sort described are bound to be applied.

DISTRIBUTION OF REWARDS

Host countries are concerned not only with the basic decisions of multinational enterprises in locating their production, research, and export facilities, but also with the internal operating rules that affect the distribution of costs and profits between the affiliate units of the enterprise. High on the list of their concerns is the question of transfer prices.

Here again, there is some initial tendency among host countries to assume that the managers of U.S.-controlled enterprises prefer to register the lowest possible profit in the host country and the highest possible profit in the United States. This assumption is widely held even though there is very little in the provisions of U.S. tax laws to encourage such a tendency. To the contrary, according to the general U.S. rule, the profits of U.S.-controlled foreign subsidiaries are not taxable under

U.S. law until they are remitted to the parent as dividends. At that time, the U.S. tax liability is calculated in such a way as to credit the enterprise with the income taxes previously paid on those profits to the host governments.* Tax considerations alone, therefore, offer no inducement to bringing profits to the United States.

There are some situations, in fact, in which tax considerations would lead U.S.-controlled enterprises to register their profits abroad to the greatest extent possible. For instance oil-producing companies would much prefer to have their profits recorded where the crude oil is produced. This is partly owing to the desire to generate the highest possible depletion allowance for U.S. tax purposes. But it is also owing to the oligopoly strategy of concentrating the profits at the stage most inaccessible to competitors, or, conversely, of discouraging competitors from entering the business at the point of easiest entry by keeping those activities unprofitable.

Various studies of the pricing practices of the automobile industry have, on the other hand, flushed up pricing patterns that could be said to understate the profits of the foreign assembly plants of U.S. enterprises. According to these studies, plants in the United States that produce components for assembly overseas have tended to charge the assembling subsidiary the full wholesale price for "completely knocked down" kits of components. This practice, by itself, has not generally been thought of as exploitative. But when any item has been deleted from a complete kit before shipment, such as a bumper or a headlight, the price of the kit has generally been reduced only by the marginal cost of the deleted item.[19] It has sometimes been remarked, not altogether facetiously, that on this pricing basis the cost of the shipping container, with all contents deleted, would generally exceed $1,000.

* There are some important exceptions to the rule, especially exceptions intended to discourage the use of foreign tax-haven companies. But these exceptions are of limited importance here.

Another well-documented case of this sort, covering imports into Colombia, indicates the same pricing bias for intermediate manufactured products shipped to the subsidiaries of
U.S.-controlled enterprises.[20] Despite various weaknesses in
the underlying data, a good basis exists for concluding that
producers of such diverse products as pharmaceuticals, consumer electrical equipment, and rubber tires were pricing their
intermediate products to their local Colombia subsidiaries at
levels well above any that would have been negotiated at arm's
length. On the other hand, the results of an Australian study
were more neutral. A survey covering pricing practices in affiliate sales to sixty-four foreign-owned subsidiaries in Australia
reported a wide range of practices, from marked overpricing to
pronounced underpricing.[21]

Multinational enterprises, therefore, transfer goods and services among affiliates at prices that are often at variance with
the results that independent buyers and sellers would reach.
But the cases so far uncovered do not create the basis for assuming that there is a systematic bias in favor of assigning the
largest profit to the parent. In the automobile illustration, the
practice of charging overseas subsidiaries high prices seems to
have been owing to internecine rivalry in the enterprise rather
than to some centralized strategy of the system.[22] The eagerness of the components export division to register the highest
possible level of profits and sales for itself even if the results
were mainly at the expense of a related subsidiary, appears to
have been the key factor. In the Colombia study, the existence
of a governmental ceiling on profit remissions by foreign subsidiaries from Colombia almost certainly affected the companies' decision on how to price intermediate products. The
Colombia data, therefore, may simply represent evidence of
the fact that when governments want to limit the level of profits
taken by multinational enterprises, they may succeed in affecting only the form in which the profits are taken and not their
size. This is a disconcerting conclusion for any host govern-

ment, but it is a conclusion that differs in its implications from the view that the profits generated by the subsidiary of a multinational enterprise tend to be awarded disproportionately to the parent.

THE JOINT VENTURE

Many host governments encourage foreign-owned multinational enterprises to share the ownership of their local subsidiaries with local interests, in the apparent hope that the benefits for the economy will be increased by such a sharing.

The economic wisdom of that decision is far from self-evident. Unless the local equity interest is given away by the foreigner as a gift, the local economy must pay for it in some way. Then the question to be asked is whether the payment could not have been better used for some other purpose in the local economy, especially if the foreigner was ready and willing to launch the local subsidiary on his own.[23]

Governments often take the view, however, that the existence of a local partner affects the style in which a subsidiary is used, with results that benefit the local economy. What does the evidence suggest on this point? The main point to be made is one that has emerged often in the discussion so far: Style depends overwhelmingly on strategy, and different strategies generate different responses on the part of multinational enterprises.

As a general rule, U.S. parents have clearly preferred to own their subsidiaries in unambiguous and unchallengeable form. In 1967, as one can see from Table 4–5, foreign subsidiaries that were wholly owned by U.S. parents were more common than those in which the U.S. enterprises had less than total ownership.* There were some countries for which the proportion of wholly owned subsidiaries was especially high, such as Canada with 85 percent, and some countries where

---

* "Wholly owned" in this context means ownership of 95 percent or more of the subsidiary's equity by the subsidiary's immediate parents in the system.

TABLE 4-5
Number of Foreign Subsidiaries of 187 U.S.-controlled Multinational Enterprises, Classified by Degree of System Ownership, 1967

AREA	BY DEGREE OF SYSTEM OWNERSHIP[a]				
	WHOLLY OWNED	MAJOR-ITY OWNED	MINOR-ITY OWNED	UN-KNOWN	TOTAL SUBSIDI-ARIES
All foreign areas	5,143	1,457	660	667	7,927
Canada	817	101	44	86	1,048
Latin America	1,195	365	197	167	1,924
Mexico	230	79	61	42	412
Argentina	115	36	20	16	187
Brazil	173	48	16	30	267
Europe and United Kingdom	2,221	651	227	302	3,401
European Community	1,025	351	137	162	1,675
France	256	133	62	42	493
Germany	293	84	26	53	456
Italy	188	70	19	33	310
EFTA	1,037	196	53	119	1,405
United Kingdom	554	129	38	79	800
Other Europe	159	104	37	21	321
Southern dominions	460	113	37	38	648
Asia and other Africa	450	227	155	74	906
Japan	72	71	65	25	233
India	29	23	28	6	86
Black Africa	112	28	20	6	166

[a]"Wholly owned" means that the subsidiary's parents in the system hold 95 percent or more of the voting stock; "majority owned," 50-94 percent; "minority owned," 5-49 percent.

Source: J. W. Vaupel and J. P. Curhan, *The Making of Multinational Enterprise* (Boston: Harvard Business School, 1969), chap. 3.

it was low, such as Japan and India with 35 and 36 percent respectively. Country differences of this sort were usually owing in part to differences in national policies. However, even if the nations that insisted on joint ventures are set to one side, considerable variations in practice remained. These variations, however, were not idiosyncratic or haphazard. Some kinds of firms and some types of industries were associated with a higher incidence of foreign partnerships than others.

Earlier, I pointed out that the breadth of the product line affected the choice of organizational structure. The same factor seemed to affect the propensity to enter into joint ventures. Organizations with broad product lines have a substantially higher proportion of joint ventures among their overseas manufacturing subsidiaries than those with narrow product lines. That tendency is illustrated by the U.S.-controlled multinational enterprises covered in earlier tables. During 1966, thirteen of these enterprises included all their overseas manufactures within a single industry—"industry," in this instance, being defined as an SIC three-digit category. Of the subsidiaries contained in these enterprises which could be classified according to ownership patterns, only 17.3 percent were joint ventures. For the forty-two multinational enterprises whose overseas manufactures fell in two industries, however, the incidence of joint ventures in manufacturing subsidiaries rose to 24.8 percent; and for the eighty-one enterprises in three industries, the figure rose further to 32.3 percent.

Apparently, enterprises with broad product lines appear to feel less need to maintain a careful uniformity from country to country in all the aspects of production and marketing.[24] Because these enterprises are under less compulsion in this regard they see relatively few difficulties in sharing management with local interests. On the other hand, organizations with narrow product lines, which base their strategies heavily on the performance qualities of a limited range of products, have understandably shown a strong preference for controlling their subsidiaries from the ground up. Such enterprises foresee a stream of day-to-day decisions involving the conflicting interests of more than one subsidiary: the maintenance of quality and uniformity, the allocation of markets, the determination of intersubsidiary prices, the allocation of products, and so on. Multinational enterprises organized on this kind of strategy, therefore, have difficulty in accommodating diverse interests in different subsidiaries. Accordingly, these enterprises have generally tried to avoid joint ventures.

Even when the product line was narrow, however, multinational enterprises were sometimes prepared to accept—even to welcome—local joint ventures, provided the bargaining position of the local partner was sharply limited. The large international oil companies have not had much difficulty with the joint ownership of chains of gasoline stations, given the dependence of these chains on the use of strong international brand names. Jointly owned refineries have generally been harder for the oil companies to accept, but they have nonetheless often been accepted *faute de mieux,* if the arrangement was the only way in which the enterprise could protect a position in a national market.

When multinational enterprises have settled for a joint venture, the evidence suggests that there are some characteristic ways in which the choice has influenced their style of management. In general, the arm's length element has been more evident in the relations between parents and joint-venture subsidiaries than between parents and wholly owned subsidiaries. The leading studies on the subject indicate, for instance, that wholly owned subsidiaries have needed U.S. parent approval and have felt the parental influence on key management questions to a greater extent than have joint ventures.[25]

The fact that joint ventures are more frequently dealt with at arm's length did not, however, reveal very much about the effects on host country interests. In general, parents are prepared to make special demands on wholly owned subsidiaries, but they are also prepared to bestow special benefits, according to the needs of the system. In sum, parents do not seem to be able or willing to impose quite the same demands or to bestow quite the same benefits on joint ventures.

In operating terms, what do these generalizations mean? One difference lies in the policies of the parent during the start-up years of the subsidiary. Occasionally, one observes quite permissive headquarters policies toward wholly owned subsidiaries during the early years: Special services are provided without cost; royalty fees are forgiven; profit remissions are postponed.[26] On the other hand, the right to call on subsidiaries in moments of need, in order to draw off cash, to reshuffle markets, and so on, is probably exercised with fewer inhibitions with regard to wholly owned subsidiaries than with regard to joint ventures.

Systematic comparisons between joint ventures and wholly owned subsidiaries suggest that, from the viewpoint of host countries, wholly owned subsidiaries may be a slightly more attractive bargain.* Some studies indicate that dividend payments in relation to profits were lower for the wholly owned foreign subsidiaries than for the joint venture subsidiaries of U.S. parents.[27] Wholly owned subsidiaries drew their imported materials and equipment from their U.S. parents to a greater extent than did joint ventures, but the reliance on imported inputs relative to total needs was not distinguishably different for the two groups.[28] As for formal restrictions on the right of subsidiaries to export, these seemed to be somewhat more extensively applied to the joint-venture subsidiaries than to the wholly owned subsidiaries, a not very surprising result.[29]

The conclusion suggested by these sketchy statistics will be encountered more than once in the pages ahead. In cold and narrow economic terms, there is no a priori basis for assuming that a greater measure of local control is associated with policies that yield a higher level of benefit for the host country; the opposite could well be the case. But the introduction of control as an end in itself changes the calculus of benefit and

* An extremely informative source on this subject and on other practices of foreign parents toward subsidiaries is M. Z. Brooke and H. L. Remmers, *The Strategy of the Multinational Enterprise* (London: Longman, 1971). Though the book was published too late for systematic inclusion of its results in this chapter, the results are generally consistent with our findings.

cost to a degree that depends on the perceived value of the control.

The Men of the Enterprise

Underlying the expectations of governments with regard to the behavior of multinational enterprises is the assumption that, in the crunch, U.S. nationals will favor the United States; Frenchmen, France; and Kenyans, their own native soil. The assumptions are, as usual, simpler than the facts. Sometimes, nationality does matter. More often, it produces results that are unrelated to national interests or that are altogether irrelevant.

Consider, first, the nationality of the stockholders of the U.S. parent companies. The stock ownership of parent firms of U.S.-controlled multinational enterprises is overwhelmingly in the hands of U.S. nationals. Only a very few of the outstanding shares of the parent firm—something on the order of 2 or 3 percent—are owned by foreigners.[30] This concentration of ownership in U.S. hands is not by choice of the managers of these enterprises. Few have explicitly considered the question, but there have been occasional conscious efforts to increase the ownership of foreigners in large U.S. companies. Now and then, in fact, U.S. corporate leaders have painted an image of an international peoples' capitalism, in which the equity in all the great enterprises of the world would be "owned" by investors located everywhere.[31] As Berle and Means observed nearly forty years ago, however, the possession of stock in publicly held enterprises has long since ceased to carry the traditional connotations of ownership. It is doubtful whether the management of any large U.S. firm would be much affected if it suddenly learned that 6 or 7 percent of its stock was registered in foreign names. Business leaders are no doubt sincere when they react warmly to the possibility of more foreign ownership in the parent company. At the same time, however, such proposals come all the easier from management because there is little expectation that their implementation would actually have much impact on management practices.

If nationality has much to do with corporate policy, it is the nationality of the governing board and the topmost echelons of management that matters, not that of the minority stockholders. All but a trivial fraction of the governing boards and officers of the U.S. parents are U.S. nationals. Even if executives uprooted from abroad and transferred to the United States are included among the foreigners, the total is still miniscule. Here and there one finds a few well-advertised exceptions to the general pattern; a survey of 1,029 directors conducted in the course of this study, for instance, turned up nineteen foreigners in the group, of whom fourteen were Canadian or British.[32] The probability is high that these exceptions will be more common in the future. For the present, however, U.S.-controlled multinational enterprises are governed and controlled primarily by U.S. nationals.

The tendency for U.S. nationals to predominate in U.S. parent companies could hardly be otherwise. As long as the parent company is located on U.S. soil and derives its juridical personality from the United States, the incentive to recruit U.S. nationals for the top echelons will be overwhelming. Yet there is ample evidence that, self-consciously or otherwise, many of these multinational enterprises would like to think of themselves as global in outlook and global in scope. "The world is our oyster" is a common house slogan. There are numerous in-house training programs aimed at suppressing a conditioned propensity on the part of U.S. headquarters personnel to think in ethnocentric or geographically nearsighted terms. (There are even more extensive and more ambitious programs designed for U.S. nationals to be stationed in foreign subsidiaries.) For the present, these globalizing activities are sometimes self-conscious and rudimentary, but they are not to be dismissed as inconsequential.

The motivations of U.S.-controlled enterprises in sponsoring these programs of global acculturation are, as a rule, quite pragmatic. A multinational enterprise requires a staff that can appraise the opportunities and risks as effectively in foreign environments as in the U.S. environment. The capacity to evaluate risk is especially important because in most countries the intrusion of powerful outsiders controlled from the United States unavoidably generates uncertainties.

When the multinational enterprise is bent on pushing outward into unconquered territories, the "world is our oyster" theme tends to dominate inside the organization. But when the object is to avoid being conspicuous in some national environment that appears threatening, the relevant ideology is "when in Rome do as the Romans do." Reconciling the two approaches is not always easy. Hard questions arise, as when choosing between two countries in which to place a new production facility, or between two currencies in which to store a pool of funds.

Still, the insistence on the two themes, all at once and together, is generally neither cynical nor disingenuous. Perhaps what reconciles the two messages in the collective mind of the multinational enterprise staff, if reconciliation is needed, is the conviction that the interplay between the enterprise and the countries in which it operates is not zero sum: one side's gain is not inevitably the other side's loss. Whereas the political philosophers of host countries often proceed from the assumption that when the enterprise gains the country loses, the ruling assumption in the multinational enterprise is that all parties gain from its operations. On this assumption, the fundamental contradiction between a global and a national view can be reduced to tolerable proportions.

The brunt of reconciling daily the conflicting interests of the global and the national view falls on the shoulders of expatriate U.S. executives in the field. Thus far, there have been only a few serious surveys of the characteristics of the expatriate executive.[33] What they suggest is that the popular caricature —a relative incompetent, shunted off by a benign headquarters to an obscure sinecure—has little to do with the facts. That portrait, no doubt, has its occasional counterpart in real life. But as a rule the U.S. expatriate executive emerges as an individual whose educational achievement is high by any standard: significantly higher than that of U.S. executives at home; higher than that of expatriates from other countries employed overseas in the same U.S.-controlled subsidiaries; and not much different from that achieved by U.S. government executives. The careers of the U.S. expatriates typically show a satisfactory rate of progression by comparison with other types of executives; if there is any difference in pattern, it consists of a tendency on the part of the expatriates not to shift their firm affiliations as often as their domestic counterparts.*

When confronted with a conflict between the interests of the multinational enterprise as a whole and the interests of his group—his product division, his regional division, or his subsidiary—the U.S. expatriate can generally be counted on to give battle in favor of his group; in such a case, his career interests are often so strongly identified with the group that he is prepared to ignore the question of conflict.[34] When the attachment is to the subsidiary, the syndrome is philosophically accepted by the head office as "going native." One old Japan hand, commenting on the experience of the typical American manager in Japan, says: "He is very likely to decide that the

---

* One study, covering the situation in Brazil and Mexico as surveyed during the late 1950s, offers a less flattering vignette; see J. C. Shearer, *High-Level Manpower in Overseas Subsidiaries* (Princeton: Princeton University Press, 1960). Various studies of the Maxwell School of Syracuse University at about the same time also were critical. But the main concern of these more critical sources is that the Americans are culturally undereducated and relatively costly. Because American executives tend to have more specialized and more vocational educations than their non-American colleagues, there may be some basis for the cultural concern.

home office is too concerned with company politics to have a proper perspective on Japan. They are demons or fools, he decides. . . ."[35]

The local national who helps direct the affairs of the local subsidiary of a multinational enterprise, however, generally has an even more difficult problem in managing his problems of conflicting loyalties. Despite his local nationality, his identification with the multinational enterprise may be fairly strong. After all, the personnel policies of most of these enterprises favor the recruitment and installation as rapidly as possible of managers of local origin.[36]

Policies in this case are buttressed by performance. A survey of U.S.-owned subsidiaries in Brazil, covering the years 1950 to 1970, shows a steady rise in the proportion of firms that were raising their Brazilian manager contingent. By 1970, 64 percent of the 450 management positions were held by Brazilians.[37] A Canadian study, done as early as 1959, shows that in 217 U.S.-controlled subsidiaries about 340 of the top 800 officers were Canadians.[38] A careful Australian study for 1962, though failing to generate exactly comparable data, found that 63 out of 105 U.S.-controlled subsidiaries in Australia had no American officers at all, and 17 had only one American employed in Australia.[39]

The prominence of local managers in U.S.-controlled subsidiaries is now in evidence practically everywhere. According to preliminary data from a 1966 census of U.S.-controlled subsidiaries in Latin America, about 10,800 of the 11,700 "managerial" personnel of these enterprises were local employees.[40] The skeptical are entitled to ask just what "managerial" means in this context. The evidence is that the term does in fact have a quite selective meaning, in that only slightly more than 3 percent of the 355,000 employees of these enterprises were in the managerial category.

The identification of local nationals with their employers in multinational enterprise can run fairly deep. There are anecdotes (perhaps aprocryphal) that suggest the depth of that identification. According to one tale, the victorious leader of a company of Nazi tanks, whose peacetime job had been the direction of the National Cash Register subsidiary in Berlin, marked his entry into Paris by pledging his unbounded cooperation to the crushed and defeated French manager of the Paris office of the company.[41]

When the conflict between the interests of the multinational enterprise and those of the local economy is apparent and overt, the personal toll on the local executive in the national subsidiary is sometimes quite high. Occasionally, one can glimpse the conflict as the local executive maneuvers between the apparent interests of his country and those of his foreign-owned firm. Like the U.S. national "gone native," the local manager tries to steer a course between these interests.[42] If a local national is lucky, however, the issue of conflict need not arise in any acute form during his working life. Besides, when it does, an alert and protective subconscious can readily fend it off by reshaping the issue in a way that suppresses the element of conflict.[43]

In sum, a set of simple assumptions gives way to a set of muddy facts. U.S. nationals in a multinational enterprise cannot be counted on unequivocally to serve the interests of the U.S. parent or the U.S. economy. Local nationals cannot be counted on for unalloyed partiality to their own home territory. The principal factor in determining the impact of the multinational enterprise on the economy of a given country is the underlying strategy of the enterprise. This strategy may have some geographical bias, but the bias is based less on a political or emotional attachment than on an assessment of risk or the existence of ignorance. "The world is my oyster" has a certain validity as a generalization of outlook, even though imperfectly and self-consciously put in practice. However, what the application of that attitude means in terms of national economic consequences is quite another question.

[5]

National Economic Consequences

NATIONAL policies toward multinational enterprises have been determined by many considerations—social, economic, psychological, and political. Concentrating on economic effects alone at this point seems to assign undue importance to one facet of the problem. Chapter 6, however, is dedicated to restoring the balance.

For fifty years or more, economists have speculated on how the economic benefits from the operations of foreign subsidiaries are distributed among "borrowing" and "lending" countries. They have never had much doubt that the operations generated advantages for one country or the other. The question has been for whom and how much. The evidence on questions of this sort has been elusive and complex, and the basis for a hard set of economic conclusions has been slow to develop. Despite the problems of measurement and analysis, however, some generalizations on the national economic effects of the multinational enterprise are beginning to emerge.

The Direct Investment Process

To assess the economic consequences of foreign direct investment, one has to know something about the nature of the resource transfer involved. The question is commonly bypassed with a simple assumption, namely, that the resource transfer can be measured as if it were a portfolio investment, that is, by the financial capital involved. The temptation to think in these terms is strong and is reflected in the fact that foreign direct investment has generally been treated in the economic literature as a slightly aberrant outgrowth of indirect foreign investment.[1] The explicit recognition of this inadequacy, so obvious from the descriptions in earlier chapters, has only belatedly begun to trickle into the mainstream of economic analysis.[2]

THE SUBSIDIARY AS TRANSFEREE

As earlier chapters suggested, the establishment of a foreign subsidiary by a U.S. parent has generally represented a strategic response to some opportunity or threat. As part of the response, parents have endowed their subsidiaries with a number of different kinds of resources and rights. If the foreign subsidiary was to be engaged in raw material extraction for export, then its dowry from the parent usually consisted of a sum of money and a cadre of managers and technicians. In addition, it acquired access to various facilities: to the parent's store of technical skills for digging mines or drilling wells; to the parent's organizational apparatus for searching out the added knowledge or resources required by the subsidiary; and to the markets provided by the parent's downstream refining or fabricating facilities. If the subsidiary was established in order to engage in manufacturing, either for the local market or for export, the list of resources and facilities provided by the parent was slightly altered, to reflect the difference in the mission of such subsidiaries.

In many cases, U.S. parents acquired overseas subsidiaries by buying out existing local enterprises rather than by building new organizations. In these cases, the resources that were transferred generally went partly to the subsidiary, partly to the former owner. Whereas the subsidiary acquired access to working capital or to the technical skills of the parent organization, the former owners generally acquired new assets in the form of cash or securities. In cases of this sort, therefore, the measurement of national impact depended partly on what the former owners did as a result of the change in their wealth and status. But the results of the transfer still had to be judged by its effects on organizations and men; the portfolio investment analogy was not very apt.

Although this description avoids the distortion of looking on the investment in a subsidiary as if it were the simple equivalent of a capital transfer, the description needs qualifications of other sorts before it can be said to correspond to reality. There is a certain danger, for instance, in characterizing the subsidiary as though it were an integral economic unit —a unit that received a set of resources, facilities, and rights that were given up by the parent. A subsidiary is not necessarily a meaningful unit in strategic business terms.[3] Some subsidiaries earn their way in a multinational system simply because they are responsible for a learning process from which the system as a whole hopes eventually to profit; a Mexican subsidiary may, for instance, be used as a staging area for eventual expansion into other countries in Latin America. Other subsidiaries may be responsible for a data-accumulating process intended to protect the system from risk, as would be the case with a subsidiary engaged in exploring for new sources of raw material. Some subsidiaries exist to reduce the system's total tax burden, others because they increase the protective coloration of the system's presence in an area.

Because the subsidiary may be an instrument for only a fragment of a multinational strategy, there is no a priori reason to relate the capital flow from parent to subsidiary with the subsequent profit of the subsidiary. The earnings of the subsidiary may be generated by resources that were never tangibly moved into the country where the subsidiary is located; this would be the case, for instance, if a subsidiary were drawing heavily on the work of a research laboratory located in another country. Contrariwise, the resources physically in the country may generate profits that are in part assigned—appropriately assigned—to other members of the multinational system, as is so often the case with subsidiaries engaged in assembly or in distribution. The capital that is nominally in the subsidiary's control may, therefore, have less than a perfect relation to what is labeled the subsidiary's profit.

One might suppose, in the abstract, that this intricate jumble of resources and profits could be properly allocated among the affiliates of the multinational enterprise by an appropriate system of transfer prices. It is true that some elements of the relationship might well be handled in this way. Some products and services can be priced objectively because they have an open market. But many of the products and services passing between parent and subsidiary do not. In this case, wherever there is joint product from any production process or wherever there is fixed cost from which several different entities benefit, the ancient and insoluble struggle over cost allocation rears its head, generating an unavoidably arbitrary response. How much, for instance, should ITT's Argentine subsidiary be charged for access to the laboratories of ITT's German affiliate, for the guarantee of its parent when borrowing from a local bank, or for the right to use the company trademark on its locally produced goods? Since subsidiaries commonly share with their affiliates throughout the world such advantages as trade names, market access, financial guarantees, research results, and similar intangibles, this issue is more than merely academic.

All this is familiar stuff. Yet its implications can easily be overlooked. The businessman who directs the strategy of a multinational enterprise, if he behaves like an economic man, gauges the subsidiary's performance by its marginal contribution to the total system, wherever that benefit may nominally appear in the system. The economist measuring social yield, if he is faithful to his discipline, will look for the marginal impact of the entire multinational system on the country in which the subsidiary is located.[4] Therefore, the yield generated by the operations of such a subsidiary cannot be calculated by reference to the accounts of the subsidiary alone; neither the capital nominally involved nor the profit nominally generated by a subsidiary need have much to do with these yields.

THE SUBSIDIARY AS RESOURCE MOBILIZER

The creation of a foreign-owned subsidiary is the signal not only for a transfer of resources across international boundaries but also—and more important—for the regroupment of resources within the local economy. When a U.S.-controlled multinational enterprise establishes a subsidiary in a foreign country, the resource-mobilizing repercussions of the decision extend quite widely. One wave of consequences can usually be seen in the mobilizing of some added local funds and local labor. These are acquired either by diverting them from other local purposes or by rescuing them from idleness. Once acquired, the local resources are put to work alongside the imported capital and labor.

By the late 1960s, according to the figures offered in Chapter 1, U.S. parent enterprises had managed to acquire control over foreign manufacturing and extraction subsidiaries whose assets were on the order of $110 billion. (Of that total, the foreign subsidiaries of the 187 U.S.-controlled multinational enterprises probably accounted for more than $80 billion.) These assets had been mobilized from several different sources. Some of the assets, including cash, machinery, and trade names, had been acquired from the U.S. parent. Just how much came from that source, however, cannot be stated with precision; a proper evaluation of these items poses all sorts of questions, such as the reasonableness of the evaluation and even the definition of "assets." For individual subsidiaries— perhaps also for individual countries—these questions of valuation could be quite significant. For crude aggregative purposes, however, they are of secondary significance. Setting definitional and data questions aside, a rough guess at the proportion of assets acquired by the subsidiary from the U.S. parent's allocation of resources and rights yields a figure on the order of 25 percent.[5]

The rest of the assets of the U.S.-controlled foreign subsidiaries came from funds generated outside the United States: through profits earned in the foreign subsidiary itself and ploughed back into the business;* through profits transferred to the subsidiaries from other foreign countries; and through sums raised from banks and capital markets outside the United States. Here again, one can only guess as to relative magnitudes. Perhaps 30 percent of the assets were acquired through funds generated by the subsidiary itself, whereas the balance, 45 percent, was acquired from other foreign sources, mostly in the form of debt.[6]

Apart from the mobilization of funds, there was also the mobilization of labor. U.S.-controlled foreign subsidiaries engaged in manufacturing and extraction employed about 49,000 Americans in 1966, but they also employed some 5.5 million local workers.[7]

As going organizations, however, the local subsidiaries of multinational enterprises are something different from the sum of the capital and labor employed in them. Any multinational

---

* One could, of course, count the funds generated by the subsidiary as if they came from U.S. resources, at least to the extent that they did not include any element of economic rent or monopoly profit drawn out of the host country. Rent in its various forms, however, should be thought of as coming from the local economy itself.

organization is likely to endow its constituent parts with the special economies, or to burden them with the special diseconomies, that go with being part of a larger organization. The problem, therefore, becomes one of measuring not merely the consequences of a simple transfer of resources but also the effects of combining these resources with others, and then operating the new mélange as an appendage of a much larger multinational system.

THE FORM OF THE QUESTION

Before the effects of U.S.-controlled direct investments on host countries can be weighed, one other kind of issue has to be confronted. Effects, as has so often been noted, can only be measured by comparing a state of being with some explicit alternative. In this case, to measure the effects of the U.S. investment one has to assume what would have happened in the countries concerned if the U.S.-controlled subsidiaries had not been created. Should it be assumed, for instance, that the local economy would have acquired equivalent foreign resources—principally capital, human skills, and access to markets—on some other basis? If so, on what basis? And what assumptions should be made about the alternative uses of the local resources mobilized by the U.S.-controlled subsidiary?

Lest queries of this sort be regarded as diversionary and captious, the reader is warned that past efforts to measure the effects of foreign direct investment have demonstrated—if nothing else—that the results are quite sensitive to assumptions of this sort. It matters very much, for instance, whether other countries would have found the means for creating the enterprises concerned if U.S. parent companies had not done so. It matters also whether the internal demand patterns of such countries can be taken as invariant or whether they are affected by the existence of a U.S.-controlled subsidiary in the country. Finally, there is the important question of national productivity in the countries involved: How different would that have been if the foreign-owned subsidiaries had not existed?

The significance of the last paragraph is much greater than the space it occupies. Each query, each alternative, opens up major avenues of speculation and raises the possibility of widely different estimates of the effect of U.S. foreign direct investment. In the studies done so far, it has not been possible to deal squarely with all these issues. Some issues have been passed by, their importance unrecognized by the analysts involved. Some have been dispensed with by the ancient formula of *ceteris paribus*. Some have been dealt with intuitively or qualitatively, simply because there was no other way. Most studies have therefore been vulnerable and incomplete. All together, however, they have pointed quite consistently to certain plausible conclusions.

The Advanced Economies

Allowing for variations in nuance and emphasis, the general view is that U.S. direct investment has on balance been helpful in the growth of the economies of the advanced countries receiving that investment. On the whole, however, questions of welfare have drawn more equivocal judgments than those of growth; guesses about long-run effects have been less favorable than those about short; and projections of the future, more critical than descriptions of the past. Several different elements have contributed to these gross generalizations.

THE RESOURCE TRANSFER

The prevailing judgment, as suggested earlier, is that in the process of creating and operating U.S.-controlled subsidiaries in the advanced countries, substantial resources have generally been transferred, adding to the supply of productive facilities in the host country.

In the case of Canada, where national growth is usually seen as constrained by a lack of domestic savings and a paucity of well-trained manpower, the main contribution of U.S.-controlled subsidiaries is thought to have been the additions to the national supply of these two factors.[8] A typical formulation of the ruling consensus is the following:

> Few would dispute the contribution and value of United States capital with respect to all the exploitation of Canada's vast natural resources, the employment opportunities for the growing Canadian labor force, and the development of the nation's economy at a more profitable and rapid rate than would otherwise be possible.[9]

There is a striking sameness in the conclusions of studies coming from other advanced countries. Some of the evidence comes from individual industry analyses, many of which have already been referred to in earlier chapters. Other indications come from broader surveys, especially those relating to Britain, Germany, and Australia. The few that have been done on Great Britain conclude, without apparent dissent, that U.S.-controlled subsidiaries in that country have been a major source of research and expertise for the economy and for the training of local personnel.[10] The Australian studies conclude that U.S.-controlled subsidiaries are the conduit of a superior technology, which is not confined to the subsidiaries themselves but is transmitted to suppliers and users of the output as well.[11] Similar inferences are drawn for Europe as a whole, based on measures that are more roundabout.[12]

Granting the existence of benefits for the recipient countries, some studies have also been concerned to assess the costs. In the advanced countries, unlike the less-developed areas, there has been a general disposition to assume that the benefits, at least as defined in narrow economic terms, exceeded the costs by some satisfactory margin. The return on investment to U.S.

parents indicated by the published data provides very little suggestion of exploitation. The apparent earnings on investment, on the order of 12 percent before U.S. taxes, are on the modest side as compared with the norms and expectations of Europe and the Commonwealth.* The fact that subsidiaries in a tight-knit multinational enterprise may have no meaningful yield on investment has not often intruded itself into the commentary. Even if it did, there would be no reason to suppose that the relevant data would suggest a grossly exploitative process.

Though studies in host countries have rarely questioned whether the benefits from U.S.-controlled subsidiaries have exceeded the costs, they have often considered the closely related question whether the benefits could be increased or the costs reduced by a change in public policy. In Canada, for instance, the question has repeatedly been raised as to whether changes in domestic policies, especially policies that generated higher internal saving rates and better educational facilities, would produce the needed capital and technology at lower cost. In New Zealand, concern has concentrated on the inadequacy of governmental criteria in granting protection and subsidies to industry. In France, the emphasis is on the need for greater national scientific effort, especially in fields that seem immediately related to industrial innovation. All over Europe there is an assumption that business schools on the American model will produce some of the needed indigenous expertise at reduced social cost.[13]

Japan's striking success in mobilizing capital and technology without giving up much equity has occasionally led the advanced countries to consider other departures in policy. Could, for instance, the benefits of foreign direct investment be made to exceed the costs by a larger margin if host governments

---

* Published statements in Europe and the Commonwealth often display lower profit levels, but the understatement of profits is common for enterprises in these areas.

insisted on local equity participation? Could the needed technology be obtained on better terms by licensing than by direct investment? Could access to foreign markets be increased if the ties between U.S.-controlled subsidiaries and their parents were dissolved?

As long as analysts in the advanced countries have weighed these questions in narrow economic terms, they have only rarely concluded that the host country could increase its net benefits by limiting the participation of the U.S.-controlled enterprises; the contrary conclusion has been much more common. The latter conclusion has generally been based on two rather obvious considerations: first, that fewer resources would be transferred into the economy if the arrangement were a joint venture or a licensing contract instead of a wholly owned subsidiary; second, that the direct and indirect payments and commitments to the foreign investor for the use of the foreign resources that were commanded by the wholly owned subsidiary seemed no less favorable in economic terms than the payments and commitments for the use of resources acquired through joint ventures.[14] The exploration of queries such as these has, however, generally led to the more general question: How efficiently do the U.S.-controlled subsidiaries make use of their resources, including the local labor and capital that are at their disposal?

EFFICIENCY IN RESOURCE USE

If technology and organization are largely what the U.S.-controlled subsidiaries bring as their special contribution to the economies of the advanced countries, then the evidence of that contribution ought to be found in the levels of efficiency with which these subsidiaries put their resources to work. Studies directed at this question have generally confronted extraordinarily difficult problems of measurement.[15] But after recognizing the difficulties, the authors who were prepared to take the leap have characteristically concluded, in appropriately guarded formulations, that the activities of U.S.-controlled subsidiaries probably raised the productivity of local resources.[16]

Many studies have, however, assumed that special national benefits were generated by certain kinds of activity. Research activities, for instance, are rated high, presumably on the assumption that the fruits of the knowledge and training that go with such activities are not fully captured by the subsidiary itself and are left in part with the labor force as a national dividend. On the research criterion, U.S. subsidiaries score fairly well. In Canada, for instance, U.S.-controlled subsidiaries did more research in relation to sales than their Canadian counterparts—though not so much research relative to sales as their parents in the United States.[17] In countries such as the United Kingdom, Germany, and Australia, one can only infer that this is the case; but the inference is reasonably strong. Elsewhere, there is no factual basis for a judgment, weak or otherwise.

Another activity on which these countries place a premium is that of the generation of exports. This is an emphasis found in studies covering practically all the advanced countries for which serious studies have been made. In the case of such countries as France, Australia, and Great Britain, the emphasis is understandable in view of the sporadic balance-of-payments crises that their economies have experienced. As a result the relatively heavy participation by U.S. subsidiaries in the export of manufactured products tends to be given rather high marks.[18] The judgment on this score is, however, rarely unequivocal. Most studies point out that the ties between U.S.-controlled subsidiaries and their affiliates in other countries have conflicting effects; that the ties to such affiliates sometimes provide an easy conduit to sales in other countries, while the parceling out of markets among affiliates sometimes creates an insurmountable block to exports. But the judgment regarding the net effect has generally been on the positive side.[19]

BALANCE-OF-PAYMENTS EFFECTS

The interest of analysts in the balance-of-payments impact of foreign-owned subsidiaries on the advanced economies has pushed them beyond the export question to every other aspect of the subsidiaries' operations: to capital flows, profit remissions, and so on. On the whole, however, it has begun to appear that the main balance-of-payments impact lies in the trade accounts of the host country—that is, in its imports and exports. Because of the orders of magnitude involved, even a modest impact on the import substitution process and on the export promotion process can readily swamp those balance-of-payments effects that are recorded by way of profit remissions.* Later on, in the context of the less-developed areas, the question will be explored whether the remissions accounts adequately reflect the U.S. parents' full income from their subsidiaries. This is an issue, however, that is much less important in the advanced country context.

The upshot is that the few comprehensive efforts at measuring the balance-of-payments effects of the U.S.-controlled subsidiaries in the economies of advanced countries have generated estimates that are overwhelmingly dependent on the underlying assumption with regard to import substitution. When the analyst assumes that the products involved would shortly have been produced within the host countries in any case, whether or not the U.S.-owned subsidiary had gone into production, then the balance-of-payments effect of the U.S. controlled investment turns out to be trivial; but when the assumption is that the goods produced by the subsidiary dis-

---

* The 1968 sales of U.S.-controlled manufacturing subsidiaries in the advanced countries amounted to about $44 billion, whereas the recorded profit remissions amounted to only $1 billion. The imports induced by changes in the income levels associated with such investment also turned out to be of an order of magnitude larger than the likely balance-of-payments effects generated by way of the remissions accounts.

place U.S. exports that would otherwise have occurred, then subsidiary operations are seen as making a net contribution to the payments position of the country receiving the investment.

Illustrative of such studies is an analysis commissioned by the U.S. Treasury Department during the mid-1960s.[20] Though the study was undertaken from the viewpoint of the United States as a capital exporter, the results offer some glimpses of the nature of the impact on the investment-receiving countries. And though based on the state of the world as it existed during the early 1960s, some elements of the analysis seem valid enough for later years. The figures in Table 5–1 indicate some of the main results of the U.S. Treasury analysis as they relate to the advanced countries.

Note that Table 5–1 offers two sets of estimates built on two different models. The critical difference between the models is this: Model A (the free choice model) assumes that if the U.S. enterprise had not made the investment in its subsidiary in the host country, the U.S. enterprise would have supplied its market in the area from its U.S. facilities;* model B is based on the assumption that the U.S. investor's decision to invest abroad is defensive, that is, that it displaces or aborts investment from a local source that would have generated an equal amount of production of the same product.

As far as Canada is concerned, Table 5–1 purports to show that the assumptions regarding import substitution determine the outcome: If the U.S.-owned subsidiaries produce import-replacing goods, then the investment strongly favors the Canadian payments balance; otherwise, it is slightly hurtful.† For Europe, the import-substitution effect is less important;

---

* Another assumption that distinguishes the two models concerns aggregate investment. In model A, U.S. aggregate investment at home is reduced by $1.00, while aggregate investment in the less-developed countries is increased by $1.00; in model B, aggregate investment is unchanged in the United States and in the host countries.

† Observe that the possibility of third country investment is by-passed in my adaptation of the U.S. Treasury figures. This possibility is of much greater importance in the less-developed area context, considered below.

TABLE 5-1

Two Models of Balance-of-payments Impact on Canada and
Europe from Transactions with the United States
Associated with $1.00 of Direct Investment
in U.S.-controlled Manufacturing Subsidiaries
(based on data of the early 1960s)

	IMPACT ON CANADA (IN U.S. CENTS)		IMPACT ON EUROPE (IN U.S. CENTS)	
	FIRST YEAR AFTER	TENTH YEAR AFTER	FIRST YEAR AFTER	TENTH YEAR AFTER
Model A: The free choice investment[a]				
Income, royalties, fees to United States	−5.7	−9.0	−9.3	−14.8
Net replacement of imports from United States	+94.0	+148.5	+14.6	+23.2
Other trade effects with United States	−34.4	−54.4	−8.1	−12.9
Total effects with United States	+53.9	+85.1	−2.8	−4.5
Model B: The defensive investment[a]				
Income, royalties, fees to United States	−5.7	−9.0	−9.3	−14.8
Net replacement of imports from United States	−1.9	−3.0	−8.4	−13.3
Other trade effects with United States	−0.6	−0.9	+0.6	+0.7
Total effects with United States	−8.2	−12.9	−17.1	−27.4
Total sales by subsidiaries	119.0	188.0	135.0	214.9

[a]See the text, p. 164, for the differences in the assumptions embodied in the models.

Source: G. C. Hufbauer and F. M. Adler, U.S. Treasury Department, *Overseas Manufacturing Investment and the Balance of Payments* (Washington, D.C.: Government Printing Office, 1968), pp. 60-63, tables 5-1, 5-3, 5-5, and 5-7.

when substitution is assumed, its favorable balance-of-payments impact just about offsets the adverse payments consequences of the investment.

However, the U.S. Treasury figures simply move the analysis back to a previous question: Are the investments by U.S.-controlled subsidiaries in the advanced countries import-substituting? In Chapter 3 some evidence was presented for the proposition that these investments somewhat accelerated a process of import substitution that would in any event have occurred. That statement is about as far as the systematic data can carry us. The clear implication is that, as far as the advanced countries are concerned, the balance-of-payments impact may not be of very much importance.

If there is much risk in this conclusion, it lies in the inability of analyses such as the Treasury study to deal systematically with the longer-run effects of U.S.-controlled subsidiaries on the balance of payments, such as the effects resulting from changes in efficiency in the advanced countries. If one can assume that the presence of U.S.-owned subsidiaries has any such consequence, and if the effect tends to cumulate over time, then the economic consequences of the presence of the subsidiaries after a decade can be fairly substantial. In balance-of-payments terms, it is hard to say whether the consequences would be favorable or adverse. Their presence could increase exports by reducing export prices, but it also could raise imports as a result of increases in income. Impacts such as these escape the analytical net of the best studies.[21]

In sum, there is nothing to indicate that the advanced countries receiving U.S.-controlled subsidiaries in their economies have much to risk in balance-of-payments terms, at least as regards long-run effects. Inasmuch as the issue has much more importance in the context of the less-developed countries, however, further elaboration of the issue is left to a later point in the chapter, where the less-developed areas are discussed.

THE QUESTION OF ECONOMIC CONTROL

The considerations that have been touched on so far—growth, efficiency, balance of payments—are dwarfed by the concern of the host countries over the question of economic control. Is the existence of U.S.-controlled subsidiaries compatible with the need to be master in one's own house?* This worry, it is clear, is composed of many elements. Part of the concern is the possibility that the U.S. government might pursue its political or economic objectives via the subsidiaries of U.S. parents; but another part of the concern has to do with the economic consequences of the U.S. parent's control, quite apart from any relation to the U.S. government.

For the managers of multinational enterprise, the host country's concern over the issue of control is sometimes a trifle bewildering. Those managers usually see themselves as wholeheartedly committed to a "when in Rome . . ." philosophy. They are determined to be good citizens: to pay their local taxes, obey local regulations, support local good works, train the local labor supply. They acknowledge that there are some well-known gaucheries with which U.S.-controlled enterprises have been associated in the past,[22] but these are generally dismissed for what they are—infrequent examples of ill-considered acts likely to occur in any large business population, foreign or domestic.

It is the "world is our oyster" theme, however, not the "when in Rome . . ." philosophy, that concerns most governmental authorities. This concern has several aspects. First, there is the assumption that the subsidiaries of multinational enterprises are more sensitive than their local competitors to changes in the comparative attractiveness of the local economy. Illustrations of this sort of sensitivity are generally of two

* A thoughtful analysis of the Canadian case, exploring the economic implications of the loss of such mastery, appears in Kari Levitt, *Silent Surrender: The Multinational Corporation in Canada* (New York: St. Martin's Press, 1970).

sorts. One has to do with the choice of production sites: If the domestic economy becomes high in cost when compared with competitive sources, for instance, local competitors are unlikely to shut down their facilities and may react simply by demanding more protection from imports; but the subsidiaries of foreign-owned enterprises, in addition to demanding more protection, may also quietly shift their production to other members of the multinational system. Another illustration has to do with responses to currency crises. Local enterprises may not be wholly averse to selling the national currency in times of crisis, as a way of hedging against foreign requirements or taking a speculative flyer. But foreign-owned subsidiaries will have even greater incentives to hedge; the fact that they are part of a multinational system that counts its obligations and reports to its stockholders in another currency will push them in that direction.

There is not much doubt that the managers of multinational enterprises are generally in a position to respond with more flexibility than the managers of local enterprises would be. These enterprises almost always have some payment obligations to the parent, past or prospective—obligations to pay for goods or technical services, to service debt, or to remit dividends. The decision to accelerate or to prepay normal obligations of this sort in a currency crisis would be a natural response for any payer, whether a foreign subsidiary or local enterprise. What distinguishes the foreign subsidiary in this respect, therefore, is simply the ease with which acceleration or prepayment of its obligations can be arranged, as well as the relative volume of its payments across the exchanges.

Clearly, foreign-owned subsidiaries have been sensitive to the risks of currency instability. In a study of thirty-nine enterprises, practically all respondents reported that they took some cautionary measures when a currency was under pressure.[23] During 1967, at the height of the crisis that preceded the devaluation of sterling, all but three of twenty-five large

U.S.-controlled enterprises with subsidiaries in Britain were hedged in some degree against devaluation.[24] It would be surprising if British-owned enterprises were found hedging to the same degree. On the other hand, there are numerous indications of a gap between the opportunities for flexible response and the actual exploitation of these opportunities. For example, the extent of the hedges, as noted in Chapter 4, was remarkably limited. And other options, such as the opportunity to borrow through one subsidiary on behalf of another, were infrequently exercised.

Apart from the question of sensitivity of multinational enterprises to changes in the comparative position of the local economy, there is also concern over their capacity to escape the regulatory net of the country once the desire to escape exists. Take the question of avoiding local regulation, for instance. The descriptions of the operations of multinational enterprises in earlier chapters make it clear that the options available for avoiding the force of local regulation by legal means are often more numerous and more effective than those available to local competitors. Where affiliates are at both ends of a transaction, credit can more easily be arranged; payments can more easily be deferred; profits can more easily be shifted. Even where affiliates are not directly involved in both ends of the international transaction, the capacity of the subsidiary to use foreign affiliates as its outside eyes and ears generates greater flexibility than locally owned enterprises are likely to have.

To all those contentions, the managers of multinational enterprises are inclined to reply that the existence of a potential for flexible response is no indication of the frequency with which the capability is actually used. Nor does the actual use of the capability imply that the interests of the host government have been harmed. No doubt, cases of all sorts exist: cases of inaction; cases of neutral or beneficial responses; cases of harmful responses. On the whole, there is no very widespread disposition on the part of government authorities in the advanced countries to assume that harmful responses are common; indeed, the contrary view is often expressed in official circles. But the existence of options, irrespective of whether or how the options are exercised, is disconcerting for some countries, especially for those that are accustomed to a sense of control.[25]

The Less-Developed Areas

The eighty or so less-developed countries of the world come in all shapes and sizes, and their cultural and historical backgrounds present extraordinary variety. Nevertheless, the standards by which they are prone to judge the effects of investment by multinational enterprises have a striking uniformity. What is more, the standards are not unlike those that the more advanced host countries tend to apply; the differences are largely those of emphasis. Those differences in emphasis, however, can produce spectacularly different judgments regarding the effects of the enterprises.

THE MOBILIZATION OF RESOURCES

If the resource transfer of U.S.-owned multinational enterprises to the less-developed countries were measured simply in terms of long-term capital movements, the activities of these enterprises would be counted as only marginally important in the less-developed world. The direct investment flow from the United States to the less-developed areas during the 1960s, for instance, came to less than $1 billion annually. This is a modest sum when compared with such yardsticks as annual gross capital formation in the less-developed countries, amounting to about $35 billion in the middle of the decade, or annual international resource flows to these countries of about

$12 billion. But these foreign-owned subsidiaries were much more than conduits for foreign capital; they were mobilizers of local resources, as well as collectors and organizers of people and information. For less-developed economies, where local institutions for the mobilization of resources were generally not very strong, this function had a significance all its own.

The degree of mobilization of resources by U.S.-owned subsidiaries is suggested by the fact that for every dollar of capital transferred from the United States to these subsidiaries in the less-developed countries, about $4 more of capital were collected by the subsidiaries from other sources, including sources internal to the less-developed areas.[26] While the subsidiaries employed about 26,000 U.S. nationals, they also had 3 million or so locally recruited employees.[27] As usual, however, the intangibles are probably the most important assets of all: information on production and marketing techniques; a commitment to the creation of a local organization; a capacity, efficient or otherwise, to search out needed inputs in the local economy or abroad.

In theory, the impact of these subsidiaries could be measured by the economic yardstick of relative productivity. In practice, it is next to impossible to find a statistical basis that allows a plausible comparison to be made. Local competitors are sometimes prepared to agree—indeed, to insist—that the productivity of foreign-owned subsidiaries exceeds their own. But in explaining the difference they tend to stress such factors as the foreign subsidiary's access to credit or its use of well-established trade names.* These factors, they argue, lead to higher sales and less variable sales than those of the local competition, thereby making

* Consistent with this view is evidence in W. J. Bilkey, *Industrial Stimulation* (Lexington, Mass.: Heath Lexington Books, 1970) p. 172. Bilkey demonstrates that in El Salvador the obstacles perceived by local entrepreneurs and those perceived by foreign-owned enterprises, when contemplating the expansion of production, were quite different. The local firms were widely concerned about the availability of credit, whereas the foreign-owned firms were much less concerned on that score.

for lower unit costs. This issue, therefore, sits in limbo until better figures can be produced. There are other fundamental issues, however, on which more can be said. One of these is the balance-of-payments impact of a foreign-owned subsidiary.

BALANCE-OF-PAYMENTS EFFECTS

The balance-of-payments issue is far more important for the less-developed areas than for the advanced countries. In the advanced countries, the need for foreign exchange varies considerably according to countries and to periods. For the less-developed areas, however, foreign exchange is widely regarded as a scarce resource that chronically inhibits growth.

The prevailing view in developing countries is that foreign-owned subsidiaries decapitalize the country that plays host to them; their operations are said on balance to reduce the supply of funds available for investment in the country and to burden the national balance of payments. The demonstration is simple enough: From 1960 to 1968, when approximately $1 billion of fresh capital was being transferred annually to U.S.-controlled subsidiaries in the less-developed areas, approximately $2.5 billion was being withdrawn annually in the form of income alone.[28] If withdrawals in the form of royalties and of the overpricing of intermediate goods were added, the figure would be still larger. The case for the decapitalization thesis, therefore, may seem fairly vigorous.

However, it takes only a moment's reflection to realize that figures of this sort are quite misleading, at least to the extent that they purport to measure balance-of-payments impact. Implicitly, the figures assume that the only balance-of-payments effect of the foreign-owned subsidiaries' operations is capital inflows and remission outflows. In reality, as was noted earlier, the presence of the foreign-owned subsidiary has an impact on every item in the balance-of-payments accounts.

The Treasury Department study throws some light on that

impact.[29] The balance-of-payments estimates, shown in Table 5-2, prove strikingly different from the popular generalizations on the subject. They offer only slight encouragement to the school that sees foreigners' direct investments as the answer to the foreign exchange shortages of these countries. And they offer no comfort at all to the school that sees foreign direct investment as a balance-of-payments drain.

In model A, it will be remembered, the U.S. investor is assumed to have a free choice in deciding whether to serve his market by means of a local subsidiary. In Latin America, his decision to invest in such a subsidiary is seen as generating a small positive payments balance for the host country during the first year after the investment, and a slightly larger positive balance during the tenth year. In other less developed areas, the positive results are somewhat larger. However, this positive outcome comes mainly from the assumption in the model that the effect of the investment is to displace imports from the United States with local production. In model B, where this assumption is absent, investment in Latin America loses foreign exchange for the host country, whereas in other less-developed areas there is a gain of foreign exchange.*

The main point of interest to be extracted from the two models is that the profits, royalties, and fees paid to the U.S. parent turn out to be much less important in determining the net balance-of-payments influence of the U.S. investment than does the import-substituting assumption.†

---

* The models fail to deal explicitly with the case in which the investment would be undertaken by another foreign enterprise if it had not been undertaken by a U.S. enterprise. The results of such a calculation would presumably come close to model B, however.

† There is a real question whether the profits and royalties figures are accurately reflected in the table. Subsidiaries are not required to pay for the services of parents in some cases. In others, high transfer prices on imports from the parent or affiliates may reduce local profits. In that case, the elevated prices would be captured in the import data, but the offset would not be perfect, owing to tax effects.

TABLE 5-2

Two Models of Balance-of-payments Impact on Less-developed
Countries from Transactions with the United States
Associated with $1.00 of Direct Investment
in U.S.-controlled Manufacturing Subsidiaries
(based on data of the early 1960s)

	IMPACT ON LATIN AMERICA (IN U.S. CENTS)		IMPACT ON AREAS OUTSIDE CANADA, EUROPE, AND LATIN AMERICA (IN U.S. CENTS)	
	FIRST YEAR AFTER	TENTH YEAR AFTER	FIRST YEAR AFTER	TENTH YEAR AFTER
Model A: The free choice investment[a]				
Income, royalties, fees to United States	−5.4	−9.0	−10.2	−23.0
Net replacement of imports from United States	+37.4	+62.5	+84.1	+190.5
Other trade effects with United States	−19.3	−32.3	--18.9	−43.0
Total effects with United States	+12.7	+21.2	+55.0	+124.5
Model B: The defensive investment[a]				
Income, royalties, fees to United States	−5.4	−9.0	−10.2	−23.0
Net replacement of imports from United States	−7.5	−12.6	+22.5	+51.0
Other trade effects with United States	+2.9	+4.9	−3.0	−6.7
Total effects with United States	−10.0	--16.7	+9.3	+21.3
Total sales by subsidiaries	92.0	154.0	111.0	251.3

[a]See the text, p. 164, for the differences in the assumptions embodied in the models.

Source: G. C. Hufbauer and F. M. Adler, U.S. Treasury Department, *Overseas Manufacturing Investment and the Balance of Payments* (Washington, D.C.: Government Printing Office, 1968), pp. 60-63, tables 5-1, 5-3, 5-5, and 5-7.

National Economic Consequences

To what extent, then, does U.S.-controlled investment in subsidiaries in the less-developed countries contribute to import substitution? There can be no serious doubt that the import-substituting effect exists and no substantial hope that the effect can be closely quantified. All one can say is that, where such investment takes place, the effect is probably to accelerate the shift from exports to local production; that the acceleration is probably more pronounced for large countries than for small,[30] more pronounced for advanced industries than for simple ones.[31] A corollary of this conclusion is that newly established subsidiaries are more likely to generate import-substituting effects than subsidiaries of long standing, especially if the subsidiaries have not been assiduous in rolling over their products or processes. The truth about import substitution, therefore, probably varies from country to country, while lying well away from the extreme assumptions of either model.

For all the complexity of analytical structures such as the Treasury model, they do not even purport to deal with the effects that operate through the impact of such investments on productivity and prices. The characteristic trigger for foreign direct investment in manufacturing facilities in the less-developed economies is a decision of the country to shut off imports and raise the domestic price level of the products concerned. The resulting rise in price level need not always be large; in a few countries governments have tried to be judicious in the selection of industries for protection. Still, there is considerable evidence in many less-developed economies that the institution of import-substituting industrialization has helped to elevate the level of internal prices and cumulatively to overvalue the nation's currency.[32] The effect of this process is eventually to place a damper on exports, as internal prices rise and as the external value of the currency lags in its adjustment to those internal changes. To the extent that foreign-owned subsidiaries have contributed to the process of import substitution, part of the resulting impact on the balance of payments is to be attributed to them.*

A second factor that can exert its force in the balance-of-payments calculations runs in just the opposite direction. The effect of the industrialization process to which the foreign-owned subsidiary has contributed is eventually to increase the productivity of the factors of the country, whether through scale and agglomeration effects, capital accumulation, or the upgrading of the labor force. This factor in time could express itself in a lower—not a higher—price level in the less-developed country than would otherwise have prevailed. A lower price level could mean a higher volume of exports; if this were the result, it could easily swamp other balance-of-payments effects. Indeed, as observed in Chapter 1, the shift in emphasis from import replacement to export development is already in full swing in some less-developed countries, and foreign-owned manufacturing subsidiaries are playing a leading role in the change. It is a commentary on the dynamic character of developments in this field that the study summarized in Table 5–2, based on the conditions of the early 1960s, barely acknowledges the possibility of manufactured goods exports by subsidiaries from the less-developed areas.†

The problems of estimating the balance-of-payments impact of U.S.-controlled enterprises in the less-developed areas, difficult enough in the manufacturing industries, have proven even more complex with respect to investments in raw materials. As has been emphasized repeatedly in earlier chapters, a considerable part of the output of raw materials in the less-devel-

---

* In the pure case of model B, the price effect of the foreign investment might be counted as benign, because the alternative to the foreigner's investment is assumed to be an investment by local producers.

† The characteristic slowness to recognize the development is even more pointedly illustrated in Keith Griffin, *Underdevelopment in Spanish America* (London: Allen & Unwin, 1969), pp. 220–244, where the extreme difficulty of developing manufactured exports from Latin America to the advanced countries is eloquently argued.

oped countries finds its way into the marketing and fabricating facilities of U.S.-controlled multinational enterprises. As far as the host countries are concerned, it is hard to place a value on this downstream tie. Would the product be marketable if those facilities were withdrawn, and if so at what price? In products such as bauxite, the effort to estimate the recovery value of the product is thwarted by the absence of a free market of any significant size; in products such as oil and copper, by the imperfect nature of the market that exists. Because of the oligopolistic character of the market, the choice of raw material sources on the part of users is only partly a question of cost. Exports depend perhaps as much on the desire of the multinational enterprises that use the materials to balance the conflicting demands of different host countries and to maintain diversified sources of supply.

In the case of raw materials produced in tightly integrated industries, the presumption is strong that U.S.-controlled investment contributes favorably to the balance-of-payments position of the host country. It would be hard to doubt, for instance, that the balance-of-payment position of such countries as Saudi Arabia, Libya, Nigeria, and Venezuela has been helped by the activities of U.S.-controlled enterprises, as compared with any plausible alternative.[33] But the kind of meticulous estimating approach implicit in models of the type described earlier is obviously even more vulnerable here. Clearly, the model A type of assumption—that local production would not take place in the absence of the U.S.-owned enterprise—is too simplistic to be very useful; so is the assumption of model B, that local production would inevitably take place whether or not the foreign-owned investment occurred. Both models imply a restructuring on radically different lines of the industries producing raw materials. Price patterns would change; tax effects would be shifted; efficiency levels would be altered; demand would be affected. In the case of raw materials, even more than in that of manufactures, the failure to handle these issues explicitly would sharply limit the credibility of the model's predictions.

Still, even in raw material industries, one cannot always say that the effect of U.S. foreign direct investment is favorable in the long run to the payments position of less-developed areas. The sustained existence of large raw material industries in some countries tends to create an equilibrium rate of exchange that blights the possibility of competitive manufactured goods exports and handicaps local import substituting industries.[34] So even here, one is reduced to equivocal statements about the long-run balance-of-payments effects of foreign direct investment.

THE STOCK OF PRODUCTIVE RESOURCES

Apart from balance-of-payments effects, another key question regarding the impact of U.S.-controlled multinational enterprises in the less-developed countries has to do with their effect on the countries' resources. That question breaks down into two parts: the effect on natural resources, and the effect on human resources.

Perhaps the most spectacular allegations that U.S. enterprises have been wasteful of natural resources relate to the role of the U.S. oil companies in Mexico during the period from the early 1920s until the time when their assets were nationalized in 1938.[35] During this period, so the allegation goes, the decline in Mexican oil production was owing in part to the wasteful cost-cutting practices of the foreign-owned enterprises. Even in this case, however, the record is uncertain. As usual, the question is whether any producer of oil, foreign or domestic, would have followed a policy of "creaming" the Mexican fields, given the decline in world demand at the time and the appearance of cheaper sources of oil elsewhere. One comes away from the question with the suspicion, but no more

than the suspicion, that the worry of less-developed governments is real, that is, that alternative arrangements extracting
more net benefit from the existing pool of natural resources
could be envisaged. But the question of articulating the
assumed alternatives still remains. We are, in short, back to
the usual question: "As compared with what?"

A judgment of the relative enrichment effects of foreign-
owned enterprise on human resources, like a judgment with
regard to natural resources, can only be based on a speculative
leap. That speculation carries the discussion back to a model
that has become familiar through repetition in the earlier
chapters.

As long as foreign-owned enterprises are introducing products or processes that are new to less-developed areas and that
would otherwise not have been introduced, there is a high
probability that such enterprises add to the capabilities and
productivity of local labor and capital.* The effects of U.S.-
controlled automobile enterprises in Latin America on local
component manufacturers, for example, are fairly well documented.[36] A more general tie between the degree of foreign
private direct investment and the rate of productivity growth
has been noted in the case of Argentina.[37] Of course, if the
advantages provided by foreign-owned enterprises could just as
well have been acquired by other arrangements, such as technical assistance contracts, then it would be hard to say that the
foreign subsidiary was making any more substantial contribution to the enrichment of human skills in the country than the
available alternatives. But the newer and more difficult the
nature of the undertaking, the less likely it is that such alternatives will be available.

---

* This assertion, of course, begs such critical questions as whether radios or
automobiles or urban agglomerations are a "good thing" for less-developed
countries, as well as the related question whether the resources used in their
making might have been used to better social purpose. Answers to these critical
issues demand a frame of analysis of a different sort, dealt with briefly in a
later chapter.

After a new product or process has been introduced, however, the usual decline in relative benefits probably sets in. The longer the enterprise operates on its original technological and organizational base, the less there is to be learned locally. What is more, the longer the enterprise operates, the more likely it is that alternative means will exist for acquiring the necessary technology and organizational skills In due course, the local personnel associated with the subsidiaries of foreign-owned enterprises, including employees and suppliers, may be gaining very little in capability and productivity.

At some stage, therefore—generally well after the foreign-owned enterprise has been established in the less-developed country—the question may arise whether the existence of the foreign-owned enterprise tends to stifle the development of human skills in the country more than it contributes to those skills. The prevailing assumption in some of the less-developed countries is that the formidable position of the foreign-owned enterprise tends to kill off the disposition of local entrepreneurs to launch a competing business, even though they would be perfectly capable of operating the business efficiently.[38]

On the face of it, this line of speculation looks plausible. If the argument has a weak link, it is to be found in the assumption that foreign-owned enterprises in the less-developed country remain unchanged in character over any long period of time. In the more advanced industries, the assumption is especially weak. Stimulated by opportunity or pushed by local government pressure, enterprises in such industries have commonly responded by continually upgrading their technological and organizational contributions. On the other hand, in other lines of economic activity, especially in lines in which oligopoly rests on the establishment of distinctive brand names and on consumers' preferences for such names, the change seems to have been slower and the risk of stifling local entrepreneurship commensurately greater.

DEPENDENCE AND DISTORTION

Practically all countries that harbor the subsidiaries of multinational enterprises suffer from a sense of dependence, a sense that is nurtured by the assumption that these enterprises may have extensive geographical options and that the exercise of these options could easily affect the local economy. Though the point may hardly seem to need repeating, this sense is especially acute in the less-developed countries because of their relative size and their relative reliance on foreign-controlled raw material exporters. The history of raw material exploitation, as is well known, is filled with cases in which those options were exercised.[39]

The economic concerns of less-developed countries, however, involve not only the familiar issues of dependence but also a group of issues that commonly go under the heading of "distortions." For instance, because those enterprises have their origins in the advanced countries, the assumption is that they are most at home with a certain kind of technology—a technology based on large scale, on cheap capital, and on relatively expensive labor.[40] This kind of orientation is thought to produce various harmful effects on the economies of the less-developed countries.[41] One of these is the misuse of local resources—misuse in the sense that too much capital and too little labor are used, given the relative price and supply of those local factors.[42]

The actual facts are, as usual, obscure. There are no comprehensive data on the degree to which multinational enterprises adapt their production processes to the conditions of less-developed countries, and scarcely any data at all on the comparative adaptive actions of local competitors. The prolonged debate among economists over factor reversals in the application of production processes in different countries has left behind a litter of conflicting and half-documented views.[43] To the extent that data exist at the individual enterprise level, they suggest that in some cases a considerable amount of adaptation actually does take place in multinational enterprises as they move their products and processes across international boundaries into less-developed areas.[44]

This is not to say that many foreign-owned enterprises approach the question of an appropriate technology with a totally clean slate. Few ask: If we were beginning from ground zero, how best would we produce in less-developed areas, given the differences in scale, factor costs, and reliability of supplies. Still, some adaptation occurs as enterprises respond to the obvious environmental differences. Following the easiest path, some enterprises have been known to fall back on the use of a product or process that they had outgrown in their more advanced markets. Adjustments of this sort generally move the enterprise toward processes that are appropriate to a smaller scale of output and to more labor-intensive methods. Of course, when multinational enterprises take this step, desirable though it may be, they court the risk of being charged with dumping second-hand machinery or obsolete products on the less-developed host economy.*

The propensity of different enterprises to adapt their technology may well be accidental in part, depending on the experience and knowledge of the production men involved. But there is some evidence that the propensity is not wholly idiosyncratic. According to one of the very few studies on the subject, the degree of adaptation depends partly on the strategy these enterprises are pursuing.[45] U.S.-controlled multinational enterprises that think of their market position as being based on product quality are loath to experiment with changes in their production processes, whereas enterprises that think of

---

* The tendency of subsidiaries of U.S. enterprises in Mexico and Puerto Rico to use second-hand equipment was quite strong during the early 1960s; see W. P. Strassmann, *Technological Change and Economic Development* (Ithaca: Cornell University Press, 1968), p. 208. But the choice seemed sensitive to the nature of the manufacturing process, and the available data were not sufficient to control for that variable.

their market positions as being dependent mainly on cost and price considerations are more prepared to make such changes. The same study suggests that adaptation is less likely to occur if production costs are a small part of the total sale price (as in pharmaceuticals) than if production costs are a large part of price (as in sewing machines). When management is scarce and overburdened, as it commonly is, first things come first.

When foreign-owned subsidiaries are unwilling to shift from capital-intensive to labor-intensive processes, that unwillingness is sometimes owing to a quite rational evaluation of the consequences of shifting, rather than to ignorance and indifference regarding the advantages of shift.[46] Sometimes, to be sure, a rationality that produces good results in private terms generates bad results by social yardsticks. When labor is unreliable and inefficient because of disease and malnutrition, it may be socially harmful to avoid its use.

At other times, however, the criteria for the private decision and the social decision are quite compatible. Cases can be found, for instance, in which engineers have deliberately designed plants and products for use in less-developed areas in such a way as to ensure that the products met acceptable quality standards abroad, or in such a way as to avoid having to rely on types of local labor that are particularly scarce, such as maintenance specialists, supervisors, and inspectors.[47] It may be, too, that production specialists are intuitively aware of what economists are just beginning to realize, namely, that when compared with the standards of more advanced countries, labor in underdeveloped areas tends to be more efficient in activities that are machine-paced than in those that are not.[48] Even when labor's efficiency has not been adversely affected by labor-intensive methods, rational decision-makers have had to consider whether such methods affect the length of the production cycle and hence the inventory costs of the process. In sum, though the assumption that labor-intensive methods are economic in labor-surplus societies may be a good starting point for generalization, it requires all sorts of careful qualification; and the qualification is necessary whether the judgment is made on the basis of social criteria or private criteria.

The issue of factor uses and proportions has implications not only for efficiency and growth but also for welfare and equity. Stated in the form of a narrow economic question, the issue is posed in terms of income and distribution: How are the income rewards of development being shared?

In many countries, including India, Pakistan, Colombia, Mexico, Brazil, and Chile, the development of the economy has gone hand in hand with the growth of government employees and of a new class of wage earners, salaried employees, and managers associated with modern industry and commerce. If too much capital and too little labor are being used in these countries, then the class associated with modern activities reaps more of the rewards than it ought to. And if they are sharing in the foreign investor's monopoly rents by means of partnerships in the foreign-owned enterprises, then the inequities of income distribution are greater still. The linkage between those that have benefited from modern economic activities and the presence of foreign-owned subsidiaries has been made particularly explicit among intellectuals in Latin America.[49]

The issue is real; the question of measurement is something else again. Data on income distribution in the less-developed countries for any point in time leave something to be desired. Data that purport to measure trends over time are even more questionable.[50] The few studies that have some basis for statistical credibility readily confirm a fact that is all too painfully visible—the vast income disparities within the less-developed countries.[51] At the same time, they suggest the relatively rapid growth in the last decade or two of an upper-middle-income class in developing Latin American economies. The economic question that remains obscure is what would have happened to local income distribution in the absence of the foreign-owned subsidiaries. Only one thing can be said with reasonable assurance regarding the operations of these subsidiaries: that they have a propensity for paying relatively high wages as compared with locally owned industry. But if this propensity goes with a tendency to employ less labor, the income distribution effects are uncertain.

The concern over economic distortions created by foreign-owned subsidiaries has taken many forms. Advertising that stimulates the demand for any product can be thought of as a distortion. It is said to distort if it creates a preference for foreign over local products that are similar in character, creating a basis by which the foreigner captures a monopoly rent. It is also regarded as distorting if it increases the aggregate demand for some products, especially for products that have an offensive connotation for the observer. The advertising of Coca-Cola or Ford, according to the views of some economists, generates distortion because it stimulates consumption without a welfare increase that they consider commensurate. Tales, real or otherwise, of triumphal campaigns for the sale of electric sewing machines among the unelectrified villages of the Peruvian *altiplano* confirm the worst suspicions of such economists.[52] But dependence and distortion are relative concepts. Dependence and distortion, as compared with what?

Irrespective of the internal role of foreign-owned enterprises in the less-developed countries, these countries are bound to rely heavily on the technology, the markets, and even the consumption norms of outside nations. The tie is particularly strong because so-called modernizing attitudes, such as the desire for more education, growth, and choice, as well as the willingness to save, are commonly found closely linked with a desire for "modern" goods.[53] If the economy is small, the reliance is likely to be great; if the economy is committed to rapid growth, the reliance may be greater still. Iran, now undisputed owner of her national oil reserves, is no less dependent on access to outside markets than she was in the days of Mossadegh, two decades earlier. Egypt, having purged itself of much of its foreign investment, still depends critcially on outside markets to find its needed foreign exchange. The issue of dependence, therefore, may be associated less with the question of foreign ownership than with the issue of income, status, and power distribution inside the less-developed countries. This is why economists who profess to see major adverse effects from multinational enterprises in the less-developed countries so commonly prescribe not only the curbing of those enterprises but also major structural changes inside the less-developed economies. As many of them see it, the curbing of the multinational enterprise is a necessary but not a sufficient condition to their economic and social objectives.

The United States and the Global Economy

Agnosticism in small doses may be tolerable; in larger quantities it becomes more difficult to abide. Yet an agnostic approach is called for once again when gauging the effect on the U.S. economy of the overseas activities of U.S.-controlled enterprises. If overseas investments by U.S.-controlled enterprises involved nothing more than a transfer of capital, there might be a case for dismissing the whole issue as trivial. In terms of resources lost to the U.S. economy through capital transfer, the effects seem minuscule. The capital that is represented in the official U.S. data as being transferred each year out of the United States is about $4 billion. If this figure were deflated in terms of U.S. opportunity cost—if capitalized knowledge were taken at zero and second-hand machinery at the going price—it would perhaps be $3 billion. This is less than 2 percent of annual gross capital formation in the United States.

When balance-of-payments effects are the yardstick, the case is changed from one of triviality to one of uncertainty. The results of the U.S. Treasury studies are consistent with almost any kind of conclusion about the balance-of-payments impact, except perhaps the conclusion that the impact is obvious and strong.[54]

When measurement effects of this sort are tested against the description of the investment process contained in earlier chapters, however, their shortcomings are striking. The decision of U.S. parents to place subsidiaries in other countries is part of a dynamic process whose effects are complex and elusive. Because the industries involved are characteristically structured on oligopolistic lines, the assumption that each firm's existence is a simple function of the capital and labor that make it up is inadequate. The decision of Kennecott or Cerro de Pasco not to search out new ore reserves in South America but to extend their existing developments on the North American continent would be a distinctive event whose effects, good or bad, could be profound. One could measure the capital and labor made idle by the decision, but the measurement would be a barren exercise. The reason, of course, is that a decision not to invest would set in train a series of consequences, benign or adverse, whose repercussions would be captured or borne by others outside the enterprise. The effect of these external economies or diseconomies may not be very large in any single year; but cumulatively, measured over a number of years, it is hard to dismiss the view that they can profoundly affect the national economy.

For the layman, there is nothing very threatening in these statements; having begun his inquiry with no particular commitment to any disciplined point of view, he has no difficulty in entertaining any proposition that seems reasonable on its face. For the economist, some of these propositions are disconcerting. What they suggest is that the impact of international investment is not necessarily measured by such figures as yield on investment, payments to labor, and tax payments. The effects recorded by these measures could be swamped by those outside the recording net, especially if the effects run over a number of years.

Despite all the ambiguity and complexity, there are some aspects of the foreign direct investment process that at first glance seem to provide simple facts leading to some equally simple conclusions. The labor union that sees a plant established abroad through the export of U.S. capital, for example, cannot fail to see a link between the establishment of the overseas subsidiary and the loss of U.S. jobs.[55] As labor sees it, capital is being moved abroad, management attention is being diverted abroad, and production is being transferred abroad. Are any clearer signs needed of prospective injury to U.S. labor?

The relation between foreign investment and U.S. jobs is not quite that unambiguous, however. To the extent that capital is transferred abroad, some of it does seem lost to the United States. But if the level of U.S. government spending is consciously reduced when domestic corporate spending is high and is increased when corporate spending is low, then the link between foreign investment and domestic employment is broken; the government's compensatory spending or compensatory saving destroys the tie. In an economy as large as the United States', investment magnitudes on the order of $3 billion are easily subject to being swamped by just such compensatory policies.

If the $3 billion figure is to be taken as uncompensated, however, then one has to reckon on two kinds of effects. The first of these is a price effect. Because capital would be slightly scarcer in the United States as a result of the export of $3 billion, the capital that remained might conceivably command a slightly higher price in the form of interest or profit. However, the earlier description of the investment motivations involved indicates strongly that the outflow would probably not be much deterred by a higher profit rate at home. Accordingly, U.S. labor would confront a shift in the share of rewards in favor of capital, a shift that would be registered through lower wages or higher unemployment rates.

Much more important, however, is—or at least ought to be

—the diversion of the attention of top management from its domestic facilities to its foreign interests. The descriptions of the operations of U.S.-controlled multinational enterprises in earlier chapters suggest that top management attention should be thought of as a scarce, rationed resource. Multinational enterprises cannot promptly expand their top management to fill a current demand. Time is needed for an appropriate response. The organizational structure of the enterprise has to be altered to accommodate an expansion in general management, and the new managers have to be familiarized with the internal resources of the enterprise, including its distinctive pool of knowledge, whatever that may be. As a result, enterprises that are expanding have a chronic sense of being short of management manpower. It is not unreasonable to assume that when the executives of a large U.S. enterprise are preoccupied with the negotiations and adaptations involved in setting up their establishments in foreign markets, the problems of improving the productivity or expanding the product line in the United States get less attention.

The issue over which U.S. labor generally expresses its concern in connection with the creation of foreign subsidiaries, however, is probably on relatively weak ground: the concern that the establishment of such facilities may shift U.S. production abroad that would otherwise have remained at home. In some cases where U.S. domestic facilities face the threat of lower costs abroad, it is conceivable that the intensive and unwavering attention of U.S. management to the domestic facilities might lead to some new cost-cutting devices that would prolong their competitive position. The product cycle analysis of Chapter 3, however, suggests that these efforts would be swimming against a strong tide.

The instinct of U.S.-controlled enterprises, as observed earlier, is to locate production of relatively young sophisticated products in the United States and to move the production abroad as the U.S. oligopoly position is impaired. This instinct may very well represent an optimal solution not only for U.S. management but also for U.S. labor. The chain of causation, however, is neither direct nor sure. It begins with the premise that the multinational enterprise adds to global welfare by its ability to communicate knowledge and resources efficiently across national boundaries. Part of the increase is captured by the host country; part by management and the stockholders; part by consumers in the United States. Is anything left for labor? That depends primarily on whether the opportunities opened up by the U.S. specialization in overseas management and by the increased incomes of its trading partners more than offset the original shift. Even if the causal chain is long, the probability that it benefits U.S. labor in the end seems pretty high, especially because the consequences have to be compared with locking such labor into occupations and into industries in which innovation was declining and competition mounting.

There are times, however, when one gains the impression that none of these worries lies at the heart of U.S. labor's concerns. The real concern, it sometimes seems, is the very same encountered in the reactions of host governments and their local élites including their labor union leaders.[56] The multinational enterprise is strong and supple. When confronted as an adversary, it seems to have options that U.S. labor does not, such as the option to move its production abroad. From labor's viewpoint, the hand of management is strengthened by the existence of the options, whether or not they are exercised. And the labor leader, whose position in his movement depends upon being able to win in the test of nerves across the bargaining table, is especially threatened by the flexibility of the adversary he confronts. This accounts for some national labor unions' efforts to pool their information and their negotiating strength when confronting a multinational enterprise, even though the economic interests of the labor groups in different countries may be directly at odds with one another.

All roads seem to lead back to a fundamental, almost primitive, issue. The men who direct the U.S.-controlled multinational enterprises find opportunity and choice through the multinational character of their operations. The nations in which these enterprises operate outside the United States probably receive a share of the benefits of the increased productivity that some of these enterprises generate. It is even possible, though it is less clear, that U.S. labor also shares in these benefits. The reaction of foreign countries and of U.S. labor is not determined solely by an estimate of benefits shared. At least as important is the sense that, where interests diverge, the multinational enterprise has numerous choices that its adversary does not share. This sense of inferiority and dependence is one of the exacerbating elements of the relationship.

[**6**]

National Élites,
Ideologies, and Cultures

So far, my emphasis has been on the economic causes and influences of the U.S.-controlled multinational enterprise. But the tension and concern that such enterprises seem to generate can hardly be explained in economic terms alone; the economic analysis, objectively viewed, generates results that are far too ambiguous to explain the observed reactions. Moreover, economic considerations do not help very much in explaining the variations in tension. Why do the Belgians or the Thais, for instance, seem so little perturbed over the presence of U.S.-owned operations, whereas the Japanese and the Mexicans seem so edgy over their presence? And why is it that the reactions of host countries have differed in different periods? If one looks at the factors that are not primarily economic, do these variations become more comprehensible?

If there are answers to these questions, they are not simple ones. The difficulties start right at the outset, with the measurement of the level of "tension." This is a condition easier felt than described. Sometimes there are overt signs that tension may exist, signs such as the threat to nationalize an existing foreign-owned enterprise or the refusal to admit a new one. But one cannot dismiss the possibility that the signs of tension are suppressed in some cases. Policy-makers in a foreign country, for instance, may reckon that their need for foreign investment is so great that they cannot afford to threaten it or to turn it away, however disconcerting its presence may be.

For all the difficulties of definition and measurement, there would not be much disagreement among observers in rating different countries on the level of tension induced by foreign-controlled investment. During the early 1970s, for instance, among the Latin American countries, Chile, Mexico, and Peru would probably be rated a little higher on the tension scale than Colombia, but not by much; Colombia would, in turn, be rated higher than Argentina or Brazil: and these latter, higher than, say, Paraguay or Honduras. In the advanced world, there would be very little hesitation in placing Japan near the very top of the scale, France somewhat below, Britain much lower, and Belgium lower still.

Apparently there is a phenomenon to be explained, elusive though its definition may be. Moreover, the observations that have piled up in the field are sufficient to push beyond the stage of pure armchair speculation into that grey area of cerebration and observation where some propositions seem more plausible than others.

The Challenge to Local Élites

There are many different ways in which to describe the sources of the tension generated by the presence of foreign-owned subsidiaries: as a clash of ideologies; as a clash of cultures; or as a rivalry among élites. None of these approaches is wholly off the mark; none by itself fully explains the phenomenon.

Viewing the sources of social tension as an outcome of the relations between competing élites is a familiar approach among sociologists. In the case of tensions associated with the presence of the multinational enterprise, the approach proves especially illuminating.

The presence of foreign investment in any local economy generally helps to bolster the strength of certain local élite groups and is usually seen as a threat to the strength of others. To some extent, the identity and the relative strength of the various élites have changed predictably with the country's growth. Various Latin American countries have, for instance, displayed parallel tendencies as they have moved from the agricultural and extractive stages of the late nineteenth and early twentieth centuries to the industrialization phase of later decades. And some of these tendencies could be glimpsed again in the less-developed areas of Asia and Africa, even though the times and the cultures were very different.

As observers in other countries sometimes have to be reminded, Latin America consists of a score of different nations, each with unique elements in its culture and history. Still, there have been certain common elements as far as foreign investments were concerned. Throughout much of the nineteenth century and into the early part of the twentieth century, the prevailing view among the élite groups of the principal countries was that foreign investment was a good thing, helpful to them and helpful to the country concerned. In some Latin American countries, this view was not very well articulated nor very well rationalized. But there were other countries in which the articulation was quite explicit.[1]

In Mexico, during the one-man rule of Porfirio Díaz from 1876 to 1910, the prevailing ideology was that the country simply could not get ahead without massive help from the "superior" cultures of Europe and North America. This help took many forms: large loans to government; huge investment in the country's railroads, power plants, and mines; a certain amount of migration of British, Spanish, French, German, and American managers and technicians; appreciable amounts of technical assistance in the establishment of fledgling breweries, metal-working establishments and textile plants. Far from being a threat to the élite groups that sat firmly in the government saddle in those years, this inflow of capital and influence was seen as an obvious boon. The economy was short of capital, technical skills, and management, so that no local group of leaders was being seriously challenged by the influx. On the contrary, the leaders, nurturing a model of "scientific" government that would eventually lead to economic growth on the pattern of the advanced countries, at first saw almost unadulterated advantages in the partnership.[2]

With variations on the theme, the same generalizations can be made for Argentina, Brazil, Chile, and Peru. For Argentina, one would have to introduce some modifications to give proper weight to the importance of the rancheros and their general hostility to efforts at local industrialization.[3] In Brazil, one would have to take note of the subtle influence of geography and culture that distinguished the expression of these views from their articulation elsewhere in Latin America.[4] In Chile and Peru, it would be hard to overlook the dominance of the raw materials industries and the special geographical difficulties that marked these countries' growth.[5] But, by and large, each of these countries went through a sustained period of many decades in which foreign investment was regarded as benign and unthreatening.

Not all countries in Africa and Asia went through a similar period. A good deal depended on the style and circumstances in which the countries had ended their colonial status. Those that had a well-developed class of "modern" local businessmen, technicians, and intellectuals at the time of independence, such as India[6] and even Nigeria,[7] were already exhibiting some of the characteristics of the Latin American model of the late nineteenth and early twentieth centuries. Those that had acquired their independence by revolt or near-revolt after World War II, such as Indonesia and the East African countries, entered into that new estate with an emotional and political conditioning that profoundly influenced their reactions to the continuation or spread of foreign investment. Some of these, having the twentieth-century socialist model to emulate—which the nineteenth-century Latin Americans had not—were determined to follow that pattern, even if they had not yet developed the trained manpower or the infrastructure to carry out their hopes: Guinea, Burma, and Ceylon, for instance, chose this route.

Still, many countries of Asia and Africa followed a pattern reminiscent of the early Latin American stage. Their élite aspired to control the government apparatus rather than to be modern businessmen, technicians, and managers. The leaders of these countries saw foreign investors as more supportive than threatening to their objectives, at least at the early stages of their development. This was the route chosen by Sierra Leone, the Ivory Coast, and the Belgian Congo, and by some of the other francophone countries of Africa, as well as by Malaysia, Taiwan, and South Korea. For perhaps a decade after its independence in 1946, one might also have described the Philippines in these terms. After the traumatic departures of Sukarno from Indonesia and of Nkrumah from Ghana, those countries also began to adopt such a point of view.

The tranquil state in which the foreign investors and the leaders of less-developed countries both saw joint opportunities in the creation of foreign-owned subsidiaries lasted longer in some countries than in others. In Mexico, the strains in the relationship could be seen quite plainly some years before the 1910 Revolution. By that time, too, Argentina, Brazil, Chile, and Peru were also exhibiting signs of the coming disaffection.[8]

Some of the sources of the tension were adumbrated in Chapter 2, where the history of raw material investment was recounted. The needs for government revenue, constantly being ratcheted upward, made the tax question an unending source of dispute. Apart from that issue, however, one could fairly describe the tension as partly, perhaps even mainly, a product of the defensive reactions of the élite groups in the less-developed countries.

A great deal has been written about the hostile reactions of the groups identified with the old order, such as the landowners and the traditional military. Less has been said, however, about the hostilities of those whom the process of economic development helped to generate and nurture. Three groups of this sort were particularly affected by the foreign investor: the government bureaucrat, as he sought to maintain power and control over an expanding local economy; the local businessman, as he aspired to shift from the role of supplier, provisioner and customer of the foreign enterprise to the status of competitor; and the intellectual outside the local establishment, as he sought to develop and promote a competing ideology.

The challenge from the government bureaucrat's viewpoint could be seen in stark form in the oil-producing countries, especially in Libya, Venezuela, Kuwait, Iran, and Iraq. The growth of the foreign oil producers in these countries had helped to generate a group of sophisticated oil specialists inside the local government bureaucracies. Unlike their fathers, these bureaucrats were familiar with the commercial and technical aspects of oil extraction and oil development. Yet, as Chapter 2 suggested, they were largely unable to parlay their familiarity into a greatly reduced dependence on the foreign companies. As long as foreign enterprises controlled the gateway to foreign markets, the dependence continued.

These indigenous bureaucrats have been torn between two powerful needs. At times, they have felt the need to safeguard the companies from the untenable demands of their colleagues, in order not to kill the egg-laying goose; at other times, they have felt the need to take a leading role in extracting added benefits from the foreign companies, in order to strengthen their claim to continued power.[9] In the course of time, the demands by the local bureaucrats on the foreign investors have tended to increase and the protection afforded to the investors has tended to decline.

A similar shift in role has occurred with respect to the local business community. Almost from the first, history suggests, foreign investors have generated some local entrepreneurial activity by their presence. Even the Peruvian guano boom of the nineteenth century, though centered on some isolated off-shore islands in the Pacific, was responsible for bringing a local contractor industry into existence on the mainland, an industry that lived off the public works that the guano boom financed.[10] The Mexican mining and railroad building boom, later in that century, helped establish a new Mexican entrepreneurial class, composed of traders, bankers, provisioners, contractors, and small manufacturers for the local market. The same phenomenon has been noted for India[11] and China.[12]

Observe, however, that in the early stages of the development of the local business class, their role was generally more complementary to the foreign investor than it was competitive; they sold their goods and services to the foreigner and acted as his mentor and guide in the local environment. If there was friction at that early stage, it arose over such questions as whether the foreign investor should buy more from local sources or pay more for what he was buying. At this stage, therefore, the complaints of the local business class were usually intended to increase the ovarian output of the foreign goose, not to displace it in the local barnyard.

In some countries, especially the newer countries of Africa and Asia, the local business class has not yet gone much beyond the stage of performing a complementary role to the foreign-owned enterprise.* In countries that have gone some distance along the development route, however, the activities of local businessmen and those of foreign-owned enterprises

---

* At this early stage, insofar as competition exists, it is between *ausländer* residents in the country and native businessmen. This rivalry has produced Ghanaianization, Nigerianization, Tanzanianization and similar programs involving the expropriation and expulsion of residents of Indian, Lebanese, and Arab stock.

are competing. In some cases, the competition has been generated by the entry of the foreigner into the local economy to produce a familiar product for local consumption, such as textiles, biscuits, or soap, his entry based on the expectation that he could produce it better or cheaper than the local competition. In other cases, however, the competition has come about because aggressive local entrepreneurs have decided to try their hand at items whose production had been introduced into the country by foreign-owned enterprises. This has been a common pattern in consumer products, such as radios and refrigerators, and in simple industrial goods, such as basic chemicals, storage tanks, and small motors.

Once competition between local enterprises and foreign-owned enterprises has begun to develop, its existence has generally signaled a visible split in the structure of the local business groups. Those whose interests have been complementary to the foreign-owned enterprises—such as the bankers, the traders, and the provisioners for such enterprises—have been inclined to cling to a policy of easy tolerance for foreign interests. Those who saw themselves in competition with the foreigners have generally tried to limit and cut back the scope of the foreign-owned subsidiary.[13]

On the whole, as development has proceeded, the local business elements that see themselves in competition with foreigners have grown in relative importance. If the making of beer, boots, and boxes was ever mysterious to local businessmen, it rapidly lost that quality. Besides, the process of development has itself tended to increase the opportunities for large-scale production and distribution in local markets faster than it has increased the opportunities in imports and exports, thereby turning the attention of businessmen inward to the national economy; as a result, local business interests that had originally emphasized the complementary activities rapidly found themselves drawn to the competitive ones. Elements of the local business community that originally had clear conflicting interests have been drawn together in common opposition to the foreigners.

The part played by the intellectual élite in the debate over foreign investment has been somewhat more complex. The universities and the mass media of most countries can generally be counted on to assume the role of the outside critic unless they are explicitly in the service of national government or pointedly terrorized into quiescence by such a government. The propensity of such groups to play an active political role varies, of course, according to the issue. Whenever official policies encourage foreigners to come into the economy in places of prestige and power, however, intellectuals outside the Establishment tend to see those policies as moves to strengthen the position of the Establishment and hence to weaken the status and influence of those outside.

In recent years, there has scarcely been an underdeveloped country in which intellectuals have not raised this issue. It has appeared with special clarity, for example, in Ghana, Nigeria, India, Chile, Mexico, Brazil, Malaysia, and the Philippines. The tension between local intellectuals and the managers of foreign-owned enterprises, however, is not confined to the less-developed world. Servan-Schreiber's *The American Challenge*[14] apparently owes its otherwise mystifying popularity in Canada and Europe to the fact that it responded to a similar kind of uneasiness among intellectuals in those countries. Indeed, the number of scholarly publications devoted to one aspect or another of this concern in the advanced countries is substantial.[15]

The reactions of the intellectuals are compounded of various elements. Some are manifestly "rational," stressing such questions as the economic and political disadvantages of relying on foreign-owned enterprises. Some appeal to such values as independence and freedom, which they see threatened by foreign-owned enterprise.

From time to time, however, notes of a more subjective and personal sort can be detected. In many countries, business is thought of as an intellectually and socially inferior pursuit. That view has become less prevalent in recent years, especially in countries where business management is becoming professionalized. But it is still strong in some countries: in Britain, for instance, where the senior businessman is generally seen as a considerable cut below the senior civil servant in terms of intellectual achievement;[16] and in Canada, where the perceived gap, though differently based, may be as large.[17] To be obliged to share position and power with a business élite, particularly when the élite is representative of outside interests, must surely contribute to the intellectuals' sense of psychic discomfort.

The Challenge to Ideologies

The stress of the past few pages on the personal elements in local responses to the foreign investor's presence is not intended to exclude another possibility, namely, that the hostility may spring more from ideology than direct self-interest. An ideological explanation seems to fit the observed manifestations of the tension about as well as an explanation based on personal interests; therefore it is hard to distinguish the two types of causation.

As the overt reason for hostility to U.S.-controlled investment, ideology seems to play a larger role in the less-developed countries than it does in the advanced. The earliest ideological basis for such opposition was, of course, Marxist in origin, based on the concept of the class struggle, capitalist exploitation, and imperialism. This form of opposition, however, made only limited progress in the less-developed countries. Even in Mexico during the 1930s—a period in which communist political theory was at the peak of its influence in that country —the Marxist-Leninist views toward foreign-owned investment were not strong enough to induce wholesale purges of the foreign investor.

After World War II, the prevailing ideological views in the less-developed countries went into a new phase. As was noted earlier in this chapter, some countries elected socialism as an ideological commitment. Even those nations that did not adopt socialism in form or substance, however, generally framed their national ideologies in terms that placed marked limits on the role of foreign investment. Insofar as an explicit ideology supported this position, the ideology tended at first to have a strong economic bias, based on the writings of such economists as Raul Prebisch and of institutions such as the Economic Commission for Latin America (ECLA). The early ECLA views were built mainly on the observation that traditional foreign-owned investment in the less-developed countries was oriented to raw materials and on the assumption that this pattern would continue. According to ECLA, the terms of trade for raw materials were unfavorable in relation to industrial products; the less-developed countries, therefore, would have to shift out of the business of specializing in the production and export of raw materials into the business of producing manufactured products for their own needs.[18] Presumably this kind of shift was not one for which much help could be expected from the foreign enterprises. Though the early articulation of this set of assumptions came mainly from Latin America, it quickly grew clear that India, Pakistan, Indonesia, Nigeria, and other countries were thoroughly in agreement.

In time, however, some of the factual assumptions of the early ECLA position began to seem questionable. The terms of trade for raw material exporters were obviously unfavorable in some periods, but quite favorable in others. Moreover, the price indexes used for terms-of-trade calculations proved to have serious weaknesses which were biasing them in the direction of the ECLA findings.[19] The underlying assumption in ECLA regarding the negotiating position of the less-developed countries also proved questionable. The less-developed economies found that they could negotiate themselves into a dominant position in foreign-owned raw material industries, at least as measured in profit-sharing terms. Foreign-owned manufacturing enterprises proved unexpectedly responsive to pressures that obliged them to set up producing facilities inside the less-developed countries and required them to increase the depth of their operations in the local economy. Even the assumption that such enterprises would resist exporting their manufactured products from the less-developed countries eventually proved at striking variance with the facts.

The ideologies of the less-developed countries have managed to assimilate these developments by a process of marginal adjustment. Many intellectuals are now prepared to assume that less-developed economies may be benefiting from the presence of U.S.-controlled enterprise and other foreign enterprises, if benefit is measured in such narrow economic terms as gross national product or national income. But the seeming benefit is thought to mask more subtle destructive forces, including increasing concentrations of income and power, as discussed in Chapter 5. Though local industrialists may sometimes appear at odds with the foreign-owned enterprises that are their rivals and their customers, both are thought to be joined in a common process of despoliation, with the foreigner as the senior partner in the process. Even the industrial workers employed by foreign-owned enterprises have become a part of the exploitative mechanism, because they have characteristically been paid wages in excess of the local norms.

As a result, the economic distortions described in Chapter 5 have been riveted into the local economy with the connivance of the local groups, the contemporary Malinches of the less-developed world. The industrial workers sharing in the foreigner's largesse have been muzzled as potential representatives of their class interest. In short, the local economy has been delivered over to the control of the foreigner. This is the *dependencia* syndrome, the final stage in the enthrallment of the local economy by the aggressive and expansive Americans.[20]

The Clash of Cultures

Though the tensions between U.S.-owned subsidiaries and the less-developed countries may be viewed in part as the result of a clash of ideologies, the tensions in the advanced countries are better seen as a clash of national cultures. It would be a mistake to push the distinction too far; obviously, cultural differences also play a role in U.S. relations with Latin American countries. But the distinction does have a certain expository value.

Each nation, propelled by cultural and historical forces that have their own unique ingredients, tends to develop its own distinctive consensus regarding the relationship of private to public power. Accordingly, the range of national attitudes, sensitivities, and expectations concerning the place of large enterprises in the economy is very wide. In the spectrum of such national attitudes, the U.S. case stands out as distinctive in many important respects. This is a fact understood by the élite of other countries, even when their knowledge of the U.S. economy is vague and prone to error. It seems reasonable to suppose that nations whose attitudes and expectations regarding business enterprises are least like those prevalent in the United States are most uncomfortable over the local presence of U.S. enterprise. This is not a testable hypothesis in any scientific sense. The concepts involved are too difficult to define and calibrate, and the cases for comparison are too few. For this exploratory probe, it may help to compare the U.S. case in a cursory way with three distinctly different national norms: those of the United Kingdom, France, and Japan.

THE U.S. CASE

For the past century two themes have struggled with each other in the United States: a fear of uncontrolled concentrations of economic power, and a respect for the contributions of big business and of the businessmen associated with it.

The United States came into her era of big business during the middle of the nineteenth century, at a time when the vestiges of certain values inherited from the colonial period could still be detected.[21] Corporations had been used by the British during the colonial period in such a way as to associate the use of that form with privilege and monopoly. A presumption against the grant of corporate charters existed widely in the new country. The right of the federal government to create corporations, even in connection with carrying out the government's constitutional obligations, was under a cloud until as late as 1819. State legislatures granted charters only infrequently. When granted, the charters had nothing like the open-ended character of the modern-day charter. Instead, they contained severe limitations on the purpose, duration, and size of the corporations they created.

One way to eliminate a privilege is to turn it into a universal right. By the middle of the century, state legislatures had begun to move in that direction. General incorporation statutes were widely adopted, making the corporate privilege available to all comers. Soon after the Civil War, the U.S. Supreme Court ruled that no state had the power to exclude a corporation created by another state from engaging in interstate commerce within its borders. With this decision, each state was able to manufacture its own brand of artificial men and to loose them on a national stage.

It was just a matter of time before the competition between the states had the effect of creating corporations without limit of power. In 1888, for example, New Jersey began to make a series of amendments to its incorporation law. In the course of that competition, corporations acquired the two attributes that made them the extraordinary vehicle for modern business they are today, namely, the right to life without limit of time, and the right to own other corporations or be owned by them.

According to some observers, the tolerance of the American public for this extraordinary use of public power was simply a reflection of the high status that businessmen enjoyed in American society, in relation to, say, the farmer, the bureaucrat, or the academician.[22] Though that esteem usually coexisted peacefully alongside a widespread distrust of private economic power, there were times when the two sets of values came into serious conflict.

Whenever the fear of private power became a dominant political force, as it did during the administrations of Theodore Roosevelt, Woodrow Wilson, and Franklin D. Roosevelt, the political action in response to that fear took a quite distinctive form, at least as compared with European responses. The U.S. effort usually consisted of attempting to liquidate the power concentrations, rather than to channel or contain them. This kind of approach lay behind the Sherman Act of 1890 and the Clayton Act of 1914. The key section of the Sherman Act states flatly: "Every contract, combination in the form of trust or otherwise, or conspiracy, in restraint of trade or commerce among the several states or with foreign nations, is hereby declared to be illegal. . . ." Though the fundamentalist view expressed in these words has since been modified by the courts, it would be a mistake to overlook the philosophical gulf between the United States and most other countries on this point.

As a general rule, business practices in the United States today are either uncontrolled or prohibited. There is a middle ground, of course, in which some practices are tolerated subject to detailed regulations. This middle ground, however, is much less important in the United States than elsewhere. And when the regulatory approach is followed, the style of such regulation is to lay down general rules, to hold down the element of governmental discretion, and to avoid the case-by-case application of the principles involved. When the regulatory style is mechanistic and nondiscriminatory, as it so often is in the United States, the chances that government and business will hold each other at arm's length are greatly increased. "Mind your own business" is the typical state of mind, if not the rhetoric, with which U.S. enterprise confronts U.S. government agencies. When one finds similar rhetoric on the lips of businessmen in other countries, as happens from time to time, the state of mind it represents is likely to be very different. In other countries, that rhetoric commonly reflects either a spirit of forlorn defiance or a sense of dominance and control on the part of business.

Despite the fundamental importance of these differences between U.S. norms and those of other countries, the differences are rarely acknowledged in any explicit way by the world's business community. U.S. businessmen commonly find it difficult to conceive of business-government relations on the French or Japanese pattern, for example, whereas businessmen in other countries generally find it hard to picture a large enterprise that can manage to maintain an arm's length relationship with its "home" government.

The style that governs the relations between U.S. business and U.S. government is also deeply affected by the curiously fragmented character of governmental authority in the United States. First, there is the division of power between state and federal authorities. Though something like that division is to be found in the constitutions of other countries, such as Canada, Australia, Germany, Mexico, and India, it has no counterpart in Britain, France, Japan, or indeed most other countries. Even where the federal form seems to exist in other countries, as in Germany, Mexico, and India, the distribution of the public powers that are important to the conduct of big business are generally more highly concentrated at the national level than they are in the United States. Besides, the federal-state dichotomy is only a small part of the fragmentation of authority in the United States. The fuzziness of the boundaries that distinguish the powers of the federal legislature from the executive, and the executive from the judiciary, has tended to diffuse and to confuse authority to a degree that has almost no counterpart elsewhere.[23] Even within the executive branch, agencies have commonly developed an identity of their own that is independent of the President, and make informal coalitions with members of the Congress on whose lawmaking the agencies depend or with the special interest groups to which they may be related.

This style of U.S. governance, partly of diffusion, partly of overlap, places a distinctive stamp on relationships between U.S. business and the U.S. government outside the United States. Seemingly simple questions begin to lose their simplicity. To what extent, for instance, do the overseas subsidiaries of the U.S. parent respond to the commands of the U.S. government; and to what extent is the U.S. government responsive to the demands of the subsidiary and its U.S. parent?

A question of this sort can be explored by examining the evidence at many different levels. One possibility is to look at relationships close up, examining the ties between government and business on foreign issues, company by company, program by program. Another is to examine the large sweep of U.S. foreign policy, searching for some indication of the basic national interests to which it seems most responsive. Either of these tasks would be excessively ambitious in the present context. But it may help to take a cursory look at the government-business relationships from each of these points of view.

Viewed close up, the relations between government and business on foreign problems appear exceedingly complex.[24]

At times, there have been the overt signs of close coordination between government and business: when the U.S. government during the 1920s struggled to gain entry for the U.S. oil companies into the areas reserved by Britain and France in the Middle East; when the marines were landed at Vera Cruz in 1914 and at Nicaragua in 1926; when the Hickenlooper amendment to the U.S. foreign aid bill, tying the continuation of U.S. foreign aid to the treatment of U.S. investors by aid-receiving countries, was promulgated in 1965; and so on.

At least as often, however, there was indifference or even hostility on the part of the U.S. government to the foreign operations of U.S. firms. The illustrations are endless. During the 1940s, the U.S. government paid some attention to the oil companies' bitter protests over the terms of indemnification of the seized American oil properties in Mexico, but its reaction was marginal and largely limited to retaliatory measures in the formulation of U.S. oil policy.[25] During the same period, the prosecution of Jersey Standard for its restrictive agreements with I. G. Farben, of DuPont for its agreements with Imperial Chemical Industries, and so on seemed to place the security of their position in world markets in jeopardy. For a time, even U.S. Export-Import Bank lending was conditioned by the principle that members of an international restrictive business agreement were ineligible to borrow. During the early 1950s, the U.S. government belied the Marxist caricature even more blatantly by blocking U.S. businessmen who were about to close agreements with the Indonesian and Liberian governments that threatened to dominate the economies of those countries. And an unending succession of proceedings against large international enterprises since that time has contributed even more to confounding any simple hypothesis concerning business-government relations.* Whatever the underlying rules of association between U.S. business and U.S. government may

* See Chapter 7, p. 238, for references to these cases.

have been—if indeed there were any—they evidently permitted frequent deviations from such simple rules as "What's good for General Motors . . ."

There is something to be said for the view, however, that a recital of individual cases and individual incidents is unhelpful, that what is needed is a much more general perusal of U.S. foreign economic policy. Yet a review of that sort proves no more illuminating in defining the influence of U.S. business on U.S. policy.

Consider the various strands of policy in the period since World War II that have a special bearing on the fortunes of the multinational enterprise. One basic U.S. position was the commitment to an open international system of economic relations, a system that would permit a relatively uninhibited flow of goods and capital among the non-communist countries of the world. The origins of that policy, the record shows, came partly out of the agricultural export interests of the American South, whose long-time reliance on exports of cotton, tobacco, and apples had rendered them especially vulnerable to the collapse of world trade in the Great Depression. Because the South was in a position to exercise more than its appropriate share of influence in key congressional committees, the interests of that area were pressed out of proportion to their importance in the U.S. economy.

The early attachment of the South to an open trading world for agricultural products would not have been enough by itself, however, to determine the general direction of U.S. trade policy in the postwar period, especially as the United States was responding to her agricultural problems by the use of strongly restrictive measures. But the U.S. desire for an open economic world was buttressed by the ideological commitment of other groups, especially of U.S. economists. Despite Keynes's impact on economic thinking with regard to domestic economic policies during the 1930s, the ruling model among U.S. economists in the international field remained neoclassical. In the economic planning that went on during the Roosevelt administrations of the 1940s, that ideological commitment mattered.

A third source of strength for the U.S. position, not to be discounted, came from the persistent strand of disinterested U.S. opinion, dating back to Wilson and earlier, that associated an open economic world with the attainment of peace. Organizations such as the League of Women Voters could be counted on for effective lobbying in favor of any bill that seemed to promote this concept.

Throughout the development of postwar policy, however, U.S. business interests were divided in their support of the concept of an open economic world. Some elements gave the policy their strong support, especially those that in past decades had felt themselves unfairly excluded from large areas of the world by the big colonial powers. Others showed little interest in the possibilities of either foreign trade or foreign investment. Still others, untroubled by the hobgoblin of consistency, were in favor of enlarging their opportunities to establish overseas subsidiaries but were against reducing the barriers to international trade. The outcome was a babel of voices from businessmen, with a mixed and diluted effect on U.S. policy.[26]

Another element of foreign economic policy of the United States in the postwar period was, of course, its early support for the various schemes that promoted European recovery and its later support for the schemes that generated European economic integration. In the end, these policies made Europe an attractive market for U.S. enterprises. But this was an outcome that scarcely anyone would have predicted during the 1940s and early 1950s. Along the way, for years at a time, these policies required the U.S. government to fend off the loud and insistent complaints of U.S. business that programs of European integration entailed measures of systematic discrimination against U.S. exports.

The early U.S. leadership in programs for aid to less-developed areas generates judgments about the role of U.S.

business that are no less ambiguous. To be sure, once the programs were well launched, U.S. business interests managed to acquire a major voice in some of the policies governing foreign aid operations. The Hickenlooper amendment—an amendment directing the termination of aid when expropriation occurred without adequate compensation—signaled the shifts. In addition, there was a strong commitment to the use of U.S. field staffs to defend and support U.S. business interests in aid-receiving countries. But it would be wrong to assume that the aid program was inspired by business interests when it was first created, or that business was at first much interested in the opportunities that foreign aid provided. The ascendant role of U.S. business in the operation of the program was a reflex action, not an initiative.

Finally, of course, there is the U.S. program for the control of U.S. foreign direct investment. This program, instituted by the U.S. government on a "voluntary" basis in 1965, became mandatory in 1968. From its inception, U.S. government agencies have been meticulous in their denial that the program was intended to inhibit the growth of U.S.-controlled enterprises in foreign countries. The object, it was repeatedly asserted, was to shift the sources of financing abroad, thereby helping to improve the appearance of U.S. balance-of-payments accounts. Whether the denial itself was disingenuous or not, the restrictions probably did not actually inhibit the growth of multinational enterprises very much. Still, U.S. business was deeply disturbed by the restrictions, and the depth of that perturbation rose sharply as the controls became mandatory. Once again, the overt signs of a close government-business relationship were not present.

Conclusions as large and general as these are rarely beyond dispute. And in this case, the disagreement on the part of some historians and political scientists is profound. Those that accept the Marxist postulates of history tend to regard the signs of debate between U.S. government and U.S. business as of no basic significance, a family quarrel among forces committed to the perpetuation of a capitalist hegemony.[27] But there are many without any particular allegiance to a Marxist interpretation of history that also regard U.S. foreign policy as totally indistinguishable from U.S. business policy.* The so-called revisionist school sees the postwar policies of the United States as a ceaseless effort on the part of the dominant political forces in the U.S. economy to achieve two ends: to extend their hegemonic reach into Europe before that continent could recover its strength and independence, and to solidify their control over the less-developed countries of the world. This is said to explain not only the U.S. leadership in promoting an open trading world but also its seeming altruism in financing the Marshall Plan and in promoting the extraordinary concept of aid to less-developed countries. Some members of the school have appealed to a conspiracy theory of history, with "good guys" and "bad guys" explicitly identified; but other interpreters have been more nearly value free, contending merely that it is in the nature of a powerful nation such as the United States to dominate others around it.

Though there is room for debate over the relative weights of the different motives in U.S. policy toward its overseas investors, there is less room for differences over the question of the dominant style of the relationship. U.S. enterprises have carried over into the international field the general style of their domestic relationships with government. That is to say, they have held the U.S. government at arm's length, neither soliciting nor receiving much guidance or advice. The U.S. govern-

* One writer, however, suggests the possibility that the military tail may be wagging the capitalist dog; that the Pentagon may be manipulating the industrialists more than the other way around. Seymour Melman, *Pentagon Capitalism* (New York: McGraw-Hill Book Co., 1970). Another suggests that the military and business establishments represent inseparable elements of a single integrated system, both committed to the defense of capitalism. Ralph Miliband, *The State in Capitalist Society* (New York: Basic Books, 1969), especially pp. 77–145.

ment's institution of voluntary controls on U.S. direct investment in 1965 and of mandatory controls in 1968 looked for a time as if it might force a new intimacy on business and government in the area of foreign investment. The government's initial willingness to consider each case of proposed investment abroad on its merits suggested the possibility of an approach based on individual consultation and ad hoc judgment. But in a few years the U.S. style reasserted itself, a style characterized by the institution of rules, the arm's length approach, the right of appeal. U.S. government agencies found themselves relying once more on newspapers and other public sources to learn about the foreign operations of these enterprises. The enterprises generally learned about U.S. government action affecting their existence from the same kind of channel.

There have been deviations from the pattern, of course, and some of them have not been trivial. Perhaps the most important have been episodes of frequent coordination between the U.S. government and the U.S. oil companies. Though the tie of the oil companies to the government cannot be compared in intimacy and continuity with similar ties in France, Japan, Italy, or even Britain, it has often been close.[28] The closeness has been disrupted repeatedly by U.S. government antitrust suits, by suits for the recovery of overcharges in the purchase of crude oil, and by quarrels over capital export controls and similar regulations, but has been restored by the recurrent need for consultation and joint action attending such crises as the closing of the Suez Canal.

There have been other exceptions as well. Regulated industries, such as the airlines, also have found close government contact unavoidable. The major defense contractors, including the aircraft companies as well as divisions of the leading communication equipment and chemical companies, have kept their intimate ties to the military establishment.[29] Still, despite all the qualifications, an arm's length quality in the relationships between business and government has persisted, distinguishing the U.S. style from that of most other countries.[30]

THE U.K. CASE

The norms that govern relations between business and government in the United Kingdom are similar in many respects to those of the United States. There are, of course, major differences between the political processes of the two countries. But the national atmosphere these processes generate in the United Kingdom is close to the norms with which U.S. business feels at home. One element in the British environment that bears a first-cousin relationship to U.S. norms is the approach to privilege and monopoly.

Britain's history, like that of the United States, has conditioned the country to a certain sensitivity over the use of the corporate form as an instrument of privilege. In Britain's case, the historical antecedents that produced this sensitivity go back to the thirteenth and fourteenth centuries. It is only necessary to recall here that by the sixteenth century the issuance of a royal charter in Britain was a vehicle for bestowing special rights and that these rights were commonly associated with some governmental purpose. Bodies created by such charters include familiar names: the Russia Company (1554), the British East India Company (1600), the Massachusetts Bay Company (1629), and the Hudson's Bay Company (1670).[31]

The tendency to link corporate charters with government purposes and to link both of these with monopoly was fixed in British history by the well-known South Sea Bubble affair. In 1711, Parliament created the South Sea Company, endowing it with a monopoly on Britain's trade in the South Seas. The intent was bizarre: to sell the company's shares in exchange for outstanding government notes, thus eliminating the national debt. What ensued was a period of wild speculation in the shares, ending in a disastrous collapse. The bursting of the South Sea Bubble, proverbial in the history of company law, led to legislation that generally restrained the use of the corporate form in Britain. Not until the early nineteenth century did Parliament even begin to consider relaxing the strictures of the Bubble Act. The needs of the Industrial Revolution finally signaled the demise of these restraints, but the remnants of suspicion against monopoly and special privileges lingered in British tradition.

Anyone familiar with the British environment will be quick to note that the British suspicion of monopoly and privilege has not always manifested itself in ways familiar to a U.S. businessman. For instance, Britain's tolerance for cartels and restrictionism until the last decade or so was the envy of the inhibited U.S. businessman; not until the passage of the Monopolies and Restrictive Practices Act in 1948 did Britain begin to confront the possibility of dealing with predatory business practices. Perhaps Britain's tolerance for these practices was owing in part to another British characteristic—the tendency to assume that any class of enterprise that has for a long time exercised some given prerogative in the economy, whether by law or custom, whether formal or informal, has an equitable claim to the continuation of that advantage. Later on, when we deal with the case of France, this theme will be encountered again. But whereas the French attitude is rationalized by reference to the sacrosanctity of legally acquired rights, the British case is built on the much more intangible and nontranslatable notion of "what's fair is fair." Quite naturally, therefore, the acquired right in British tradition is tied to still another general view: that organizations that exploit such vested rights ought to have due regard for the interests of others.

The notion that enterprises are expected to play fair suggests the basis for another policy that is distinctly British. If the standard of fairness can be defined, then, according to British assumptions, purely voluntary arrangements for its achievement stand a chance of working well. Accordingly, many of the regulatory devices to which the British economy has resorted in the past have been voluntary in form; and unlike the typical outcome in U.S. experience, such arrangements have not been predictable failures. For instance, voluntary wage-price freezes in Britain have had a somewhat greater chance of affecting the economy than they would in the United States.

This syndrome of attitudes is generally attributed in part to the élite that directs British institutions. And it is often related to another characteristic of that élite, namely, the limited character of their emotional and intellectual commitment to their business activities. Those who have the courage to generalize on the subject describe amateurism as a major characteristic of British heads of enterprise.[32] This amateurism is evidenced by the lack of vocational preparation on the part of businessmen, and by the preference of executives for a leisurely work pace and a limited degree of personal involvement. Like most clichés, these generalizations have their striking exceptions, especially in recent years. But there is not much doubt that they also retain considerable validity.

When friction has developed between the U.S. businessman operating in Britain and the British with whom he has contact, it has often been traced to the taut professionalism of the U.S. businessman interacting against the more relaxed and more tolerant attitudes of the British in business. Even if the U.S. businessman were at ease with the notion of the vested right and the implicit duty, he could not always recognize the right or the duty where it existed. But that friction, though painful at times, has proved manageable. It has proved manageable in part because it has not been exacerbated by any very great surprises in the official regulatory style of the U.K. government. In the United Kingdom, perhaps even more than in the United States, there is a marked distaste for governmental regulation that discriminates within a class of enterprise, or regulation that is specifically tailored to the individual enterprise. Though deviations occur, the prevailing rule is nondiscrimination and regulation by category. This does not mean that U.K. business, especially big U.K. business, keeps government at quite the arm's length position that is characteristic of its U.S. counterparts. The country is too small, its classes too well defined, and its "old boys'" clubs too highly developed for that outcome. Besides, the use of voluntary schemes of regulation on any considerable scale requires a fairly efficient process of interaction between business organizations and government agencies. Despite the frequent contacts between business and government, the nondiscriminatory character of U.K. regulation and the concept of fairness in U.K. administration seem to keep the tension that is generated between U.S.-controlled enterprises and their U.K. hosts at an easily manageable level.

There is one area in which U.S. norms and British norms are visibly different, however: in the relations between the government and its businessmen outside the home country. Because this is a book about U.S.-controlled multinational enterprises, the style of British business-government liaison abroad may seem of only trifling relevance. But this style does have a bearing. It highlights the respects in which the U.S. situation is distinctive. It suggests also the views that an ethnocentric Britisher might adopt as he tried to project the behavior of U.S.-controlled enterprises that had established themselves in Great Britain.

In substance, the liaison between the U.K. government and its enterprises regarding their interests outside the United Kingdom appears more intimate and more continuous, by some large order of magnitude, than is the case for the United States. Perhaps this is a vestige of British history when trade and the flag so often moved side by side into new territories. In any event, if the British practice were the U.S. norm, the political implications of U.S.-controlled subsidiaries in foreign countries might well be very different.

THE FRENCH CASE

In sharp contrast to Great Britain, relations between business and government in France contain few elements of familiarity for the U.S. businessman. When Salvador de Madariaga in 1929 was looking for a single word to epitomize the French national culture, he chose *le droit,* a distinctively French concept that somehow mingles law and right in a harmonious confusion.[33] Since then, political scientists and sociologists have been validating that semantic choice. In Great Britain an enterprise may acquire rights by mere precedent, including the kind of precedent that lies at the base of common law. But in France the gap between law and right is narrower. Rights are not easily acquired without specific law, but once acquired, they do not need to be justified by standards of nondiscrimination or tested by abstract concepts of fairness.

One can rarely be sure when to interpret historical events as cause, when as effect. But the tendency of the French to specify rights and obligations in detail, to reduce the scope for ambiguity or ad hocery, was evident in their earliest enactments relating to business. The tendency was to spell out every function, attribute, responsibility, and right of each legal entity created by the statutes.

Related to this tendency was an apparently intense need on the part of French society for stability and permanence. Practically every observer of the spirit of historical France comments in one way or another on the constant drive of the French business classes for equilibrium and harmony. Profits, so the formula repeatedly goes, are less important than the protection of principal; change is less important than the preservation of status. To be sure, as some economic historians have delighted in pointing out, the amount of change in the structure of French business during the nineteenth century cannot have been much less than that of the British or

German or Italian. But this change could well have occurred in spite of the desires and efforts of the French élite, not because of any tolerance for change. Even in peacetime France was not shut off from outside forces. And in war her openness as aggressor or as victim was even more in evidence. If France underwent considerable change, it may have been in spite of the aspirations of her élite, not because of them.

Just why the French businessman should have placed so heavy an emphasis on stability is not immediately clear. Some seem to ascribe it in part to the influence of Saint Simon during the pre-Napoleonic and Napoleonic periods in applying the state apparatus to the job of national development; but that fact, by itself, would not distinguish the French case from others that did not produce a special need for stability, such as the Japanese. Other suggested causes have been the chronic shortage of business credit in France, as well as the contempt in which business was held by the aristocracy.[34] Whatever the cause, the result was evident. Even when individual Frenchmen were brilliant technical innovators, as was commonly the case during the nineteenth century, their innovations were often first applied abroad.

The drive of businessmen for stability in France suggested a number of distinctive things about French business, not only throughout the nineteenth century but also in the succeeding years up to World War II. Cartels, of course, were extraordinarily common. True, cartels were hardly unique to France; they existed all over Europe during that period. But in Britain, the existence of cartels was generally justified by the standard of fairness more than by an appeal to the virtues of security. And in Germany the cartel was perceived partly as a means of increasing efficiency and was related intimately to plans for rationalization. In France, on the other hand, it seemed sufficient that the cartel should provide a means for stability in order to justify it in social terms.

Despite all the paraphernalia for the avoidance of change

in France, the country nevertheless has managed to evolve; the penchant for stability has been no guarantee that stability would be maintained. It was evident long before the era of modern planning in France that change could appropriately be induced from the top, provided it was done by some ordered and regulated process. During 1860, continuing the Saint Simon tradition, Emperor Napoleon III produced a national development plan, nearly a century before such plans were fashionable. Again, in 1882, France promulgated a national development plan. Both these efforts proved stillborn, but not for reasons of ideology.

Moreover, major French policy decisions in the economic field were not always sterile. The French government's decision of the 1920s to reduce its reliance on the Anglo-Saxon oil companies for the country's supply of petroleum was rapidly converted into action by the creation of Compagnie Française des Pétroles. And by the time World War II had ended, governmental intervention in the daily affairs of French business had spread through many sections of the economy.

Jean Monnet's general rehabilitation plan of 1946 was notable for the fact that, for perhaps the first time in France, change became a major objective of the French government. But the instrumentalities of the plan had a quality that neither the United States nor Great Britain could be said to share.

This difference in quality manifested once again the French need for balance and control. Industries that were to be modernized, such as steel and public energy, took their cues primarily from the government, whether they were government-owned or privately-owned properties; and the execution of modernizing policies covering all major industries was carefully monitored by the relevant ministries of government. Later, during the mid-1960s, when France decided that her computer industry needed strengthening in the national interest, the government played the same initiating and monitoring role.

Apart from the question of the source of initiative, there was also the question of style of implementation. The concepts of stability and harmony could be seen repeatedly in the details of the plan. In the case of steel, for instance, ownership of the two huge mills at the heart of the modernization program was under government guidance painstakingly shared out among the scores of existing firms in the French steel industry. On similar lines, the French decision to modernize the computer industry expressed itself through an elaborate Plan Calcul. Change, it seemed, was to be managed with minimum disturbance to the existing balance.

It may be that all these simple generalizations have been losing their validity for France during the past decade or two, or perhaps that they were not thoroughly justified in the first instance. In any event, observers of contemporary France have struggled with the question of relating the recent operational patterns of business and government under the various national four-year plans to the large historical generalizations that seemed to apply for the century or more before. Big business and government have developed a tolerance for consultation and for give-and-take through negotiation that does not seem to fit the historical pattern. It could be that the concept of the acquired right has been impaired a little in France, perhaps as an unintended consequence of the sustained emphasis on modernization and change.

Though the accent on change is probably appropriate and necessary for describing the France of the early 1970s, there is one aspect of the French style that has endured, emphasizing the gap between U.S. and French norms. The need for centralization of governmental power, a persistent theme in French history, continues as strong as ever. This centralization is strong both in a geographical and in a functional sense; it is located in Paris and it resides in the bureaucracy. Though the French find it hard to contemplate a public authority that does not feature such centralization, the Americans find it unpalatable to contemplate a public authority that does. Accordingly, the gap between the French norm and that of U.S. business remains very large. The expectation that initiative will come from the state, the insistence on order and stability, the emphasis on control, the subordination of profit as an objective, all represent a source of tension between the two cultures. The realities of actual governmental functioning in France and the United States are not quite so starkly different; there is plenty of centralization of governmental power in Washington and a certain amount of decentralization in France. But the propensity for generating tension may depend on the norms and expectations of the actors rather more than on the quality of the performance.

THE CASE OF JAPAN

In the spectrum of industrial countries, the norms of business and government in Japan seem about as far removed from those of the United States as one can find. Unlike the United States, the United Kingdom, and France, Japan developed her operating norms as a modern state over a period of little more than 100 years.[35] No doubt the speed of that development was partly illusory. The system that emerged was certainly conditioned by the events that preceded the modern era. Nevertheless, after the Meiji restoration in 1868, Japan set about consciously copying the forms that other cultures had produced. One of these was the corporate form.

Borrowing an instiutional form does nothing to ensure that it will be infused with its original spirit. Once in Japanese hands, the corporate form had rather different implications than in the countries from which it was borrowed. And the relations between the Japanese enterprise and Japanese society, which drew on the values of a culture distinctly different from those of the West, were infused with their own special set of characteristics.

Some of the key values that dominate Japanese society today were shaped by the centuries of feudal rule that ended in 1868. The government of this premodern era was built on rigid feudal lines. Unquestioning loyalty to one's local lord was the over-riding obligation, and the social structure within each lord's domain was fixed in a tightly prescribed hierarchy. But Japan had also developed some group values that distinguished her from other feudal societies and that would later stand her in good stead. One was the commitment to goal attainment, a commitment so strong in Japanese society as to gladden the heart of any *n*-achievement devotee. A second was the concept of shared responsibility within any group for the achievement of a task assigned to the group, a concept that somehow managed to survive side by side with a rigid hierarchy within the group.

A Westerner would be hard put to say with unerring sensitivity how feudal Japanese defined the limits of the "group" for any given purpose. Some things, however, are clear. The limits of the relevant group were flexible. In the family context, for instance, the group was much more a social entity than one based solely on blood ties. Once linked to a Japanese family or group, one shared its responsibilities and its successes, its honor and its disgrace.

The Japanese managed to draw another social characteristic into their distinctive feudal mix, a characteristic whose utility for an industrial society is self-evident. Despite the emphasis on group responsibility and the existence of a rigid pecking order within any given group, Japanese institutions managed to reward obvious individual merit and Japanese society to tolerate considerable mobility between the classes. This was achieved by allowing for a highly competitive selection process at a very few key points in the careers of ordinary Japanese. Bright young men of low degree, for instance, could hope to make it to the best universities simply on the basis of their ability; if they bested the competition in the universities, they could hope for appointment to the most promising jobs in industry. Even formal adoption by one of the leading families was a real possibility. At critical times, too, the hierarchical structure of Japan was allowed to weaken and social mobility was given an almost free rein. This seems to have happened extensively during the two great crises of Japan's modern existence: the Meiji restoration and the Allied occupation.

The compatibility of some of these social values with an industrial society became evident when Japan moved out of the smothering restraints of feudalism. In the case of Japan, unlike that of Europe, the transition from feudalism to a modern society was very swift; it occurred over decades rather than centuries. As a result, the élite of Japan were able to draw on some of the surviving preindustrial Japanese characteristics of group loyalty, shared group responsibility, and task-achievement orientation when managing the process of transition.

Almost from the very first years of the modern Japanese era, the political and business élites had a common cause, using the instrumentalities of both the public and the private sectors to industrialize quickly.[37] In order to lubricate the process, the government set up a number of public enterprises to act as recipients of Western technology and as prototypes of Western business organizations. Inasmuch as there were no obvious ideological boundaries defining the respective roles of the public and the private sectors, the question could be considered on wholly pragmatic grounds. When by 1880 the need for direct government participation in the industrializing process was no longer so obvious, there was no ideological block to a wholesale divestiture of these corporations. In the divestiture process, the companies were often acquired by private entrepreneurs at bargain prices.

The social organization that emerged to take over the task of managing Japan's industrializing society represented an extraordinary blend of the feudal family structure, the government agency, and the modern corporation. These elements have persisted in Japanese industrial society to the present, though the relative strengths of the components have shifted somewhat in the 100 years or so of evolution. Still, if one were to generalize regarding the direction of the shift, it would be that the private and public élites have become even less differentiated than they were 100 years ago.

The sense of group participation and group responsibility has shaped not only the ties between the public and private sectors in Japan, but also the internal organization of the private sector itself. From the first, Japan's industry has been dominated by a small number of large business groups, in whose hands have been concentrated most of the banking and manufacturing activities in the modern sector. Before World War II, the leadership of each of the major groups was expressed through family holding companies, which characteristically controlled a cluster of subsidiaries. As a rule, each such cluster included one or more banks and insurance companies, conduits for marshaling public savings to finance the other members of the family group. Managers for the affiliates were generally recruited through the family holding company as they emerged from the university; thereafter, they spent the whole of their business lives within the family system. Because managers were readily transferred among sister affiliates, they could be thought of as a common pool of élite manpower for assignment within the system. The same flexibility could be seen in the deployment of capital. The banks in any system regularly loaned sums to their affiliated companies of a size that no prudent banker would consider committing in an arm's length transaction, and the affiliated companies incurred debts to their sister banks that seemed utterly out of proportion to the companies' equity.

No two of the family groups were quite alike in industrial composition, but practically all of them were widely diversified, running the range from textiles to steel. This fact was apparently no accident; the rivalry among the groups for equal and balanced participation in the Japanese economy was intense.

The stress on equality of status was so strong, in fact, that during World War II the five major holding companies paid identical amounts of income tax to the Japanese government. Both their ability and their desire to negotiate with the tax authorities for such identical payments suggest how large the gap has been between the social norms of Japan and those of the United States.

After World War II, job mobility inside Japan's industrial structure was greatly accelerated. A period of galloping inflation, coupled with occupation measures curbing the role of the old industrial families, opened positions for new business talent. The rapid growth of Japan's economy during the 1950s and 1960s helped that talent to get well launched. New companies not intimately related to the old family groups managed to elbow their way into the industrial structure, among them Sony, Honda, and Matsushita Electric. The connection between family ownership and family management of big enterprises became somewhat attenuated. The emergence of a professional management class, already a visible tendency in the Japan of the 1920s, became a dominant trend during the 1960s.

Despite all these changes, however, certain basic aspects of Japanese industrial life appeared to remain unchanged. The propensity for group identification, the acceptance of group goals and group responsibilities, did not seem to diminish. Though Japan managed to accommodate a new crop of Schumpeterian innovators, these innovators showed no philosophical attachment to Western individualism. Like their predecessors, they emphasized group goals and teamwork. The tendency to think of the firm as a group to which owners, managers, and workers attach a common loyalty has expressed itself in numerous ways. Such things as company songs and company shrines, which may seem incongruous by Western standards, have real power and meaning in contemporary Japan. The solemn resolutions defining the joint national responsibilities of the various industrial associations might be interpreted as trivial image-building or pious nonsense in a Western setting, but they are not to be dismissed so lightly in Japan.[38]

The sense of group identification might conceivably have divided Japan's internal social structure on lines comparable with Western political ideologies, such as the public-private or labor-management dichotomy. Divisions of this sort have been of no great importance, however. The gap that separates the public from the private sector in Britain or the United States, for example, has never been evident in modern Japan. On the contrary, the heads of the leading industrial families have taken portfolios as cabinet ministers without a hint of the conflict-of-interest queries that accompany such appointments in the United States. Senior civil servants, at the retirement age of fifty, have "descended from heaven" to the nether regions of industry and commerce. Private banks have worked hand-in-glove with public credit institutions. Indeed, public policy such as that of the Ministry of International Trade and Industry (MITI) has sometimes been indistinguishable from the private policy of the national trade associations.

Still, Japanese society has been no more exempt from internal policy struggles than any other complex society. An internal struggle of special relevance to the future of multinational enterprise in Japan has been the struggle between Japan's Fair Trade Commission (FTC) and MITI. The FTC is a remnant of the occupation, entrusted with the quixotic task of preventing monopoly and preserving a competitive economic structure in Japan under authority of the Antimonopoly Act. MITI, on the other hand, took its task from its title; and, predictably, it saw group commitment and group cooperation as the best way to achieve that task. The inevitable clash developed almost immediately. The only surprising element in the clash has been the stubborn ability of the FTC to survive. Evidently, the Japanese spirit of group decision still allows for the utility of struggle between groups. It may also be that the FTC has been seen as having some value inside Japan in maintaining the internal equilibrium among the groups.

In relations with foreign investors and foreign governments, however, MITI has been the dominant Japanese institution. For external purposes MITI has put up a common front, constructed by a group process in which its influence has dominated. It has been MITI, therefore, that has signaled the areas of foreign technology that members of the group should try to mine. It has been MITI also that has screened foreign proposals to enter Japan. In the process, the squabbles between MITI and others in Japan were internal matters, and foreign investors could not hope to exploit those internal differences to anything approaching the extent possible in other countries, such as France. Here and there, perhaps, a foreign business interest has managed to develop a special tie to some internal group, especially if the foreigner offered a source of technology or markets that the group felt it could use in its internal struggles. Close and intimate ties have, however, been quite exceptional.

When Japanese enterprises have established their subsidiaries abroad, the close-knit character of Japanese society has come to the surface once again. In many ways, indeed, the overseas ventures of the Japanese have come close to conforming with the Marxist assumptions about the ties between imperialism and capitalism. Japanese businessmen must have the Japanese government's formal permission to make the investment. Even if formal approval were not required, the propensity of Japanese business to rely very heavily on borrowed funds means that any such step would be screened by a Japanese banking institution. As in the case of France, the liaison between these institutions and the central bank of Japan is so intimate that any such venture must pass through an official screening that is more than perfunctory.

As this description suggests, there is a great difference in the relations between business and government to which Japanese conform when they invest abroad and the relations that exist in the case of the United States. The Japanese may be aware of the difference in an intellectual sense, but it is doubtful that they are capable of giving it much credibility. For them, as for the revisionist historians, U.S.-controlled enterprises are part of an integral national system called the United States.[39] Their ties to the United States make loyalty to Japanese goals out of the question. When representatives of the system establish a foothold inside Japan, they violate the integral character of the Japanese culture.

In sum, the existing level of tension generated by U.S.-controlled subsidiaries in host countries cannot be explained merely in terms of conflicts of economic interest. Cases of such conflict exist; but they are too tangled and the results too obscure to explain the universality and depth of the reaction. In a search for prime causes, one is pushed off economics to the political, social, and cultural variables. Variables of this sort, of course, are difficult to distinguish and difficult to measure. The viscera prove more important than the cerebrum as the instrument for analysis. All one can say on the basis of the discussion is that the concepts of clashing élites, clashing ideologies, and clashing cultures seem to add an important dimension to understanding the host countries' reactions to U.S.-controlled enterprises. If this is where the causes of the tension lie, then measures that do no more than redistribute the economic benefits of multinational enterprise may have very little to do with the easing of international tensions.

[7]

National Thrust
and National Riposte

THE modern world of nation-states, it will generally be agreed, is hardly a model for tidy organization. Each of a 100-odd nations is concerned with the achievement of its own distinct national, social, and political goals. Yet each feels the need to accept a certain measure of contact with the others through investment, trade, tourism, and the exchange of ideas. During the last few decades, national goals have grown progressively more ambitious and more refined, as states have assumed responsibilities inside their borders for such complex matters as health, welfare, economic security, and the equitable distribution of income. At the same time, contacts between the states seem to have multiplied inexorably, propelled by continuous improvements in transportation and communication.

Just at the stage when the need for national control has increased, therefore, the national ability to maintain that control has declined. The interests and responsibilities of nations, which once might have been delineated explicitly by the surveyor's theodolite, have lost their geographical tidiness and spread outward into the areas of other nations. For the United States, the outward spread has been much more evident than for others, epitomized not only by the interests of its multinational enterprises but also by its pace-setting position in scientific achievements and in consumption norms. But practically all countries, whether leaders or otherwise, have found themselves increasingly involved with the internal affairs of the others. One result has been a steady increase in questions of overlapping and conflicting jurisdiction.[1]

The Jurisdictional Conflict

"It is settled law," said Judge Learned Hand in his 1945 opinion in the landmark Alcoa antitrust case, "that any state may impose obligations, even upon persons not within its allegiance, for conduct outside its borders that has consequences within its borders which the state reprehends; and these liabilities other states will ordinarily recognize."[2] As far as the reaction of other states to U.S. extraterritorial measures is concerned, however, the statement has proved rather too sanguine. As a rule, other states have resented any reaching out by the United States into their own jurisdictions.[3] Indeed, resentment has been quick to develop even when the U.S. command was issued in the first instance to someone who was also within the jurisdictional reach of the United States. More and more cases have appeared in which the commands of the U.S. government, even though directed unequivocally to U.S. nationals, have produced major international reverberations. The increase in situations of this sort stems out of two ineluctable facts: first, that every transaction across international borders has two sides, hence involves two national jurisdictions; second, that nationals who control assets outside their own country generally find themselves confronting two sets of obligations—one to their home country, the other to the country in which their assets are located.

The fact that every international transaction is subject to the control of two jurisdictions has been producing frictions in international relations for as long as there have been international transactions—in short, long before the multinational enterprise could be conceived of as an institution. The United States restricts copper exports in order to hold down the domestic price of copper; as a result, the supply of copper for European countries is curtailed. The United States restricts the importation of oil in order to protect her domestic industry; as a consequence, the price commanded by Libyan oil in Europe is depressed. The United States lays restraints on the exportation of capital because she thinks such restrictions are needed to protect her balance-of-payments position; as a consequence, the demands for credit from European capital markets rise sharply. The U.S. government prohibits the export to some friendly country of materials that are intended for processing and reexport to a cold war "enemy"; as a result, the intermediary country that is to process the material is prevented from doing useful business. Inasmuch as the presence of U.S.-controlled subsidiaries in any foreign country generally leads to a higher level of transactions between that country and the United States than would otherwise exist, their presence also connotes an increased vulnerability on the part of the local economy to the regulatory measures of the United States.

It is true, of course, that the problem is symmetrical, that the same generalizations would apply to the foreign subsidiaries of British or French or Japanese enterprises. The fact that the aluminum industry of Greece is controlled by a Pechiney subsidiary, for instance, exposes that country to the regulations of France more than would otherwise be the case. But there is a difference in degree between the United States and other economies that host nations cannot easily overlook. The subsidiaries of U.S. parents are in the aggregate many times larger than those of any second-tier investor country, such as Britain or Japan. The issue, as far as most host countries are concerned, is of a wholly different order of magnitude.

The fact that every international transaction has two sides

is less troubling to host countries, however, than the fact that the local personality of the U.S.-controlled multinational enterprise—the local subsidiary—is subject to the commands of two masters. The U.S. government can direct the U.S. parent to take measures that determine the actions and plans of its foreign subsidiaries, while the local governments can direct their ukases at the subsidiary with equal readiness.

In this case, once again, the force that the U.S. government is in a position to exert is matched, at least nominally, by a force in the other direction. Though the U.S. government can command a U.S. parent to take action affecting the subsidiary, the local government can command the subsidiary to take action affecting the parent; when the Mexican government directs the Mexican subsidiary of the Ford Motor Company to find ways of exporting its products to other countries, the message is intended for Dearborn, Michigan. Nonetheless, host governments tend to assume that the capacity of the U.S. government to influence the conduct of the subsidiary is much greater than the host's capacity to influence the U.S. parent. Because the struggle is generally thought of as a zero-sum game—a game in which the gain of one side is the loss of the other—the difference in persuasive power between the United States and the host country assumes a critical importance.

There is another aspect of government influence that can be stated in formally symmetrical terms. Though the U.S. government can influence International Harvester in ways that affect the management of its British subsidiary, the British government can surely influence British Petroleum, or the Italian government Olivetti, with regard to the management of their U.S. subsidiaries.[4] Once again, however, the symmetry is one of form not of substance. In this case, the U.S government's role is relatively less potent than the formal symmetry might imply. The influence of the U.S. government on the overseas subsidiaries of U.S. enterprises is much less, as a rule, than the influence of other advanced countries over the foreign subsidiaries of their home enterprises. It is nearly inconceivable for a leading company in France or Japan to make some major move abroad without first consulting a tutelary ministry at home; it is unlikely that a large enterprise in Great Britain, Italy, or Germany would take such an action without some serious consultation; yet a U.S. company would probably make no more than the most perfunctory disclosure to the U.S. government—if it made any disclosure at all—before taking a similar step.

Nevertheless, the U.S. government has at times reached through the U.S. parent to the foreign subsidiary in ways that represented a flat challenge to the policies of host governments. Cases of this sort have stimulated a torrent of publicity as they have come to light. The fact that it was the United States whose will was being imposed on the local subsidiary generally added a special piquancy to the situation, reminding the host government of the overwhelming potential for interference that lay in reserve behind the individual case. These cases have been documented elsewhere in considerable detail. Sometimes they have been described with a disinterested objectivity, sometimes with embellishing flourishes of a less objective sort.[5] Perhaps the most sensitive group of such cases is the one that involves U.S. efforts to extend its network of economic cold war measures so that they cover the activities of U.S.-controlled foreign subsidiaries.[6] A classic incident involved Ford of Canada's tentative exploration in 1957 of the possibility of shipping trucks to mainland China. This was a time when Canada was eager to build up that trade while the United States was bent on discouraging it. Accordingly, when a U.S. government frown of displeasure stopped Ford in its tracks, the Canadian reaction was predictably bitter. On similar lines, the U.S. government tried to stop the British from selling some British Viscount aircraft to China because the aircraft were equipped with U.S. navigational equipment.[7]

As provocative as the cases involving Canada and Britain

was one in 1965 that involved Fruehauf's majority-owned joint venture in France. In this case, the U.S. government tried to prevent the French company from selling its vans to another French company that would incorporate them in products destined for mainland China, but the effort was thwarted by French minority interests through resort to their own courts. Another provocative case occurred in 1964 when the U.S. government refused to allow U.S. IBM to export some specialized computer equipment to its French subsidiary. The justification for that refusal was that the United States, as signatory to the nuclear nonproliferation treaty, would be violating her international obligations if she helped France improve her nuclear capabilities.[8] From the French viewpoint, this was a case of one sovereign state using its economic force to dominate another. There is a widespread well-grounded assumption that many other measures of this sort have been taken by the U.S. government without publicity.

Applications of U.S. government power through the foreign subsidiaries of U.S. parents have had a strong impact on public opinion abroad. In economic terms, however, they have probably been less important than U.S. government controls over the flow of funds between U.S. parents and their subsidiaries. In form, these controls were directed at the parent; in substance, they represented commands that deeply affected the behavior of the foreign subsidiaries. By 1970, after several years of tightening and formalizing those controls, the U.S. government's program had produced telling effects—largely unanticipated effects—upon the financing patterns of U.S.-controlled subsidiaries in Europe. More than ever before, for instance, the capital needs of those subsidiaries were being raised from sources outside the United States.[9]

One way of characterizing the U.S. program of control over capital exports is that it was an effort to improve the appearance of the U.S. balance-of-payment position at the expense of other advanced countries. For a short period, it generated a furious reaction abroad, including official complaints from Australia, Canada, and Japan.[10] But the reaction was not sustained, and it never involved the Europeans very deeply. That the controls failed to generate much direct reaction from the Europeans is to be attributed to various circumstances. For one thing, most European nations would not have hesitated to use very similar restrictions for the same ends; for another, the adverse balance-of-payments consequences for Europe generated by the U.S. program, to the extent that such consequences existed, could not be very easily detected and measured. Besides, there was hesitation in Europe about protesting against U.S. capital export controls at the very time that so many Europeans were expressing misgivings over the growth of U.S.-controlled enterprises in Europe. So the issue has been allowed to smolder underground, probably to break out at a time when the conflict of interest is more evident.

The conflict between U.S. objectives and the objectives of other governments appears in many other settings. For example, governments often try to restructure national industries inside their borders to meet some pressing national needs. These efforts commonly affect the structure of multinational enterprises. When that happens, the probability of generating conflicts with the policies of other countries is high.

As far as U.S. measures to shape the organization of industry are concerned, they generally appear as part of a well-articulated antitrust policy, in which the object is to avoid the impairment of national competition. But a policy for the maintenance of competition is less than complete if it overlooks the restrictions on imports. This is especially the case for industries in which the enterprises are large and few in number and in which the markets of different countries are closely interrelated. As a result, the U.S. policy for the maintenance of domestic competition inexorably pushes U.S authorities into the business of scanning the economies of other countries, and it focuses attention especially on those industries in which multinational enterprises play their largest role.

At times, the U.S. authorities' probing of the activities of U.S.-controlled enterprises abroad has benefited some foreign countries in which these enterprises operate. For instance, the U.S. government's various cases against the United Fruit Company during the 1950s and 1960s, charging that company with monopolistic practices in the world banana trade, could reasonably be supposed to have helped the banana-raising countries.[11] There have been many other cases of a similar sort: a 1960 proceeding against General Foods and a number of other large enterprises, alleging collusion in the importation of coconut products from the Philippines;[12] several proceedings against drug companies, alleging numerous restrictive practices in exports to foreign countries;[13] a 1953 action against the major lead producers that enjoined them from restricting U.S. imports or exports of primary lead;[14] private and governmental actions against the leading U.S. radio manufacturers to break up their restrictive arrangements in the British Commonwealth;[15] various actions during the 1960s directed against leading U.S. chemical companies, designed to put an end to restrictions on the exportation of phosphate products;[16] and other actions of a similar sort. The record fails to disclose any expressions of appreciation by other countries for such U.S. efforts. And expressions of appreciation could hardly have been expected. The actions in those cases were taken because the U.S. government had concluded that they were in its own interests. The main psychological impact on other countries, predictably, was to remind them of their vulnerability to initiatives coming from the United States.

There is hardly any part of the U.S. antitrust program that cannot affect the overseas activities of U.S.-controlled multinational enterprises in some respect. But there is one provision in particular that has a special potential for bringing such enterprises into conflict with the policies of other countries. This is section 7 of the Clayton Act, which enjoins enterprises subject to U.S. jurisdiction from acquiring other enterprises wherever "the effects of such acquisition may be substantially to lessen competition or to tend to create a monopoly."[17] Under this provision, a merger by any part of a multinational enterprise, wherever it may occur, is subject to the steely scrutiny and possible intervention of U.S. antitrust authorities.

It should not be supposed that the United States is the only country concerned with maintaining competition inside its national markets. Canada and Great Britain have developed programs to promote the maintenance of domestic competition. Both the European Community and some of its constituent countries have gone a considerable distance in the same direction.[18] But nations rarely go so far as to require potential exporters in their economy to compete for the markets of other countries. On the contrary; most national statutes, including those of the United States, eschew the Golden Rule by incorporating an exemption that permits their national firms to limit their competition when exporting from home territory. Any country that relies heavily on outside suppliers must therefore fall back on the principle of self-help if it is to protect itself from their agreements to restrict competition.

Here, of course, is where the difficulty lies. Many countries in Europe feel that their local enterprises are too small to operate efficiently in a modern world. Accordingly, while U.S. authorities ponder how to keep the foreign subsidiaries of U.S.-controlled enterprises from colluding with other enterprises that might be potential exporters to the United States, these nations are busy exploring the possibilities of promoting mergers among the potential exporters in their economies.* Even the nations which assume that competition may be worth encouraging in certain circumstances are sufficiently eclectic in their approach

---

* The usual roles were reversed when the Algerian government in 1969 refused to recognize the merger of Sinclair Oil and Atlantic-Richfield, even though the merger was legal under U.S. law. See "Algeria Takes Control of Oil Properties Held by Atlantic Richfield," *The Wall Street Journal*, January 27, 1970, p. 12.

to also contemplate the desirability of creating larger firms by way of merger.[19] This is why it is possible for Britain to operate two seemingly incompatible programs side by side: one devoted to the promotion of competition, the other to the encouragement of mergers. France has had a paramount policy for a decade or so to squeeze the leading companies of each industrial sector into a smaller number of larger undertakings.[20] In Japan, some government officials have put extraordinary pressure on some branches of industry, such as the automobile producers, to combine in larger units.[21]

A clear confrontation of these conflicting national policies is visible on the horizon. The U.S. government's intervention in Gillette's acquisition of an electric shaver company in Germany and in Litton's acquisition of a German electric typewriter company are an indication of things to come.[22]

Apart from the fact that the Clayton Act antimerger provision leads U.S. authorities to reach out into the jurisdictions of other countries, there is the even more painful fact that it inhibits the Europeans from setting up their enterprises in the U.S. market by means of merger or acquisition. When British Petroleum first tried to break its way into the U.S. market by acquiring various chains of gasoline stations, it looked for a time as if the strictures of the Clayton Act might prevent the move; some highly convoluted accommodations and compromises on the part of the Department of Justice finally saved the day.[23] And when two Swiss drug firms, Ciba and Geigy, decided to unite their operations in the United States as part of a worldwide merger of the two companies, the Clayton Act once more appeared as a threat to consummation.[24]

A European of an unduly Machiavellian turn of mind might well suspect that the Clayton Act was a bogey deliberately invented by the Americans to prevent European mergers, especially if these mergers might threaten either the strength or the independence of U.S. enterprises. This interpretation would, of course, be a gross misreading of U.S. intentions. Whether a misreading or not, however, the sentiment is bound to be a growing factor in the relations between the United States and other advanced countries.

Restraining the Foreign-Owned Subsidiary

Bit by bit, without any grand design or general policy, host governments have been responding to the growing presence of the foreign-owned subsidiary. Despite the absence of a grand design, there have been consistent elements in the reaction. Nations have been whittling away at the concept that foreign-owned businesses are presumptively entitled to nondiscriminatory treatment, substituting a much more qualified set of rights for the national treatment standard.

The qualifications have not been uniform from one country to the next. For one thing, as pointed out in Chapter 6, different countries have exhibited different levels of sensitivity to the issue. For another, even when the sensitivity was the same, the problems generated by the presence of the foreign subsidiaries have differed. Finally, some countries have felt less inhibited than others about curtailing foreigners' rights because the price to be paid by limiting the scope of foreign-owned enterprises seemed relatively low.

Most countries, when confronting the implicit trade-offs in a policy that restricts foreign-owned subsidiaries, have chosen to limit such subsidiaries to some extent, groping toward a balance that took cognizance of both the gains and the costs.[25] Most of them, including the United States, have had no hesitation in deciding that it was worth any price to keep foreign-controlled interests out of certain sensitive national industries. Accordingly, practically every country limits the right of foreign-owned subsidiaries to participate in industries such as ordnance and aircraft, public broadcasting, coastwise shipping, banking, and minerals exploitation on public lands. France and Japan, exhibiting the special degree of chariness that has for so long characterized their responses to foreigners, have gone further still. In France, for instance, as far back as the 1920s, foreign oil companies were limited in their refining and distribution activities;[26] and during the early 1960s, a systematic screening of all proposed enterprises by foreigners was instituted.[27] In Japan, by that time, the only industries for which foreigners had unrestricted establishment rights were fifteen or so sectors that foreigners could be counted on to avoid, such as brewing, ice manufacturing, cotton spinning, and steel.[28] For all other purposes, highly rigorous screening criteria and drastic limitations were the general rule. Great Britain, despite her long tradition of maintaining a liberal regime on capital movements for nonresidents, has exhibited occasional misgivings over the acquisition by U.S. firms of enterprises in "sensitive" industries and has been imposing special conditions in some cases.[29] Even Germany, despite her insistent commitment to a free, open economy, has shown occasional nervousness over foreign takeovers of domestic oil enterprises.

The insistence of some governments that foreign-owned subsidiaries should be subject to special rules of the game is sometimes motivated by questions of public policy. At other times, however, the object is simply to show preference for a national group over foreigners, without much regard for national economic consequences. Whatever the nature of the national benefits may have been, provisions of this sort have frequently been at variance with the general principle of national treatment of foreign-owned subsidiaries, a principle widely adopted in bilateral treaties.[30] But the internal compulsions to apply the restrictions have usually been so strong that the existence of a conflicting treaty commitment has been of no great moment. The U.S. government itself has not been wholly free of that tendency. U.S foreign aid programs, for instance, have made various distinctions between U.S. enterprises that were "substantially beneficially" owned by Americans and enterprises created under U.S. law that were not so owned: True-blue Americans are entitled to have their investments abroad guaranteed against risks such as war and expropriation, whereas *ersatz* Americans are not. The U.S. armed forces have made similar distinctions of this sort in the acquisition of materiel involving classified information, probably more on commercial grounds than on genuine security grounds.

Other governments have gone a great deal further, however. Many seem determined to broaden the range and scope of the discriminations to be applied against foreign-owned subsidiaries, especially when those subsidiaries are controlled by U.S. parents. One common form of discrimination has been in the selection of suppliers to government agencies. In many countries, the application of buy-at-home practices, already a well-established tradition among government procurement officers, has been embellished by an added admonition—"except from foreign-owned subsidiaries."[31] The practice of distinguishing local producers according to the nationality of their owners, especially producers in advanced industries such as computers, has become well established.[32]

Practices such as these can be expected to spread into other areas of national policy. It is quite clear, for instance, that governmental organizations such as Britain's Industrial Reorganization Corporation[33] and France's Institut de Développement Industriel, will be less ready to extend a helping financial hand to U.S.-owned subsidiaries than to locally controlled competitors. European governments that are subsidizing research will surely raise questions over the ownership of local corporations that apply for subsidy; otherwise, they may find themselves financing IBM's research in fourth-generation computers. In countries where access to local capital markets is a licensed privilege, the same sort of ownership consideration is being taken into account.[34] In the administration of national antimerger laws, the tolerance for monopoly by national companies seems greater if the company is not foreign owned.[35] In sum, governments are gradually extending and solidifying the principle that local corporations, even though created by domestic law, have rights and privileges that are determined in considerable measure by the identity of their stockholders.

The urge of host countries to place special restraints on foreign-owned enterprises has struggled brutally at times with the need of those countries to use such enterprises as a means for achieving some badly wanted national ends. For example, U.S.-controlled subsidiaries have often been more responsive than their locally owned competitors to the local programs of governments for the development of lagging regions. Governments have offered cheap public loans and tax exemptions to enterprises prepared to settle in backward areas, such as France's Ardèche region or Italy's Calabria, only to find that rootless foreign-owned subsidiaries could respond to such incentives more easily than well-established local enterprises already located in, say, Nancy or Milan. As a result, U.S.-controlled subsidiaries have sometimes been placed in a seemingly favored position in relation to their local competition, rather than in a position of handicap.

The response to this problem has varied from country to country. A few, such as Mexico, have simply refused to allow foreign-owned subsidiaries to have access to the benefits of some of their special subsidy programs.[36] Others have exacted special conditions from the foreigners, more stringent than they would have required of locally owned enterprise.

In one kind of situation, however, countries have been content to maintain their special inducements to prospective investors even if foreign-owned enterprises were the beneficiaries. Nations that were part of a common regional market, such as the European Community or the Central American Common Market, have seen themselves in competition with the other members to attract strong producers into their national territory.[37] As a result, national programs to induce investment have sometimes been used by members of a common market area as a competitive weapon. The object of the competition, as often as not, has been to persuade a U.S.-owned subsidiary to make its home in one of the competing countries. As a result, one more source of resentment against such subsidiaries has been generated.

The development of common market schemes has tended to raise questions about the position of the subsidiaries of U.S.-controlled enterprises in a number of other contexts. Even where the member governments involved in such arrangements have not offered special inducements to prospective investors, U.S. enterprises generally seem to have responded to the opportunities with much greater alacrity and commitment than have the enterprises owned by nationals of the participating states. The willingness of enterprises such as IBM and Ford to specialize and cross-haul among their subsidiaries in the European Community, for instance, has not been matched by many similar responses on the part of European-owned enterprises. The disposition of U.S. enterprises to take the Latin American common market arrangements seriously and to plan for the area on an integrated basis has been much greater than that of the indigenous enterprises in Latin America.[38]

Here, too, however, the very responsiveness of U.S.-controlled enterprises may yet lead to their undoing. Member governments in the EEC and in the Latin American Free Trade Area have flirted repeatedly with the idea of subjecting outside enterprises to special area-wide discriminations and restraints. In the European Community, from time to time, France has proposed that other member countries adopt some common policy of restraint embodying the features of the French national policy.[39] This view has repeatedly struck a sympathetic chord in the Commission of the European Community, as well as among some of its technical working parties. When in 1964 the commission was struggling actively with the formulation of a common oil policy, the idea of granting special rights and subsidies to "European" oil companies under such a policy—a national extension of the French approach—kept coming to the surface.[40] Since then, the European Community's projects for reducing the barriers to industry among the countries of the common market, such as policies for the creation of a European company and for the creation of a European patent,[41] have generally included provisions that could limit the availability of the new institutions as far as U.S.-owned subsidiaries in Europe were concerned.*

Until 1970, despite the number of efforts of this sort, only one important project for the achievement of joint restrictions within a common market area had actually materialized. This was an agreement adopted by the so-called Andean group of countries, a group of five nations on the western shores of South America that constitute a part of the larger Latin American Free Trade Area. That group, spurred by the studies of an outstanding secretariat and bolstered by the populist revolutionary bent of the Peruvian government, adopted a common requirement that will oblige new foreign investors to accompany their initial proposals with a plan for later divestiture. The objective of the requirement is to reduce foreign investors to a minority position in their local subsidiaries within a period of twelve to fifteen years after entry. Agreements of this sort have to be tested in the crucible of conflicting national interests, and that test still lies ahead. But the adoption itself represented a precedent of consequence.

There is no reason to expect, however, that measures which formally restrain the U.S.-owned subsidiaries will do much to

* As a rule, the limitation is created by a definitional link whose implications are not immediately apparent to the layman's untutored eye. Only "nationals" of an EEC country as defined by local law are to have access to the new European facilities. But in five out of six EEC countries "nationals" so defined are limited to companies which maintain their *siège social* in the country. Eric Stein, "Conflict of Laws by Treaty: Recognition of Companies in a Regional Market," *Michigan Law Review*, vol. 68, no. 7, June 1970, pp. 1327–1354. This threatens the position of many foreign-owned subsidiaries with parents outside the EEC.

reduce the tension that is created by their presence. What host governments badly want is not only a sense of control over foreign-owned subsidiaries but also access to the resources they think some of these subsidiaries can provide. As long as governments feel that they need those resources, they are likely to be vulnerable. And being vulnerable, they will continue experiencing the discomfiture that foreign-owned enterprises have so commonly produced.

[8   ]

A Choice of Futures

THE evidence summarized in the last few chapters makes a fairly solid case for a few key propositions.

The multinational enterprise as an economic institution seems capable of adding to the world's aggregate productivity and economic growth, as compared with the visible alternatives. In some kinds of industries, its contribution to productivity and growth seems less than in others. There may even be industries in which the existence of multinational enterprise is stifling to growth, though these situations are probably exceptional.

Conclusions regarding the distribution of the benefits of that growth are more uncertain. However, the idea that the "lending" country captures all the benefits while the yield to the "borrowing" country is zero or negative seems altogether improbable.

As for the distribution of benefits within the countries, it is difficult to say how the operations of multinational enterprises are affecting the outcome. For instance, the question as to whether existing inequalities of income are enlarged or reduced in host countries by the operations of multinational enterprises depends partly on the alternative economic system one has in mind. There is no evidence that economies which retain elements of a decentralized enterprise system, such as the Japanese, the Mexican, and the Yugoslav economies, have managed to develop more egalitarian income distributions by placing special limitations on the scope of multinational enterprises.

Although it is hard to say just what effect multinational enterprises have had on national income distribution, some other effects of the multinational enterprise have been clear. As a rule, the presence of multinational enterprises has generated tensions in the foreign countries where they appear: not much in some countries, but a great deal in others. When such enterprises are headed by U.S. parents, that fact generally tends to increase the level of tension associated with their presence. As a rule, the tension is a manifestation of powerful psychic and social needs on the part of élite groups in host countries. These needs include the desire for control and status and the desire to avoid a sense of dependence on outsiders.

Different value systems lead to different definitions of the problem of the multinational enterprise. As I see it, the problem contains several elements. Sovereign states have legitimate goals toward which they try to direct the resources under their command. Any unit of a multinational enterprise, when operating in the territory of a sovereign state, is also responsive to a flow of commands from outside, including the commands of the parent and the commands of other sovereigns. Moreover, the multinational enterprise as a unit, though capable of wielding substantial economic power, is not accountable to any public authority that matches it in geographical reach and that represents the aggregate interests of all the countries the enterprise affects. As long as these two issues remain unsolved, the constructive economic role of the enterprise will be accompanied by destructive political tensions.

Patterns of Future Growth

A useful first step in any prescriptive exercise is to attempt a projection based on the assumption that events will be allowed to run their course, without the conscious intervention of new policies. That done, one can pinpoint the aspects of the future that one finds distasteful.

There are times in history when a plausible projection of the future can be built up simply by extending the trends of the past. There are other times, however, when a projection of past trends involves more than the usual risks. As far as the future of multinational enterprises is concerned, simple projection seems risky. As tension builds, more Chiles and more Cubas could easily develop. How tensions are managed involves some of the most elusive issues of politics. The observations that follow, therefore, may be thought of more as a reconnaissance than as a projection, a process in which some critical variables are identified and some possibilities tentatively explored.

Some of the elements for the projection of the growth of U.S.-controlled multinational enterprises have been scattered through the pages of this volume. However, not all of them have contributed to a common view. Some suggest a relative decline in the future scope of such enterprises, some an increase. What is needed, therefore, is to assign weights to the various forces involved and to generate some net judgment regarding their impact.

Recall some of the asserted regularities in the patterns of growth. Products commonly move through a cycle from birth to senescence. During this cycle, the demand for the product grows, the technology associated with its production is diffused and appropriated, and the specifications defining the product become more standardized. As demand grows, the threat of new entrants into the industry also tends to grow. This threat can be staved off for a time if the optimal size of the production unit or the optimal size of the distribution system also grows, in pace with the growth of demand. This sometimes occurs, as the case of the automobile industry suggests. More often, however, the growth of demand outpaces the growth in economies of scale. When the threat of new entrants becomes acute, the established leaders in the industry sometimes respond through measures that try to distinguish their standardized products from those of others. Using various forms of advertising and minor product differentiation, industry leaders have sometimes managed to produce this result. At other times, however, the leaders have sloughed off products as they have lost their distinctive characteristics and have turned to the generation of new products.

Another relevant sequence has been occurring, especially in industries involving raw materials. As demand has grown, the well-established multinational enterprises have constantly sought to avoid being dependent on actual or potential competitors for either markets or raw materials. On the whole, leaders in the raw material industries have succeeded in these efforts. But their success has been less than perfect, especially in industries in which international demand has been growing rapidly. In these cases, the growth in demand has opened up strategic opportunities for new marketers and new producers, somewhat weakening the hold of the established leaders on their respective industries.

Forces of this sort will operate in the future, as they have in the past. But some of them almost certainly defy rational projection. Who can say, for instance, how rapidly scale economies in production and distribution are likely to grow relative to total demand? And who can say how effectively producers will succeed in differentiating standardized products in order to generate the desired response from prospective buyers? Still, the future of U.S.-controlled multinational enterprises is not all that indeterminate. As far as their future in other advanced countries is concerned, some expectations seem more plausible than others.

The extraordinary improvements in international communication and transportation seem destined to continue, accompanied by more Intelsats, Concordes, IBM 370s, and all the other modern instruments for shrinking time and space. The relative decline in the costs of communication and transportation is likely to increase the advantages of large-scale producing units and to increase the size of manageable enterprises.

It seems likely also that the cost of generating and launching major industrial innovations will continue to grow, relative to the other costs associated with the production and marketing of the products concerned. On the other hand, it also seems likely that the rate of adoption of innovations by industrial users and consumers will continue to accelerate, when compared with historic norms. So will the rate of appropriation and imitation on the part of the producers that pursue a follow-the-leader strategy. These tendencies, taken in combination, suggest that those multinational enterprises that base their business strategy on an innovational lead will have to plan even more than in the past for the speedy exploitation of any industrial advance over the largest possible market. This means that such enterprises will continue to place a high value on quick and easy access to overseas markets and that they will constantly try to extend the geographical reach of their distribution network.

There are a few other critical projections that ought to be assigned a high probability. If the European Community grows larger and more cohesive, as seems likely, the tendency of large European-owned enterprises inside the area to think of their market as pan-European rather than as national—a tendency already well advanced in automobiles and electronics—will probably grow stronger. The size difference between the large U.S.-controlled enterprise and the large European-controlled enterprise could very well decline a little, though many elements of asymmetry can be expected to persist for a considerable time.

Where the asymmetry is likely to linger longest is in one of the most sensitive areas of all, the genuinely high-technology industries. Though Europe may yet find the institutional means for assembling the disconcertingly large quantities of resources that seem necessary for major advances in such fields as airframes, nuclear reactors, and so on, progress on this front is likely to be slow. Inasmuch as fields such as these involve the most difficult political and military issues and generate the most sensitive national responses, this source of tension and strain may continue undiminished.

Still, even if the governments of the advanced countries continued to follow a policy of grudging tolerance for the growth of U.S.-controlled multinational enterprises, as most of them have in recent years, it seems quite unlikely that such enterprises will increase their relative position in the world's industry and trade at the rate that has prevailed since the early 1950s. History may eventually attribute part of the growth of U.S.-controlled enterprises during the past few decades, especially the growth in the advanced countries, to two special factors: a belated introduction of the stream of innovations that U.S.-based enterprises had managed to accumulate in the war and immediate postwar period; and a temporary acceleration in Europe's demand for the products and processes in which these innovations were incorporated, generated partly by the postwar catching-up process and partly by the special stimuli associated with the creation of the European Community. If the product cycle concept has any validity, the Europeans and the Japanese can be counted on to elbow their way into these U.S.-dominated preserves, appropriating the designs or other elements of novelty embodied in the innovations and eroding the oligopolistic position of the U.S. leaders. The size and multinational character of U.S.-controlled enterprises, which may have been an advantage in earlier stages of a product's life, will afford less advantage at the later stages. As the product is standardized and as demand grows, local enterprises in the advanced countries may be in a position to exploit all the potential economies of scale that then exist, without having to bear the costly overhead involved in maintaining an international organization of communication and control, and without having to generate the funds needed for the development of a crop of new products.

The production of standardized goods can be expected to shift to Europe and Japan, as it has in the past, whether under the aegis of multinational enterprises or of local producers in those areas. What, then, are the consequences for the United States, especially if new products are not so readily forthcoming from the U.S. economy as they were during the 1940s and 1950s? There is every reason to suppose that the classical Marshallian response would apply, that is to say, that the shift of production to Europe and Japan would prove self-arresting. If production moved away from the United States and if she were unable to fill the economic hole with new innovations, then the mix of products and the type of process in the other advanced countries would begin to resemble that of the United States more closely. In this case, one major reason for the higher labor productivity of the United States would disappear, and with its disappearance, labor costs in Europe and Japan—which have provided one of the main advantages of those areas in producing standardized goods—would probably converge toward the U.S. level. The patterns of trade among the advanced countries might then begin to move closer to the pattern that has long prevailed between, say, the United Kingdom and Germany—that is, an exchange of specialized products based not so much on differences in factor costs as on differences in specialization and scale. Indeed, as one reviews the recent history of Europe and Japan in their trade relations with the rest of the world, there are a number of indications that the self-arresting factors are already hard at work.

Japan is distinguished from Europe, however, in a number of different respects. Until very recently, Japan had managed her spectacular industrial growth without appearing to increase her dependence on the resources of the U.S.-controlled enterprises. This stage of Japan's development could conceivably be coming to an end. The spectacular rise of Japan's living standards and of her industrial capabilities has begun to move her toward the position of Great Britain, Germany, or France in terms of her technological needs. Until very recently, these needs could generally be satisfied by industrial technology that had already been in existence for some years—hence, by innovations that were not very closely held among foreign enterprises outside Japan. As long as the Japanese were bidding for technology that was well known and widely dispersed in other countries, their bargaining position was relatively strong. Paradoxically, however, as nations approach the industrial innovation frontier, their bargaining position tends to weaken in certain respects; the technology they are reaching for is much more closely held. Except perhaps for the United States, there is no advanced nation in the world capable of generating more than a fraction of the technological elements needed for a highly advanced society. As Japan approaches that frontier, therefore, her negotiating position in relation to U.S.-controlled enterprises could well decline.

A serious projection of the future position of Japan involves numerous other elements, of course. One of these is whether Japan will appear as quite so much a threat to U.S.-controlled enterprises as she has in the past, capable of mobilizing low-cost labor to perform high-cost manufacturing tasks. Another is whether Japan herself will need increased access to the advanced countries in order to market home-produced goods of an increasingly sophisticated sort. If Japan's labor grows scarce and costly and if U.S.-based enterprises feel they have less to fear from the capacity of Japanese enterprises to draw on low-cost labor, one incentive for developing alliances with these potential rivals will be weakened. And if the Japanese need overseas markets for their industrial products so urgently as to oblige them to open their own home markets to the foreigners, another element in the strong Japanese bargaining position will be somewhat weakened. There is a possibility, therefore, that success will spoil Japan's independence as an industrial power by reducing the country's capacity for extracting advantageous bargains from U.S.-controlled enterprises.

Turning from the advanced countries to the less-developed areas, some added factors are brought into play. If the issues were mainly economic, some fairly plausible assumptions could be made about the future of multinational enterprises in such countries. In the raw materials industries, it could be foreseen that these countries would continue to press foreign-owned enterprises for a repartitioning of the rewards and that the outcome would depend on the bargaining position of the two parties. In industries in which the foreigner's role was most dispensable—whether because of capital requirements, technology considerations, or questions of market access—the erosion of the foreigner's position would be most rapid.

In the manufacturing sector, foreign-owned enterprises might be expected to exhibit continued strength. The capacity of multinational enterprises efficiently to manage international logistical systems has been growing, stimulated by relative declines in international transport costs and by absolute shrinkages in transport times. The growth in the logistical capabilities of these enterprises has been matched by the growing needs of the less-developed countries for organizational skills and export markets. The result has been that the underlying hostility and tension in those countries toward the multinational enterprises have been held in check, and multinational enterprises have been allowed to expand their local activities. True, less-developed countries in the position of India, Mexico, and Brazil—nations that have made some progress toward industrialization—have placed unremitting pressure on the more conspicuous multinational enterprises, compelling them to give up lines of local activity as rapidly as national entrepreneurs can take them over, and this sort of pressure can be expected to continue. But there is nothing to prevent multinational enterprises from continuing to do what they have done successfully in the past—adding new activities of increasing complexity, even as they slough off the old.

The Political Uncertainties

Though the last few pages have been intended as a reconnaissance of the economic aspects of the future, the political questions have obviously been lurking just offstage. These questions, implicit in any projection of the future position of U.S.-controlled enterprises, are infinite in number. Any selection involves an arbitrary choice, but there are a few that need special attention.

One set of issues bearing on the future of the multinational enterprises has to do with the social goals of the advanced nations. Will nations continue to emphasize such goals as the redistribution of personal income, the promotion of laggard regions, the provision of social services, and the enlargement of guarantees against economic vicissitudes? The odds seem high that they will—indeed, that the emphasis will increase rather than otherwise. If it increases, the need of governments to feel that the main facets of the national economy are under their control will also grow. They will want to feel able to determine the conditions of the labor market, the supply of money, the balance of payments, and so on. It would seem to follow that if multinational enterprises appear less controllable than national enterprises in the eyes of national officials, that perception —whether justified or not—will constitute a growing source of agitation and perturbation.

Is one to assume, therefore, that multinational enterprises are bound to confront increasingly hostile national administrations in the advanced countries? There is no inevitability in the response. It is always possible for the political view of the European nations toward U.S.-controlled enterprises to be affected by new political initiatives. Responsibility for such policies may be shifted to the European Community, with new outcomes. Common Atlantic interests may form the basis for new political coalitions, broader than the European Community. Today, with NATO declining in relevance and U.S. leadership in an Atlantic community at very low ebb, this possibility may seem a poor starter. But the possibility is not to be dismissed. Improvements in international communication and transportation continue to generate common norms and problems among the advanced countries. Monetary and fiscal problems grow increasingly interrelated among countries not merely within Europe but also across the Atlantic; so do issues of employment and unemployment. These interrelations probably will not decline even if the multinational enterprise is curbed; the form of the relations and the productivity increases they generate will mainly be affected. As long as an increase in these relations grows, the possibility of new Atlantic initiatives is real.

All these issues and many others are involved in projecting the political forces that are likely to affect the position of U.S.-controlled enterprises not only in the advanced countries but in the less-developed countries as well. During the early 1970s, however, these questions seem dwarfed by an even larger one: Are the less-developed countries likely to adopt some form of economic system, socialist in character, that could be expected grossly to limit the role of the multinational enterprise? With the experience of Chile, Peru, and Bolivia fresh in mind, questions of this sort are hardly avoidable.

The risk of making projections on the outcome in the tug of war among competing ideologies is very high: first, because recent events tend to blot out those that went before, sometimes creating the illusion of a major trend where none exists; second, because the ideologies themselves and the institutions on which they rely have been changing with such rapidity. The innocent observer from Mars would have some difficulty comprehending why the system that Lenin defined as "socialism" is applied to the present group of "socialist" states, and why the system that Marx confronted as "capitalism" is thought to be related to the contemporary political economies of the United States and Western Europe.

The fact that many less-developed countries associate themselves with some form of socialism needs no detailed documenting. The number may even have increased somewhat in the course of time. It is not clear, however, just what that espousal means for the role of the multinational enterprise. During recent years, several genuinely socialist countries have been exercising enormous ingenuity to find a way of assigning a role to foreign-owned enterprises in their economies. The Yugoslavs, of course, have moved furthest in this direction; by 1970, foreign-owned enterprises were in a position to negotiate for rights that were the de facto equivalent of those available in such nonsocialist states as Mexico or Brazil.

Many other less-developed countries—for example, Pakistan, Tunisia, and Iraq—though committed to socialism of some sort, have nevertheless cultivated a certain deliberate ambiguity over the future position of multinational enterprises in their economies. As India edges her way toward national identification with socialism, it is not at all clear that the country's policies toward foreign investors will grow any more restrictive. Besides, the actual shift of less-developed countries toward state ownership of the means of production has not been irrevocable—witness the cases of Indonesia and Ghana. Neither is it clear that the countries that do not yet see the future in these terms will eventually make the shift. Mexico, with her abiding coalition of local big business, bureaucracy, and a single party of ambiguous ideology, seems as likely a model as Guinea; Yugoslavia, with her bent for improvisation and pragmatism, seems no less likely a model of the future than Cuba.

There is one characteristic of the less-developed world,

however, that it does seem safe to predict. This is an endemic condition of political instability. One authoritative compilation covering the period from 1945 to 1965 notes that there were successful coups d'état in seventeen of twenty Latin American states, in half a dozen North African and Middle Eastern states, and in half a dozen African states.[1] Each year from 1960 to 1965, more than forty insurgencies, revolts, coups, or uprisings were reported around the world, mostly in less-developed areas.[2]

If political instability is to be anticipated as the normal state of being in the less-developed world, however, there is a corollary that does bear on the future of the multinational enterprise. There is generally a learning period following any coup, in which the new leaders confront the question of conflicting national objectives. Is independence, for instance, to take a place ahead of growth? Is long-term growth to be subordinated to short-term recovery? And by what means are the chosen priorities to be achieved? Whatever the trend of ideology may be in the less-developed world, therefore, uncertainty will be the lot of the foreign investor.

There is another corollary that goes with the prospect of instability. Situations will be frequent in which one side or another in a local political struggle will need some issue on which to rally local support. One of the most reliable issues for that purpose in less-developed countries is a show of firmness toward the foreign investor. This phenomenon, so common in the life of multinational enterprises, is overwhelmingly likely to endure.

Some Familiar Proposals

The problems relating to multinational enterprises have evoked scores of proposals for action. The variety and range of these proposals emphasize the validity of a venerable homily: Problems are in the eye of the beholder. What the managements of multinational enterprises have seen as a problem, governments sometimes have seen as a solution, and vice versa. Most of the proposals, therefore, have generally been special in outlook and limited in objective.

THE MULTINATIONAL ENTERPRISE VIEWPOINT

To the extent that multinational enterprises see a problem, it is the unremitting nipping at their flanks by governments, as the enterprises try to expand and prosper in the world environment. The U.S. government's insistence on maintaining a system of controls over the flow of funds between U.S. parents and their overseas subsidiaries represents one set of hurdles. The conditions that other governments impose on entry represent another. Even after these obstacles have been surmounted, the discriminations practiced against U.S.-owned subsidiaries established in host countries represent still another source of difficulty.

As far as U.S. government controls are concerned, the views of U.S. parent companies have been straightforward enough. There has been near unanimity that U.S. controls do nothing to strengthen the U.S. balance of payments and are probably hurtful to U.S. economic interests in the longer run. The evidence in the course of this study suggests that they may be right; at any rate, a persuasive case to the contrary has yet to be made. Certainly, as long as the U.S. objective in maintaining such controls is that of dressing up the balance of payments, it is doubtful that the retention of controls is contributing to the objective.[3]

As for the difficulties created by other countries, there is remarkable unanimity among large U.S.-controlled enterprises that such problems will not be greatly helped by governmental action. The seeming passivity of the affected enterprises, even when treaty rights are being impaired, largely reflects the basic fact so often emphasized in these pages: U.S. business interests feel most comfortable in their relations with the U.S. government when they are holding the government at arm's length.

There are times, of course, when governmental help is wanted, even demanded. Managers of the larger multinational enterprises are aware, however, that their organizations have displayed a remarkable capacity for surviving in an environment of uncertainty and risk. They have been aware that trying to pit government against government in an effort to solve their problems could have a price in terms of ill will and retaliation. Even when pressure on behalf of a multinational enterprise has been applied by so powerful an advocate as the U.S. government, one could not be sure it would work. Accordingly, when U.S.-controlled enterprises have felt foreign governments breathing down their necks, the disposition has been to find some formula to relieve the pressure locally without inviting the U.S. government into the fray. Strategies that involve intergovernmental threat or collaboration have taken a very low place in the list of possible responses.

Despite their general aversion toward governmental action, enterprises concerned with international business have been known to support intergovernmental agreements where they felt such agreements could be held to carefully limited and selected goals. After all, the International Convention for the Protection of Industrial Property—a convention safeguarding the rights of inventors and their assignees to obtain patent protection in foreign countries—has been operating for eighty-five years or so. Protective clauses in the field of trademarks have been in force for almost as long. Bilateral treaties of establishment—guaranteeing national treatment to foreign businessmen and defining their local rights in other respects—have been negotiated between pairs of nations for many years; bilateral treaties for the avoidance of double taxation have been sponsored by business interests where needed. These agreements, however, have been seen as far less equivocal in effect and intent than any governmental initiative would be with regard to the more general problems of multinational enterprises.

Because explicit, well-defined bargains have proved useful in times past, managers of multinational enterprises have on occasion proposed that the United States should negotiate bargains of this sort in order to strengthen the rights of U.S. enterprises abroad. The United States might, for instance, exchange reductions in U.S. tariff schedules for guarantees that would benefit U.S.-owned subsidiary operations in foreign countries. Nations are free to apply their bargaining power to any end they choose: for air bases in Spain, for landing rights in Delhi, for guarantees in favor of their investing nationals in Japan, or for any other purposes. In the end, the selection turns on a subjective view of what is important and desirable, and what is less so. The exchange of tariff concessions for investment guarantees, however, seems less than wholly appropriate, given the character of the U.S. interests involved.

Anyone evaluating proposals of this sort from a global point of view would probably begin by assuming that the growth of multinational enterprises makes a positive contribution. In terms of U.S. economic welfare, however, the case is more qualified: clearer for management and for stockholders than for labor. In terms of the political objectives of the United States, the case is more qualified still; the tension generated by the presence of U.S.-controlled subsidiaries abroad can hardly be thought of unequivocally as a positive contribution to the foreign relations of the United States.

To be sure, when the United States trades her tariff reductions for tariff reductions from other countries, there are also some uncertainties concerning who benefits in the United States and by how much; import-competing industries may be hurt, for instance, while exporters are helped. But there is firmer ground for the assumption that, in the end, the United States as a whole benefits in economic and political terms.

The question as to whether the United States benefits from the foreign activities of her multinational enterprises is complicated not only by the disparate U.S. interests associated with the investment, but also by the question whether the interests should be regarded as American. Remember what the overseas commitments of U.S.-controlled multinational enterprises consist of. Measured by equity ownership, they are 90 percent or more American; by sources of funds, perhaps 25 percent American; by the identity of employees, less than one percent American; and by the identity of the governments that receive their taxes, practically 100 percent foreign. Though the contribution of these enterprises to global welfare suggests that their rights and interests would still be worth fostering ana protecting, notwithstanding any ambiguities regarding national identification, it is questionable if the appropriate means for providing these safeguards is for one nation—the United States—to bargain with its tariffs to that end.

Though some U.S. businessmen have been prepared to accept a U.S. government role in negotiating for international rights, most have preferred to handle their problems principally by exhorting governments to be more reasonable. When they have supported any more specific approach, it has been the promulgation of a code of fair conduct to which multinational enterprises would adhere.[4] This type of proposal contemplates that businessmen would subscribe to a set of general standards of behavior by which they would be guided in host countries. The commitments proposed to be taken by these enterprises generally include the usual list of good things: a careful adherence to local law; a meticulous respect for local custom; a willingness to train local workers for responsible jobs and to support local social projects; perhaps even an undertaking to plough back some proportion of local profits and to engage in local research activities.

There is nothing wrong with an approach of this sort. But it

A Choice of Futures

is trivial by comparison with the malaise with which it deals. Commitments in the form of general codes of behavior could not be expected to affect the host countries' prevailing perceptions of the effects of multinational enterprises.

THE HOST COUNTRY VIEWPOINT

All the rhetoric to the contrary, many political leaders and members of other élite groups in host countries are generally well aware of the willingness of most U.S.-controlled multinational enterprises to adhere to the "when in Rome . . ." principle. There is fairly widespread recognition of the fact that an explicit intent to depart from the principle is not very frequent. There may be occasional haggling over just what the "when in Rome . . ." principle requires in its operational details. But this is not where the real problem lies. The crux is to be found in the inherent nature of the multinational enterprise, as the leaders in the host countries see it. These enterprises draw their special strengths from the ability and opportunity to think in terms that extend beyond any single country and to use resources that are located in more than one jurisdiction. These characteristics are seen as posing a threat for government leaders bent on control, for local businessmen who aspire to compete, and for intellectuals who are hoping to challenge the status quo.

The measures that host governments have taken in response to their worries have already been described in earlier chapters. One of the common reactions, it will be remembered, has been to insist on joint ventures. The discussion in Chapter 4 suggests that measures of this sort have had some of their desired effect, tending to alter the style of the parent by creating more formal relationships with the subsidiary. But there has also been a price connected with that achievement; a lesser flow of resources from abroad, a more meticulous insistence by the parent on the payment of royalty fees and dividends, a tighter control over exports, and so on. Besides, the creation of a favored class in the host country, specializing as partners of foreigners, has been looked on with increasing misgivings.

Nevertheless, the inescapable fact that multinational enterprises represent a challenge to local control and interests means that host governments have repeatedly been drawn to schemes for sharing ownership and control in the subsidiaries of these enterprises. Such proposals have been much more common with respect to subsidiaries in the less-developed countries than those in the advanced countries;[5] but they have had adherents in all areas. One of these proposals even has been developed to the point of proposing an intergovernmental aid mechanism that would finance the divestiture process.

The assumption in proposals of this sort is that multinational enterprises may well perform some useful economic function at the time they set up their subsidiaries in foreign countries, but that the usefulness of any given subsidiary declines in the course of time. Divestiture is generally thought of as a remedy in two senses: It reduces the economic costs to the host country by setting a terminal payment lower than the equivalent value of the future flow of payments from the subsidiary to the parent; and it reduces a source of political tension between the host country and the country identified with the parent enterprise—that is to say, the United States. It is generally implicit in these proposals that the multinational enterprise may find divestiture of the subsidiary less attractive than continued ownership, but not so unattractive as to discourage its continuing to set up subsidiaries even when divestiture is probable.

The description of the operations of multinational enterprises presented in earlier chapters is not wholly incompatible with these assumptions. A U.S. enterprise could be pictured establishing a radio assembly plant or a food-processing plant in a less-developed country in order to replace existing imports. Given the costs of capital and technology from alternative sources, the initial contribution of capital and technology might seem a good bargain for the host country. It is also possible to envisage that at some point the technology would have been absorbed and appropriated by others in the country, and that payments for the continued use of the foreign capital would seem exorbitant. In this case, divestiture on some reasonable basis would not be excluded as a constructive response.

The trouble with this hypothetical case is that it probably does not correspond to the circumstances of more than a small minority of U.S.-controlled subsidiaries in the less-developed countries. As a rule, foreign-owned subsidiaries have continually altered the scope of their activities, pushed by the threats of new local competition or government pressure, or stimulated by the discovery of new opportunities in the local economies. Plants that began with a given product line have had to slough off their old products, such as radios and small motors, while taking on new products, such as television sets; and they have had to deepen their processes from simple assembly and packaging to the manufacture of complex components and ingredients. Some subsidiaries that originally had nothing to offer in terms of market access because they were selling only in the local market have turned to exports, using the intelligence network and the distributing machinery of their affiliates in the multinational enterprise structure. In such cases, therefore, a constant process of divestiture and renewal has been going on inside the organization. There is no basis in these instances for an a priori assumption that the benefits to the host country have declined in time; the contrary could just as well be true. In narrow economic terms, a program of more formal divestiture could prove hurtful rather than otherwise.

There are other aspects of a systematic divestiture program that limit its applicability. One of these is the fact that the value of a going subsidiary to a multinational enterprise system may be substantially different from the value of the same entity set up as an independent local enterprise. Why is there such a difference?

The usual commitment of multinational enterprises to their subsidiaries is to include them in a global organization and strategy. This commitment may allow for a great deal of local independence or for very little, according to the character of the enterprise. Except in unusual circumstances, however, the relationship entails the sharing of knowledge, resources, skills, and goals.

It follows that the establishment of a new subsidiary generally requires the parent to restructure and adapt the organization, so that it can assume a block of career commitments, train a cadre of key men, and transmit a store of information. After this process is completed, what appears on the parent's books as its investment is determined by conventional accounting practice, in turn based on the misleading and inappropriate analogy to the portfolio investment. This accounting figure often has very little relationship to the parent's perception of the real value of its investment or to the reproduction cost of the resources involved in creating the subsidiary. Moreover, the value of the subsidiary to the parent will depend on its marginal contribution to the multinational organization's strategy, which may be quite different from the profits nominally recorded on the subsidiary's books.

If a subsidiary's function were only remotely related to the global strategy of the enterprise and if its resources consisted mainly of those recorded on its books—that is to say, if it came close to satisfying the portfolio concept of direct investment—presumably its value would not be much altered by its being separated from its parent through divestiture. A canning plant operating under local trade names in local markets, for instance, might be little changed in value by a change in ownership. But the assembly plant of an international automobile company could lose most of its earning capacity after divestiture. This fact would in practice be a nasty impediment to the achievement of a reasonable divestiture price.

A difficulty of still another sort would handicap any divestiture policy. Multinational enterprises might be persuaded to suppress their hostile reactions to such a policy, provided that divestitures were to be limited to those cases in which the investor and the host government had foreseen and prearranged the dénouement at the time of the original investment. But this proviso would be hard to guarantee. A divestiture by a consenting enterprise in any country could easily whet the country's appetite for another divestiture in which the enterprise was less willing, especially if the domestic political situation suggested the usefulness of such a step. And the example of one country could generate pressures for similar action by others. Some domino theories may be implausible, but foreign investors would not be wholly unreasonable if they feared that this one had a certain validity.

None of these considerations, however, is of such a quality as totally to destroy the utility of a scheme that provided for foreseeing and prearranging the eventual divestiture of the subsidiary of a multinational enterprise. To be sure, when measured in standard economic terms, a scheme of this sort would probably be hurtful to host countries. It would tend to scare off those foreign investors who had a long-term view of their investment. It would probably repel those investors who had genuinely scarce capabilities rather than some widely available standardized skills. And it would almost certainly discourage those investors who were planning to use the subsidiary to produce for export to other affiliates rather than to supply the local market. Still, if the arrangement were between consenting parties—that is, if it were a condition of entry laid down by an informed host government and accepted by the enterprise—outsiders could hardly object. The existence of the arrangement could serve some of the political and psychological needs of the host country by blunting the government's sense of being irrevocably blocked from controlling a major facility in its own economy, and it could reduce the political cost to the United States associated with the protection of foreign investments.

One of the main problems to be guarded against in arrangements of this sort is that both parties would come to regret a commitment they were no longer free to change. This could easily occur, for example, if a subsidiary that was in a position to continually move on from old lines to new was inhibited by the divestiture commitment, or, alternatively, if the local capital involved in the buy-out arrangement could be put to better use when the date of the acquisition approached. Problems of this sort could be dealt with if divestiture schemes were framed in terms not of inevitabilities but of options—renewable options exercisable at the termination of relatively long periods of time.

To speculate in too much detail about arrangements of this sort would lead to rapidly diminishing returns. One other issue, however, can be foreseen. The proposals that have so far been advanced by others usually call for partial divestiture, that is, for the conversion of wholly owned subsidiaries into joint ventures. The uncertain value of such arrangements from the viewpoint of both multinational enterprises and host governments has already been suggested in earlier chapters. Situations that might seem appropriate for a joint venture at the beginning of the option period may change sufficiently to make a joint venture intolerable at the time that the option was exercised. Options could be arranged on such terms, however, that the parties are not thrown together into a joint venture that one or the other prefers to avoid. If, for instance, local interests were given an option to buy a one-half interest in a subsidiary at the end of some stated period, the foreign parent could be given the right to "put" the remaining half-interest to the buyers in the event the local interests actually exercised the buying option.

A Choice of Futures

Arrangements along the lines just described would provide an interesting experiment with limited risks, but at best such arrangements would generate limited benefits as well. The problems associated with the growth of the multinational enterprise are much too profound to respond to some light and incidental pruning. One fundamental problem stems from the fact that multinational enterprises have something to offer that host countries badly want and that the acceptance of these offerings generates problems of overlapping jurisdictions, accompanied by a sense of loss of national control. Can remedies be suggested that might leave the multinational enterprise to perform its creative functions, accompanied by more tolerable levels of tension and by the needed sense among governments of more effective control?

In the best of all possible Panglossian worlds, the writ of every government would extend as far as the interests that might affect it. But this possibility, it is all too clear, cannot exist in a system of nation-states without generating jurisdictional overlap and jurisdictional conflict. Because multinational enterprises have global interests and these affect many nation-states, only a global government could provide the essential geographical symmetry. This simple concept lies at the heart of the many proposals for a world corporation or a U.N. corporation.[6] According to proposals of this sort, an enterprise that expects to establish itself in many jurisdictions ought not to consist of an agglomeration of artificial persons, each created by the notarial seal of a different sovereign and each responsible to its mandates. Instead, that enterprise should be a single entity, responsible in the first instance to a world body. According to the usual assumption in these proposals, where supplementary obligations are imposed by national jurisdictions, the global corporation will be accountable to these obligations as well.

Proposals of this sort may satisfy the intellectual need for symmetry between the governor and the governed. In other respects, however, they are out of joint with the times, especially when stated in the bold and pristine terms that have been used here. The solution in such approaches consists essentially of assuming the problem away. The underlying assumption is that nations can be persuaded to delegate the rules of corporate behavior to an international body and that the conflicts of national interest resulting from the operation of the rules will be allowed to work themselves out without direct interference by nation-states. There is also an assumption that where the mandates imposed by the nation-states and those imposed by the higher global authority are in direct conflict, the mandate of the nation-state will give way to that of the global authority. One day, these assumptions may seem plausible, but not at present.

Yet the problem is important; it may even be acute. Do any approaches exist that are sufficiently realistic to be relevant over the next decade, yet sufficiently ambitious to measure up to the size and nature of the problem?

Shaping the Future

When choosing among courses of action, personal values are of overwhelming importance. I personally am mistrustful of any large concentration of economic power, on the grounds that Lord Acton so aptly summarized: Power corrupts. Men with power have an extraordinary capacity to convince themselves that what they want to do happens to coincide with what society needs done for its good. This comfortable illusion is shared as much by strong leaders of enterprise as by strong leaders of government.

I assume that the manifest technical advantages of large

enterprises and of strong governments will lead men in the future to insist on both. The possibility that societies may be organized in small units with limited power seems implausible. Adam Smith's model of a world of little firms and Karl Marx's model of a society of benign utopian proletariats both seem to me grotesquely implausible.* The challenge in social organization is to ensure that the large units on which our future societies are likely to be based act as countervailing political powers, not as mutually reinforcing ones. That critical series of judgments powerfully shapes the direction of the recommendations that follow.

THE CASE FOR ACTION

Anyone with a respect for the continuity of history would be inclined to guess that the basic rights and obligations of multinational enterprises will not be altered in any organic way during the next decade or so. Such enterprises, chary of governmental action, are likely to continue to make their own way in the international environment, tempering their eagerness to expand with judiciously applied self-restraint. Local governments, unwilling to consider any broad international approach to their tensions, will probably respond piecemeal to the existence of the foreign-owned enterprises by bolstering their locally owned industry and discriminating against the foreigners in their jurisdiction. Now and then, a disconcerting incident may lead to protest and confrontation: an uncompensated expropriation of a U.S.-owned subsidiary by some host government, an egregious discrimination against such a subsidiary in the application of local law, an untoward "interference" by the United States in the internal affairs of some host government

* But not to others, including some sober and serious scholars. See, for instance, Ralph Miliband, *The State in Capitalist Society* (New York: Basic Books, Inc., 1970) p. 277, who still hopes that "the working class and its allies in other classes will . . . bring into being an authentically democratic social order, a truly free society of self-governing men and women, in which, as Marx also put it, the state will be converted 'from an organ superimposed upon society into one completely subordinated to it'."

through such means as the application of U.S. antitrust law or trading-with-the-enemy legislation or capital export controls.

But the problem will not stand still. Despite the recrudescent nationalism in the policies of the U.S. government and other advanced countries during the early 1970s, the factors that have been increasing the economic and political interaction between national economies during the 1950s and 1960s are still hard at work. The flow of international communications is still increasing exponentially, stimulated by mounting efficiency and declining cost. Though international trade may be somewhat inhibited by tariffs and quotas, the movement of knowledge and capital resources is quite another matter. Attempts to control the international movement of ideas or capital by means of national border restrictions seem an increasingly quixotic pursuit. With these elusive elements moving more readily across international boundaries and blunting many of the purposes of national trade controls, a key question for the future is how long it will take for governments to find the level of tension unacceptable.

When the tension does come to be unbearable, the time for substantial action may be at hand. At this stage, apocalyptic projections vie with mundane possibilities. If the mundane prevail, as I think more likely and more desirable, a number of steps can be envisaged.

THE TAX ISSUE

Taxes are the root of much tension. From the viewpoint of many local governments, the taxes extracted from the local subsidiaries of U.S.-controlled enterprises constitute an act of grace on the part of such enterprises. As local governments are well aware, their own ability to gauge the appropriateness of the taxes that are paid is fairly limited. This fact does nothing to contribute to their sense of assurance and control over the operations of multinational enterprises.

The question of local taxes is also one in which the multinational enterprises themselves take a detailed and continuous interest. Because of the interrelated character of the operations of the subsidiaries of many multinational enterprises, the division of the profits of such enterprises among different national jurisdictions almost always involves unavoidably arbitrary allocations. As long as multinational enterprises have felt that the freedom to allocate their profits among jurisdictions offered them net advantages, they have preferred to let the problem rest in obscurity. This freedom, however, shows signs of being reduced. The curiosity of governments over how allocations are made and how they affect tax liabilities is growing speedily. Questions of international transfer pricing, overhead allocation, the use of debt in lieu of equity, and similar esoteric issues are rapidly becoming a familiar part of the concerns of many national tax officials.

As noted earlier, the response of multinational enterprises to international tax pinches has been to call on governments to negotiate bilateral tax agreements; agreements of this sort could be tailored narrowly to the particular needs of the enterprise in particular jurisdictions. As government tax authorities grow more sophisticated and more aggressive, however, the complex and tortuous process of tailoring each tax jurisdiction to every other by way of bilateral agreements could prove inadequate. General principles, coupled with an adjudicating mechanism, may seem more attractive to both business and governments. At this stage, the case for a multinational approach would be very strong.*

A multinational approach to tax problems could take several different forms. A relatively easy response would be to enunciate some general principles applicable to all tax jurisdictions, such as principles that relate to transfer pricing and to the use of debt in lieu of equity, and to develop a means for settling

---

* In July 1970, the Organization for Economic Cooperation and Development took cognizance of the problem, agreeing to launch a study of the international aspects of company taxation.

disputes in the application of the principles. If the principles were adopted by a sufficient number of countries, they would accomplish two things: They would reduce the chances that a multinational enterprise, caught between the scissor blades of two taxing jurisdictions, would be unfairly taxed; at the same time, they would increase the assurances that such enterprises were not using their flexibility to slip between the national taxing authorities.

Still another approach directed to the same general ends is possible, an approach more fundamental in character and more ambitious in reach. The operations of the individual subsidiaries of multinational enterprises are inescapably interrelated; the profits assigned to each of them are unavoidably arbitrary. Therefore, it can be argued, the assessment of tax liability in any jurisdiction should be based on the proration of the consolidated profit of the multinational enterprise as a whole, according to an agreed proration formula. The analogy of this approach to corporate tax formulas promulgated by the several states of the United States is obvious. The states, recognizing the meaninglessness of profits generated in their territory by a large national corporation, have been content to accept arbitrary allocating formulas, thereby reducing one source of tension that otherwise would be associated with the presence of the national company.

The analogy to the U.S. interstate system, however, also suggests the fundamental character of the proposed change. If the change were adopted, it would require the United States and other countries to look on the taxable profits of their multinational enterprises in a wholly new light. Instead of regarding the profits of the multinational enterprise as taxable only when they were returned home in the form of income to the parents, as many now do, the jurisdictions involved would have to regard such profits as taxable as soon as they occurred anywhere in the system. Germany then would share in the profits generated by General Motors in the United States, while the United States would share in the profits generated by a subsidiary in Germany. The experience would be novel for both: for Germany because she has so far been entitled to look only to the German subsidiary for taxes, and for the United States because she has up to now confined her tax reach mainly to the parent's dividends from foreign subsidiaries.

THE PROBLEM OF OVERLAPPING JURISDICTION

Another problem that will commend itself for international collaboration is the question of joint jurisdiction over subsidiaries. A solution to problems of this sort is more complex than might be supposed on first impression. To achieve any forward motion, a set of agreements based on several interrelated principles would probably be involved.

In essence, countries would have to be prepared to give up a precious right—the right to reach into the jurisdiction of others in order to influence actions that they feel affect their national interests. Quite clearly, no nation would be prepared to subscribe to self-denying ordinances of this sort on a wholesale basis. The prospects for joint action would be greatest among countries that thought of themselves as having a common interest and a common viewpoint, and greatest with respect to those fields in which consultation appeared easiest. On these criteria, the United States would find collaborative efforts easiest with the advanced countries of Western Europe, perhaps with the European Community itself. And the fields of possible collaboration might be expected to include national policies with regard to restrictive business practices and mergers, trading-with-the-enemy policy, and the control of capital movements. In these fields, one could picture the adoption of treaty commitments under which governments would be proscribed from trying to shape the behavior of the overseas subsidiaries of their national companies, whether by means of direct injunction or by coercion of the parent.

At the same time, however, there would almost certainly be need for a joint commitment to a continuous process of policy harmonization in the fields in which restraints on the exercise of sovereign power were being assumed. The harmonization process in any field could hardly be expected to lead to identical national policies in that field. Experience suggests, however, that in practice substantial differences in national levels of control are readily tolerable. The United States, for instance, has long since resigned herself to the fact that the controls of other countries over trade with the communist countries are likely to be considerably more relaxed than her own and is prepared to permit activities on the part of overseas subsidiaries that impair the objectives of U.S. policies in this area.[7] The same is also true of the antitrust field; the United States is by now ruefully aware that she must move with a certain restraint when she reaches into the jurisdictions of other countries to enforce her antitrust objectives. Consultation with foreign governments of the advanced countries is now the rule, rather than the exception, before actions of this sort are undertaken.* The formalization of consultation procedures and the commitment to harmonization efforts, therefore, would represent no giant departure from the direction toward which circumstances already have pushed the United States.

Undertakings of the sort just described might conceivably enlist some support from multinational enterprises. But there is a corollary of these proposals that is likely to encounter much heavier going from that quarter. If sovereigns agree to refrain from trying to control the overseas subsidiaries of their national enterprises, the corollary proposition is that the sub-

* An informal agreement on such a procedure was reached among OECD members in 1968. The United States and Canada have since agreed more explicitly on close antitrust cooperation; see "United States and Canada Agree on Closer Antitrust Cooperation," *The New York Times*, November 4, 1969, p. 63. In a recent Justice Department suit against Westinghouse Electric Corporation charging an illegal conspiracy with major Japanese companies, the suit is said to have been filed with the foreknowledge of the Japanese government; see "Patent Protection," *The Economist*, June 6, 1970, p. 50, and "Trustbusters Challenge U.S. Firms' Dealing with Concerns Abroad," *The Wall Street Journal*, July 30, 1970, p. 1.

sidiaries themselves should be treated as nationals by the host governments; if such treatment is guaranteed, these subsidiaries should give up access to diplomatic support from the government of their parent companies. This set of principles has cropped up repeatedly in the diplomatic history of international investment, but it has evoked unrestrained hostility on the part of U.S. enterprises. Known as the Calvo Clause after the Argentine minister who first advanced them, these principles have been pushed hard by Latin American governments in their efforts to cut off U.S.-controlled subsidiaries from the support of the United States. As Latin American governments generally frame the principles, they would deny all local rights and remedies to any foreign-owned subsidiary if the subsidiary called on a foreign government in a dispute with its host government.[8]

At first glance, the package of principles seems wholly reasonable. It has to be remembered, however, that the presumption that governmental authority will be applied on a nondiscriminatory basis to enterprises, whether local or foreign, is far from universal; under most systems of jurisprudence, governments are free to distribute rewards and penalties to their nationals according to less obvious criteria, without running afoul of their own laws, expectations, and customs. A guarantee of "national treatment" in such cases is a guarantee without much content. Instead, some minimum guarantees based on the concept of equitable treatment would probably have to be substituted.

If the concept of equitable treatment were adequately defined, there would still be the problem of defining the position of very large enterprises established in very small economies. Because of the unique position of such enterprises, identifying and applying concepts of equitable treatment involve special difficulties. It would not be surprising, therefore, if the formulation of guarantees for the protection of certain kinds of subsidiaries proved impossible as a practical matter.

Defining the concept of equitable treatment would be difficult; enforcing it would be more difficult still. Given the nature of the judicial process in many countries, it would be infeasible to leave the enforcement problem wholly to national legal systems. More likely than not, some sort of international tribunal would have to be charged with the adjudicating function. And even that step, quite understandably, would leave some residual doubts in the minds of foreign investors.

The objective of disentangling conflicting jurisdictions, therefore, will not be easily attained. According to this analysis, it will require a series of international commitments: some self-denying ordinances on the part of sovereigns to prevent their reaching into other jurisdictions, a means of international consultation in order to bring about some degree of harmonization where governments have accepted jurisdictional constraints, a denial to foreign-owned subsidiaries of the right to call on the governments of their parent companies for diplomatic support, and a means of providing and enforcing commitments for the equitable treatment of the subsidiaries concerned. This is an ambitious package of agreements, one that may well have to wait on a more propitious conjuncture of events in the field of international relations.

The chances are that such a conjuncture, when it appeared, would permit some forward motion among a group of advanced countries long before it permitted similar action with the countries of the less-developed world. The refusal of Latin American governments in the late 1960s even to sign a relatively innocuous multilateral Convention on the Settlement of Investment Disputes suggests how far those countries are from any willingness to consider joint action in this general field.[9] Nor does the fact that so many African countries have gone along with the agreement offer any basis for greater hope. In many cases, that acquiescence was much more a recognition of weakness than an expression of collaboration; eventually, a more independent line of response is to be expected from this quarter as well.

However, all these problems could probably be surmounted for a considerable number of enterprises in a substantial number of countries, especially advanced countries. In this case, some sources of tension might be reduced. To be sure, a large part of the problem would still remain. Indeed, it could even be argued that the ultimate problem—the fact that multinational enterprises seem to have options that are largely unmatched by the interests that bargain with them—would be essentially unaffected.

THE ULTIMATE PROBLEM

Consider a world that has adopted some of the suggestions strung out in the preceding pages. The United States has suspended her controls over the flow of funds between U.S. parents and their foreign-owned subsidiaries and has loosened her jurisdiction over the subsidiaries. The foreign-owned subsidiaries and their parents have waived rights of diplomatic support on the part of the parent's government, while the host countries have extended guarantees of equitable treatment to the subsidiaries, including the right to establish themselves and conduct their business in any industry on the same terms as a locally owned enterprise.

Make still another set of assumptions that lie just inside the bounds of plausibility. Agreements not to impose controls on outward flows of direct capital investment, let it be assumed, have been developed among the major advanced countries. Undertakings of this sort could be made subject to the familiar caveats covering balance-of-payments difficulties and "vital national interests," and under a procedure that envisioned the possibility of complaint and adjudication; the provisions of the General Agreement on Tariffs and Trade and of the International Monetary Fund provide ample precedent for such an approach. Assume, too, that the division of taxes has been made a matter of joint commitment and interest among major governments. Would these measures be enough to eliminate the problems generated by multinational enterprises, as seen by those they confront?

The answer is clearly no. The capability of multinational enterprises to exercise flexibility and choice would still seem oppressive in the eyes of many that had to deal with them. What more could be done?

There have been some cautious and tentative proposals for making a beginning on this difficult issue. As befits first steps in so uncharted an area, these proposals have generally been based on the assumption that international requirements for more and better disclosure of the global affairs of multinational enterprises might narrow the issues and eventually might concentrate attention on the problems that really mattered.[10] But the hope has generally been expressed in a spirit that was wistful and hortatory. There have been other proposals which have argued persuasively for the creation of an international organization whose first order of business would be to build up ground rules for dealing with the problems covered in the last few pages.[11]

This is one of those areas of international tension, however, in which constructive international action may be called for on a more rapid timetable than these cautious proposals suggest. Though the obstacles to major action now seem formidable, pressures for some sort of move at the national or international level also seem to be growing.

Of the various pressures that may spur international action on an accelerated timetable, the most telling is the threat of considerably more unilateral actions by the individual states requiring multinational enterprises to justify major decisions in the allocation of production or of markets among facilities located in different national jurisdictions. Proposals that this sort of practice be greatly increased are being generated from many sources.[12]

The prospect that a number of states might expand such practices, unilaterally and on an uncoordinated basis, would be slightly nightmarish from the viewpoint of the multinational enterprise. Yet if governments do not take cognizance of the problem on a collective basis, the prospect of unilateral action is not to be excluded. In industries where such action is not uncommon, such as the oil industry, the experience of conflicting government commands already hurts at times. The international regularization of such commands might be less intolerable than the growth of unilateral actions by states.

How could one envisage the ground rules by which an international organization might become party to the major allocative decisions of multinational enterprises? If the broad interests of all nations are to be considered, a major decision of such enterprises that was otherwise consistent with the laws and policies of the nations concerned ought not to be subject to the veto of parties that felt threatened, unless the project was based on some patently "artificial" factor, suitably defined. The definition would presumably include various kinds of cases: the existence of a subsidy or of a threat coming from one of the signatory governments; or the existence of a private market-sharing agreement among enterprises.

Some kinds of "artificial" factors, it seems clear, ought to be prevented from providing the basis for a major decision on the part of multinational enterprises. Others, however, should be subject to international agreement that permitted their use in certain circumstances. Nations cannot put off much longer some joint understanding over the conditions when subsidies and tax concessions were appropriate in the international movement of industry. The competition among advanced countries in making lavish capital grants to industry and among less-developed countries in extending broad tax exemptions to industry could be brought under some measure of control. If all host countries were to reduce or eliminate the benefits, it is improbable that foreign direct investment would decline very much or that global welfare would be impaired.

Another implication is that governments—especially the U.S. government—will be obliged to convert issues they had once thought domestic into issues of international concern. U.S. labor interests, for instance, would find themselves in an international forum if they were seeking to block the establishment of the Taiwan subsidiary of a U.S. parent. Initially, this outcome may seem a trifle strange. Its strangeness declines rapidly, however, if one accepts the view that the accountability of multinational enterprises is international for certain purposes, rather than national. This adjustment in viewpoint is no greater than the adjustment that has led nations to accept the fixing of tariffs as a proper function of international agreements.

The direction of these suggestions is clear. The basic asymmetry between multinational enterprises and national governments may be tolerable up to a point, but beyond that point there is a need to reestablish balance. When this occurs, the response is bound to have some of the elements of the world corporation concept: accountability to some body, charged with weighing the activities of the multinational enterprise against a set of social yardsticks that are multinational in scope.

If this does not happen, some of the apocalyptic projections of the future of multinational enterprise will grow more plausible.

Notes

CHAPTER 1

1. The U.S. Department of Commerce reports that 90 percent of U.S. foreign direct investment in 1967 and 1968 is accounted for by 561 U.S. parent-companies; see *Foreign Affiliate Financial Survey, 1967–1968* (Washington, D.C.: U.S. Department of Commerce, July 1970), p. 1. Within the group of 561, according to various indications, the distribution is very highly skewed; see Samuel Pizer and Frederick Cutler, U.S. Department of Commerce, *U.S. Business Investments in Foreign Countries* (Washington, D.C.: Government Printing Office, 1960), pp. 144–145.

2. The measures presented in Table 1–1 and related measures mentioned elsewhere in the text were designed and computed by J. W. Vaupel.

3. Tests of the significance of the difference between means were conducted for all measures representing the "187 enterprises" group and the "Rest of *Fortune*'s 500 enterprises" group, using conventional *t* tests. It is uncertain what tests of significance may mean in this context. Nevertheless, the results of the tests are consistent with the main conclusions reported in the text.

4. Efforts to measure the oligopolistic position of the 187 enterprises directly were thwarted by the fact that each is engaged in so many different lines of production. The number of products manufactured by the median enterprise in the group, for instance, came to twenty-two in 1965, "product" in this instance being measured by SIC five-digit categories. A "concentration index" was established for each enterprise by (1) calculating the ratio of sales of the four largest enterprises in each five-digit industry as a percentage of the industry's total sales, and (2) combining in a single average the industries in which the enterprise was engaged, weighting each such industry by its sales. The results were 43.2 percent for the 187 enterprises, 40.8 percent for the rest of *Fortune*'s 500, and 37.9 percent for U.S. industry as a whole.

5. An index was calculated for every pair of products, measuring the extent to which the pair was encountered together in the product mix of the companies on the 1964 *Fortune*'s 500 list. "Product" in this

context was defined in terms of SIC five-digit categories. If the two products were invariably found together, the index value was +1.00; if invariably found apart, −1.00. For the 187 multinational enterprises the average measure for the list of products reported by the enterprises was +.36; for the rest of *Fortune*'s 500, +.51.

6. M. T. Bradshaw, "U.S. Exports to Foreign Affiliates of U.S. Firms," *Survey of Current Business*, 49, no. 5, pt. 2 (May 1969): 37.

7. G. C. Hufbauer and F. M. Adler, *Overseas Manufacturing Investment and the Balance of Payments* (Washington, D.C.: U.S. Treasury Department, 1968), pp. 36–38. Though the Hufbauer-Adler figures are the most recent comprehensive estimates of the relative importance of U.S. subsidiary activities in other countries, more recent figures are available on the sales of such subsidiaries. These figures, which cover each year from 1961 to 1968, indicate that the relative contributions by the various industry groups is quite stable. See *Survey of Current Business*, October 1970, p. 19.

8. Report of the Task Force on the Structure of Canadian Industry, *Foreign Ownership and the Structure of Canadian Industry* (Ottawa: Queen's Printer, 1968), p. 422.

9. Hufbauer and Adler, *Overseas Manufacturing*. The group of 187 multinational enterprises probably accounts for as much as four fifths of the sales activities of all U.S.-controlled manufacturing subsidiaries in that area.

10. Further evidence of the high concentration of U.S.-controlled subsidiaries in the more advanced industrial sectors of host countries is to be found, for the United Kingdom, in J. H. Dunning, "The Effects of United States Direct Investment on British Technology," 1969, mimeograph; for France, in Gilles Bertin, *L'Investissement des firmes étrangères en France* (Paris: Presse Universitaire de France, 1963); for Belgium, Belgian Ministry of Economic Affairs, *Investissements étrangers en Belgique* (Brussels, 1966); for Canada, Dominion Bureau of Statistics, *The Canadian Balance of International Investment Position* (Ottawa, August 1967); for Japan, *Gaishi Donyu Nenkan* (Tokyo: Zaidan Hojin Shoko Kaikan, 1965), discussed in Whatarangi Winiata, "United States Managerial Investment in Japan, 1950–1964," unpublished Ph.D. thesis, University of Michigan, 1966, p. 28.

11. Alberto Mucci, "The Investment Challenge," *Succèsso*, February 1968, p. 99.

12. Christopher Layton, *Trans-Atlantic Investments* (Boulogne-sur-Seine: Atlantic Institute, 1966), p. 19.

13. These figures are roughly in line with preliminary data from the U.S. Department of Commerce census of U.S. foreign investment for 1966. See Council for Latin America, *The Effects of United States and Other Foreign Investment in Latin America* (New York, January 1970).

Notes

CHAPTER 2

1. A classic source for the period is I. M. Tarbell, *The History of the Standard Oil Company,* 2 vols. (New York: Macmillan, 1925). Also of great assistance is Mira Wilkins, *The Emergence of Multinational Enterprise* (Cambridge: Harvard University Press, 1970). Because of the large number of sources used in the preparation of this chapter, references are confined to major works.

2. For industry data covering this period, see especially G. H. Barrows, *The International Petroleum Industry* (New York: International Petroleum Institute, 1965), vol. 1.

3. A. D. Chandler, Jr., *Strategy and Structure* (Garden City, N.Y.: Doubleday, 1966), p. 210; the reference in this source is to the policy of Jersey Standard.

4. For brief accounts of the early international developments in oil, see E. T. Penrose, *The Large International Firm in Developing Countries* (London: Allen & Unwin, 1969), pp. 53–62; see also U.S. Federal Trade Commission, *The International Petroleum Cartel* (Washington, D.C.: Government Printing Office, 1952), p. 37 ff.

5. D. D. Martin, "Resource Control and Market Power," in Mason Gaffney, ed., *Extractive Resources and Taxation* (Madison: University of Wisconsin Press, 1967), contains some systematic tests of the relation of vertical integration to market strength for firms in a number of raw material industries. The results are provocative but do more to indicate the complexity of the relation than to confirm its strength.

6. J. L. Enos, *Petroleum Progress and Profits: A History of Process Innovation* (Cambridge: MIT Press, 1962), and "Invention and Innovation in the Petroleum Refining Industry," in R. R. Nelson, ed., *The Rate and Direction of Inventive Activity: Economic and Social Factors* (Princeton: Princeton University Press, 1962), pp. 299–322; Harold Williamson et al., *The American Petroleum Industry: The Age of Energy 1899–1959* (Evanston, Ill.: Northwestern University Press, 1963), pp. 795–821.

7. R. R. Nelson et al., *Technology, Economic Growth and Public Policy* (Washington, D.C.: Brookings Institution, 1967), p. 50.

8. Two outstanding treatments of the motivations of the principal participants in the world oil market of the 1960s, including the state-owned exporters, are found in Penrose, *The Large International Firm,* pp. 213–219, and M. A. Adelman, *The World Petroleum Markets 1946–1969* (Washington, D.C.: Resources for the Future, 1971).

9. M. S. Brown and John Butler, *The Production, Marketing and Consumption of Copper and Aluminum* (New York: Praeger, 1968); Sterling Brubaker, *Trends in the World Aluminum Industry* (Baltimore: Johns Hopkins Press, 1967); M. J. Peck, *Competition in the Aluminum*

Industry 1945–1958 (Cambridge: Harvard University Press, 1961);
U.S. Federal Trade Commission, *Report on the Copper Industry* (Washington, D.C.: Government Printing Office, 1947).

10. For an account of this period, see U.S. Federal Trade Commission, *Report on the Copper Industry*, pp. 214–238; O. C. Herfindahl, *Copper Costs and Prices: 1870–1957* (Baltimore: Johns Hopkins Press, 1959), pp. 96–111; E. S. May, "The Copper Industry in the United States," in W. Y. Elliott et al., *International Control in the Non-Ferrous Metals* (New York: Macmillan, 1937), p. 537.

11. For a description of the system, see remarks of H. S. Houthakker, "Copper: The Anatomy of a Malfunctioning Market," August 11, 1970, mimeograph; see also "Report of the Subcommittee on Copper to the Cabinet Committee on Economic Policy," May 13, 1970, mimeograph.

12. O. C. Herfindahl, *Copper Costs*, p. 210 ff.; Markos Mamalakis and C. W. Reynolds, *Essays on the Chilean Economy* (Homewood, Ill.: Irwin, 1965), pp. 213–216; C. E. Julian, "Copper: An Example of Advancing Technology and the Utilization of Low-Grade Ores," in F. G. Tyron and E. C. Eckel, eds., *Mineral Economics* (New York: McGraw-Hill, 1932), pp. 123–124; Alex Skelton, "Copper," in Elliott et al., *International Control*, pp. 376–377.

13. The account that follows draws on Brown and Butler, *Production, Marketing, and Consumption*, pp. 3–6; Peck, *Competition;* OECD, *Gaps in Technology Between Member Countries: Non-Ferrous Metals* (Paris, 1968).

14. Jean-Bernard Berthelon, "La grande bataille de l'aluminium," *Entreprise*, 473 (Dec. 6, 1969): 57–71.

15. The figures for copper and aluminum are from M. S. Brown and John Butler, *Production, Marketing, and Consumption*, p. 5; and for oil from *OPEC Bulletin*, September–October 1969, p. 1.

16. Mira Wilkins and F. E. Hill, *American Business Abroad: Ford on Six Continents* (Detroit: Wayne State University Press, 1964), p. 162.

17. "Alcan Goes More International," *The Economist*, September 6, 1969, p. 48.

18. Henry Cattan, *The Evolution of the Oil Concessions in the Middle East and North Africa* (New York: Oceana Publications, 1967); E. E. Murphy, Jr., "Oil Operations in Latin America: The Scope for Private Enterprises," *International Lawyer*, 2, no. 2 (April 1968): 455–498. More generally, see Raymond Vernon, "Long-Run Trends in Concession Contracts," *Proceedings of the American Society of International Law*, April 1967, pp. 81–89.

19. This point is carefully analyzed in R. F. Mikesell, "Conflict in Foreign Investor-Host Country Relations: A Preliminary Analysis," in R. F. Mikesell, ed., *Foreign Investment in the Petroleum and Mineral*

Notes

Industries: Case Studies on Investor-Host Relations (Baltimore: Johns Hopkins Press, 1971), chap. 2.

20. D. H. Finnie, *Desert Enterprise* (Cambridge: Harvard University Press, 1958), pp. 155–168; Government of Mexico, *Mexico's Oil* (Mexico City, 1940), p. 50; Stacy May and Galo Plaza, *The United Fruit Company in Latin America* (Washington, D.C.: National Planning Association, 1958), p. 183 ff.; Benjamin Higgins et al., *Stanvac in Indonesia* (Washington, D.C.: National Planning Association, 1957), pp. 62–90; W. C. Taylor and John Lindeman, *The Creole Petroleum Corporation in Venezuela* (Washington, D.C.: National Planning Association, 1955), pp. 32–60.

21. See, for example, M. L. Kilson, Jr., *Political Change in a West African State* (Cambridge: Harvard University Press, 1966), p. 42.

22. For a perceptive analysis of the Chilean case, see T. H. Moran, "The Relations Between Chile and the World Market in Copper," Santiago, 1969, mimeograph; see also "Dark Cloud with a Copper Lining," *Forbes*, March 1, 1970, pp. 26–36.

23. Council for Latin America, *The Effects of United States and Other Foreign Investment in Latin America* (New York, January 1970), pp. 54, 56.

24. Ragaei El Mallakh, *Some Dimensions of Middle East Oil: The Producing Countries and the United States* (New York: American-Arabian Association for Commerce and Industry, 1970), p. 8.

25. Sources differ somewhat on the exact figure, presumably because of differences in definitions. See W. G. Harris, "The Impact of the Petroleum Export Industry on the Pattern of Venezuela Economic Development," and Henry Gomez, "Venezuela's Iron Ore Industry," in Mikesell, ed., *Foreign Investment*, chaps. 6 and 12.

26. Adelman, *The World Petroleum Market*, in press.

27. Adelman, *ibid.*, estimates the average figures at about 72 percent in 1970. Newspaper estimates, following the Teheran agreement of 1971, placed the new share at 80 to 90 percent.

28. The Venezuelan and Saudi Arabian data are from P. E. Church, "Labor Relations in Mineral and Petroleum Resource Development," in Mikesell, ed., *Foreign Investment*, chap. 4. The Caltex data are based on personal interview in Indonesia.

29. G. G. Edwards, "The Frondizi Contracts and Petroleum Self-Sufficiency in Argentina," in Mikesell, ed., *Foreign Investment*, chap. 7.

30. J. E. Zinser, "Alternative Means of Meeting Argentina's Petroleum Requirements," in Mikesell, ed., *Foreign Investment*, chap. 8. Zinser's measures, based on 1958–1963 performance, reflect net balance-of-payments effects and net contribution to domestic product.

31. W. H. Bortsch, "The Impact of the Oil Industry on the Economy of Iran," in Mikesell, ed., *Foreign Investment*, chap. 10, table 23.

32. Adelman, *The World Petroleum Market*, documents this view with particular force.

CHAPTER 3

1. Mira Wilkins, *The Emergence of Multinational Enterprise* (Cambridge: Harvard University Press, 1970).

2. For an extended discussion of the ties between market conditions and industrial innovation, see Jacob Schmookler, *Invention and Economic Growth* (Cambridge: Harvard University Press, 1966).

3. A. T. Knoppers, "American Interests in Europe," in Eric Moonman, ed., *Science and Technology in Europe* (Harmondsworth, Middlesex, Eng.: Penguin Books, 1968); W. P. Strassmann, *Risk and Technological Innovation* (Ithaca: Cornell University Press, 1959), pp. 32–34, 221; D. A. Schon, *Technology and Change* (New York: Delacorte Press, 1967), pp. 19–41, 103–111; OECD, *Gaps in Technology between Member Countries: Sector Report, Plastics* (Paris, 1968), p. 102; P. R. Lawrence and J. W. Lorsch, *Organization and Environment: Managing Differentiation and Integration* (Boston: Harvard Business School, 1967), pp. 88–96; A. J. Harman, "Innovations Technology, and the Pure Theory of International Trade," unpublished Ph.D. thesis, MIT, September 1968, p. 131.

4. This is, of course, a familiar point elaborated in George F. Stigler, "Production and Distribution in the Short Run," *Journal of Political Economy*, 47 (June 1939): 305 ff.

5. H. M. Croom and R. J. Hammond, *An Economic History of Britain* (London: Christophers, 1938), p. 293; H. O. Meredith, *Outlines of the Economic History of England* (London: Pitman & Sons, 1908), p. 352; S. B. Clough and C. W. Cole, *Economic History of Europe* (Boston: Heath, 1952), p. 662. In France, wages and prices followed a roughly similar trend; wages rose rapidly whereas prices scarcely increased over the period. Institut National de la Statistique et des Études Économiques, *Annuaire statistique de la France, 1966: Résumé rétrospectif* (Paris, 1967), pp. 373, 422, 425.

6. W. H. Gruber, Dileep Mehta, and Raymond Vernon, "The R & D Factor in International Trade and International Investment," *Journal of Political Economy*, 75, no. 1 (February 1967): 24–25; G. C. Hufbauer, "The Impact of National Characteristics and Technology on the Commodity Composition of Trade in Manufactured Goods," in Raymond Vernon, ed., *The Technology Factor in International Trade* (New York: Columbia University Press, 1970); W. H. Gruber and Raymond Vernon, "The Technology Factor in a World Trade Matrix," in the same source; J. H. Dunning, "European and U.S. Trade Patterns, U.S. Foreign Investment, and the Technological Gap," *Proceedings of*

Notes

the International Economic Association, September 1969, mimeograph.

7. H. S. Houthakker and S. P. Magee, "Income and Price Elasticities in World Trade," *Review of Economics and Statistics,* 51, no. 2 (May 1969): 111–125; F. M. Adler, "The Relationship between the Income and Price Elasticities of Demand for U.S. Exports," Columbia University, November 1969, mimeograph; W. H. Branson, *A Disaggregated Model of the U.S. Balance of Trade,* Federal Reserve System Staff Economic Study (Washington, D.C.: Federal Reserve System, 1968).

8. Rolando Polli and Victor Cook, "Validity of the Product Life Cycle," *Journal of Business,* 42, no. 4 (October 1969): 385–400.

9. L. T. Wells, Jr., "Test of a Product Cycle Model of International Trade," *Quarterly Journal of Economics,* 83 (February 1969): 152–162.

10. R. B. Stobaugh, "The Product Life Cycle, U.S. Exports, and International Investment," unpublished D.B.A. thesis, Harvard Business School, June 1968. See also OECD, *Gaps in Technology* (Paris, 1968), six industry sectoral studies; also studies on the plastics, electronics, and chemical process plant industries, respectively, all directed by Christopher Freeman, *National Institute Economic Review,* 26 (November 1963), 34 (November 1965), and 45 (August 1968).

11. See R. S. Basi, *Determinants of United States Private Direct Investments in Foreign Countries* (Kent, O.: Kent State University Bureau of Economic and Business Research, 1963); A. N. Hakam, "The Motivation to Invest and the Locational Pattern of Foreign Private Industrial Development in Nigeria," *Economic and Social Studies,* 8, no. 1 (March 1966): 50; G. L. Reuber and Frank Roseman, *The Takeover of Canadian Firms, 1945–1961: An Empirical Analysis,* 1968, mimeograph; National Industrial Conference Board, *U.S. Production Abroad and the Balance of Payments* (New York, 1966), p. 63; Arthur Stonehill and Leonard Nathanson, "Capital Budgeting and the Multinational Corporation," *California Management Review,* 10, no. 4 (Summer 1968): 39–55; R. F. Mikesell, ed., *U.S. Private and Government Investment Abroad* (Eugene, Ore.: University of Oregon, 1962), p. 89; *Overseas Operations of U.S. Industrial Enterprises, 1960–1961* (New York: McGraw-Hill, 1960); National Planning Association, *Case Studies of U.S. Business Performance Abroad* (Washington D.C.: National Planning Association, 1955–1961), eleven case studies; H. J. Robinson, *The Motivation and Flow of Private Foreign Investment,* Investment Series no. 4 (Menlo Park, Calif.: Stanford Research Institute, 1961), p. 24; D. M. Phelps, *Migration of Industry to Latin America* (New York: McGraw-Hill, 1936), pp. 43–87; Michael Kidron, *Foreign Investments in India* (London: Oxford University Press, 1965), pp. 253–256; B. L. Johns, "Private Overseas Investment in Australia: Profitability and Motivation," *Economic Record,* 43 (June 1967): 257–261; Whatarangi

Winiata, "United States Managerial Investment in Japan, 1950–1964," unpublished Ph.D. thesis, University of Michigan, 1966, p. 110.

12. Especially fruitful sources are Yair Aharoni, *The Foreign Investment Decision Process* (Boston: Harvard Business School, 1966), esp. chaps. 3–7; E. P. Neufeld, *A Global Corporation* (Toronto: University of Toronto Press, 1969); Mira Wilkins and F. E. Hill, *American Business Abroad* (Detroit: Wayne State University Press, 1964). For a good source of business histories repeatedly consulted, see L. M. Daniells, *Studies in Enterprise* (Boston: Harvard Business School, 1957).

13. Mordechai Kreinin, "The Leontief Scarce-Factor Paradox," *American Economic Review*, 55 (March 1965): 131; T. R. Gates, *Production Costs Here and Abroad* (New York: National Industrial Conference Board, 1958), pp. 26–27.

14. See G. C. Hufbauer, *Synthetic Materials and the Theory of International Trade* (London: Duckworth, 1966), p. 59; OECD, *Gaps in Technology between Member Countries: Plastics* (Paris, 1968), p. 104; R. B. Stobaugh, "Systematic Bias and the Terms of Trade," *Review of Economics and Statistics*, 49 (November 1967): 617–619; R. B. Stobaugh, "Away from Market Concentration: The Case of Petrochemicals," Marketing Science Institute working paper, October 1970.

15. This phenomenon is being explored by F. T. Knickerbocker in a D.B.A. dissertation at the Harvard Business School.

16. For background, see D. S. Landes, *The Unbound Prometheus* (Cambridge: Cambridge University Press, 1969), p. 41 ff.; Nathan Rosenberg, "The Role of Technology in American Economic Growth," in *A New American Economic History* (New York: Harper & Row, 1971); "Technological Change in the Machine Tool Industry, 1840–1910," *Journal of Economic History*, 23, no. 4 (December 1963): 414; Nathan Rosenberg and Edward Ames, "The Enfield Arsenal in Theory and History," *Economic Journal*, 78 (December 1968): 827; and Nathan Rosenberg, "Introduction," in Nathan Rosenberg, ed., *The American System of Manufactures* (Edinburgh: University Press, 1969). Other well-known sources have also helped greatly, esp. J. H. Habbakuk, *American and British Technology in the Nineteenth Century* (Cambridge: Cambridge University Press, 1962); W. P. Strassmann, *Risk and Technological Innovation;* Robert Gilpin, *France in the Age of the Scientific State* (Princeton: Princeton University Press, 1968); A. L. Levine, *Industrial Retardation in Britain, 1880–1914* (New York: Basic Books, 1967); and D. H. Aldcroft, ed., *The Development of British Industry and Foreign Competition, 1875–1914* (Toronto: University of Toronto Press, 1968).

17. For an extended discussion of the ties between market conditions and industrial innovation, see Jacob Schmookler, *Invention and Economic Growth*.

Notes

18. Joseph Ben-David, *Fundamental Research and the Universities* (Paris: OECD, 1968), p. 21.

19. See Walter Adams and J. B. Dirlam, "Big Steel Invention and Innovation," *Quarterly Journal of Economics,* 80, no. 2 (May 1966): 169–171; T. A. Wertime, *The Coming of the Age of Steel* (Chicago: University of Chicago Press, 1962), pp. 284–297.

20. The background of the German chemical industry pre-World War I is drawn mainly from Ernst Bäumler, *Ein Jahrhundert Chemie* (Düsseldorf: Econ-Verlag, 1963), and Wilhelm Vershofen, *Die Anfänge der chemisch-pharmazeutischen Industrie,* vols. 1 and 3 (Berlin: Deutscher Betriebswirte-Verlag, 1949); Archibald Clow and N. L. Crow, *The Chemical Revolution* (London: Batchworth, 1952); L. F. Haber, *The Chemical Industry during the Nineteenth Century* (Oxford: Clarendon Press, 1958); P. M. Hohenberg, *Chemicals in Western Europe: 1850–1914* (Chicago: Rand McNally, 1967).

21. Jacob Viner, *The Customs Union Issue* (New York: Carnegie Endowment, 1950), p. 23.

22. D. C. Coleman, *Courtaulds: An Economic and Social History* (Oxford: Clarendon Press, 1969), p. 105.

23. See Ervin Hexner, *International Cartels* (Chapel Hill: University of North Carolina Press, 1945).

24. For evidence on Britain, see Levine, *Industrial Retardation*, pp. 88 ff. For a generalized theory of skills related to machine processes, see Strassmann, *Risk and Technological Innovation*, p. 173.

25. The data in this paragraph are from Ben-David, *Fundamental Research*, pp. 21, 40–41.

26. Adams and Dirlam, "Big Steel Invention"; G. S. Maddala and P. T. Knight, "International Diffusion of Technical Change—A Case Study of the Oxygen Steel Making Process," *Economic Journal*, 77, no. 307 (September 1967): 531–558.

27. For striking evidence of the relative unimportance of distance in determining the level of U.S. exports of tobacco products and aircraft, see W. H. Gruber and Raymond Vernon, "The Technology Factor in a World Trade Matrix," in Vernon, ed., *The Technology Factor in International Trade*, p. 259, table 9. Among twenty-four industries studied, exports of these two exhibited the least sensitivity to distance.

28. *The Final Report of the Anglo-American Council on Productivity* (London, 1952), p. 13; Graham Hutton, *We Too Can Prosper: The Promise of Productivity* (London: Allen & Unwin, 1953), pp. 18, 32; British Productivity Council, *Policy and Progress, 1954–1955* (London, 1955), pp. 8–9.

29. For similar generalizations by others, see Bela Balassa, "American Direct Investments in the Common Market," *Quarterly Review* (Rome), 77 (June 1966): 134; S. H. Hymer, "The International Operations of National Firms: A Study of Direct Foreign Investment," un-

published Ph.D. thesis, MIT, 1960; C. P. Kindleberger, *American Business Abroad* (New Haven: Yale University Press, 1969), pp. 1–36.

30. The leading cases, summarized in Kingman Brewster, Jr., *Antitrust and American Business Abroad* (New York: McGraw-Hill, 1958), embrace a very wide range of products, principally affecting the modern industries, that is, chemicals, machinery, and electrical and electronic products. Primary metals also are included.

31. Various efforts at trying to isolate by statistical means the gross "EEC effect" on U.S. investment have so far failed to turn up anything significant. All that such studies seem to demonstrate is a correlation between the level of U.S. direct investment in Europe and the size of the gross product of the area. See A. E. Scaperlanda and L. J. Mauer, "The Determinants of U.S. Investment in the EEC," *American Economic Review*, 59, no. 4, pt. 1 (September 1969): 558–568; V. N. Bandera and J. T. White, "U.S. Direct Investments and Domestic Markets in Europe," *Economia Internazionale*, 21, no. 1 (February 1968): 1–19; Ralph d'Arge, "Note on Customs Unions and Direct Foreign Investment," *Economic Journal*, 79, no. 314 (June 1969): 324–333.

32. International Statistical Year for Research and Development, *The Overall Level and Structure of R & D Efforts in OECD Member Countries* (Paris: OECD, 1967), vol. 1; *Statistical Tables and Notes* (Paris: OECD, 1968), vol. 2. For a detailed interpretation of these data and other material on the same subject, see OECD Committee for Science Policy, Secretariat Report, *The Conditions for Success in Technological Innovation* (Paris: OECD, 1970), mimeograph.

33. Illinois Institute of Technology (IIT) Research Institute, *TRACES: Technology in Retrospect and Critical Events in Science* (Chicago: IIT Research Institute, 1968, 1969), vols. 1 and 2.

34. Edwin Mansfield, *The Economics of Technological Change* (New York: Norton, 1968), pp. 84–86.

35. The point is made, for example, in A. T. Knoppers, "American Interests in Europe," pp. 101–116. See also J. J. Servan-Schreiber, *The American Challenge* (New York: Atheneum, 1968); "Technological Gaps: Their Nature, Causes and Effects," *OECD Review*, 33 (April 1968): 18–28; R. R. Nelson, *The Technology Gap: Analysis and Appraisal* (Santa Monica: Rand, 1967); and Gilpin, *France in the Age of the Scientific State*, pp. 125–146.

36. W. F. Mueller, "The Origins of the Basic Inventions Underlying DuPont's Major Product and Process Innovations, 1920 to 1950," in R. R. Nelson, ed., *The Rate and Direction of Inventive Activity* (Princeton: Princeton University Press, 1962), pp. 337, 340.

37. J. L. Enos, "Invention and Innovation in the Petroleum Refining Industry," in Nelson, ed., *Rate and Direction of Inventive Activity*, pp. 311–312.

38. "Concorde's Growing Pay Load," *The Economist*, August 16–22,

Notes

1969, p. 51, and "Who Will Take Rolls-Royce On?", *The Economist*, November 14–20, 1970, p. 67.

39. J. L. Enos, "Invention and Innovation," pp. 307–308.

40. IIT Research Institute, *TRACES*, vol. 1, pp. 29–98.

41. A fuller argument for this conclusion, together with bibliographical references, appears in my "Organization as a Scale Factor in the Growth of Firms," in J. W. Markham and G. F. Papanek, eds., *Industrial Organization and Economic Development* (Boston: Houghton-Mifflin, 1970). See also A. M. Weinberg, "Scientific Teams and Scientific Laboratories," *Daedalus*, 99, no. 4 (Fall 1970): 1056–1061.

42. See Landes, *The Unbound Prometheus*, chap. 7.

43. See for instance, Mansfield, *Economics of Technological Change*, pp. 69–98; see also John Jewkes, David Sawers, and Richard Stillerman, *The Sources of Invention* (New York: St. Martin's Press, 1958), pp. 162–166. This may be one reason why even a firm as much oriented to science as DuPont was said to be basing "three out of five" important new products or processes on the ideas and discoveries of other firms. See Mueller, "Origins and Basic Inventions," p. 323.

44. W. S. Comanor, "Market Structure, Product Differentiation, and Industrial Research," *Quarterly Journal of Economics*, 8, no. 4 (November 1967): 639; Daniel Hamberg, *R & D: Essays on the Economics of Research and Development* (New York: Random House, 1966), pp. 69–112.

45. A good analysis of IBM's performance appears in A. J. Harman, *The International Computer Industry: Innovation and Comparative Advantage* (Cambridge: Harvard University Press, 1971). For the organizational side of the story, see William Rodgers, *Think: A Biography of the Watsons and IBM* (New York: Stein & Day, 1969), pp. 228–245.

46. Edwin Mansfield, "The Speed of Response of Firms to New Techniques," *Quarterly Journal of Economics*, 87, no. 2 (May 1963): 290–311.

47. F. M. Scherer, "Firm Size and Patented Inventions," *American Economic Review*, 55, no. 5, pt. 2 (1965): 1097–1123. The research effort in the firm and the sales generated by the firm are not firmly linked by the statistics; unfortunately, the tie can only be inferred.

48. M. M. Postan, *An Economic History of Western Europe, 1945–1964* (London: Methuen, 1967), p. 110.

49. S. H. Hymer and Robert Rowthorn, *Multinational Corporations and International Oligopoly: The Non-American Challenge*, Economic Growth Center Discussion Paper, no. 75 (New Haven: Yale University, 1959), tables 5 and 6.

50. Jean-Jacques Salomon, "European Scientific Organizations," in Moonman, ed., *Science and Technology*, pp. 64–86.

51. Gilpin, *France in the Age of the Scientific State*, p. 387.

52. Frank Lynn, *Technology and the American Economy* (Washing-

ton, D.C.: Government Printing Office, 1966), vol. 1, pp. 3–4; Gilpin, *France in the Age of the Scientific State*, p. 24. For a more reserved view, see Mansfield, *Economics of Technological Change*, pp. 130–131.

53. Frank Lynn, "The Rate of Development and Diffusion of Technology," in H. R. Bowen and G. L. Mangum, eds., *Automation and Economic Progress* (Englewood Cliffs: Prentice-Hall, 1966), pp. 99–113; Stobaugh, "The Product Life Cycle," App. D.

54. The national automobile industries of Latin America offer a classic illustration of this tendency. For Argentina, see Jack Baranson, *Automotive Industries in Developing Countries* (Baltimore: Johns Hopkins Press, 1969), p. 46.

55. Council for Latin America, *The Effects of U.S. and Other Foreign Investment*, pp. 29–39.

56. GATT Secretariat, "Engineering Export Patterns," *International Trade Forum*, 6, no. 1 (February 1970): 17–26. A recent survey of India's engineering goods industries underlines the key role of foreign-owned subsidiaries in their growing exports; see R. K. Singh, "Engineering Goods Export and Foreign Collaboration," *Calcutta Statesman*, 1970.

57. For an interesting analysis comparing and analyzing the export propensities on the part of foreign-owned and locally owned manufacturing enterprises in El Salvador and Costa Rica, see W. J. Bilkey, *Industrial Stimulation* (Lexington, Mass.: Heath Lexington Books, 1970), pp. 63–108. For a similar study covering Colombia, Mexico, and Nicaragua, see José de la Torre, "Exports of Manufactured Goods from Developing Countries: Marketing Factors and the Role of Foreign Enterprise," unpublished D.B.A. thesis, Harvard Business School, 1970, esp. chaps. 4 and 5.

58. See Baranson, *Automotive Industries*, pp. 13–42.

59. National Council of Applied Economic Research, "Collaboration between Indian and Foreign Firms," New Delhi, September 1969, mimeograph, pp. 88–90.

60. Canada, for instance, has developed an arrangement with its foreign-owned automobile enterprises, conditioning their right to duty-free import of motor vehicles and original equipment on their export of Canadian-built components; see Abraham Chayes, Thomas Ehrlich, and A. F. Lowenfield, *International Legal Process* (Boston: Little Brown, 1968), pp. 307–338. Britain and France have quietly applied similar conditions in selected cases; see J. H. Dunning, *The Role of American Investment in the British Economy*, PEP Broadsheet no. 507 (London 1969), pp. 160–161.

61. Harman, "Innovations," pp. 131–134.

62. Royal Commission on Farm Machinery, *Special Report on Prices* (Ottawa: Queen's Printer, 1969), p. 92; "A Ford Aide Fears Minicar Cost Rise," *The New York Times*, August 21, 1970, p. 1.

63. For articulation of a typical set of such views on the part of businessmen, see F. G. Donner, *The World Wide Industrial Enterprise* (New York: McGraw-Hill, 1967).

64. For a factual summary of foreign direct investments in the United States, see J. P. Daniels, "Recent Foreign Direct Manufacturing Investment in the United States: An Interview Study of the Decision Process," unpublished Ph.D. thesis, University of Michigan, 1969.

65. Royal Dutch/Shell Petroleum Company, *1911 Annual Report* (The Hague, 1911), pp. 20–21, and *1912 Annual Report* (The Hague, 1913), p. 33.

66. "The Game That Two Could Play," *Forbes,* 94 (December 1, 1964): 41. See also "Pechiney Multinational," *Entreprise,* 679 (September 14, 1968): 36–45, where some added motives are suggested.

67. As is usual in such cases, the motivations of British Petroleum for investing in the U.S. market were rather complex, the existence of a crude oil surplus being only one element in a tangled situation. See "B.P.'s Spring Double," *The Economist,* March 8, 1969, p. 62.

68. Charles Wilson, *Unilever 1945–1965* (London: Cassell, 1968), vol. 2, p. 228. See also pp. 231–232.

69. *Ibid.,* p. 83.

70. *Ibid.,* pp. 7, 70, 150.

71. R. M. Moore, "The Role of Extrazonally Controlled Multinational Corporations in the Process of Establishing a Regional Latin American Automotive Industry: A Case Study of Brazil," unpublished Ph.D. thesis, Fletcher School of Law and Diplomacy, Tufts University, 1969.

72. "German Building Steel Mill in U.S.," *The New York Times,* January 26, 1969, sect. 3, p. 1.

CHAPTER 4

1. The usual list includes J. K. Galbraith, *The New Industrial State* (Boston: Houghton Mifflin, 1967); Peter F. Drucker, *The Age of Discontinuity* (New York: Harper & Row, 1969); and C. I. Barnard, *The Functions of the Executive* (Cambridge: Harvard University Press, 1938) More satisfying for economists are K. J. Cohen and R. M. Cyert, *Theory of the Firm* (Englewood Cliffs: Prentice-Hall, 1965); E. T. Penrose, *The Theory of the Growth of the Firm* (Oxford: Blackwell, 1968); Robin Marris, *The Economic Theory of Managerial Capitalism* (New York: Basic Books, 1968); and Martin Shubik, "A Curmudgeon's Guide to Microeconomics," *Economic Literature,* 8, no. 2 (June 1970): 405–434.

2. For a typical argument on this score, see Maurice Byé, trans. by Elizabeth Henderson, "Self-Financed Multiterritorial Units and Their Time Horizon" undated, *International Economic Papers,* no. 8.

3. These are Martin Shubik's words in "A Curmudgeon's Guide," p. 413.

4. For illustrative materials, see J. L. Bower, *Managing the Resource Allocation Process: A Study of Corporate Planning and Investment* (Boston: Harvard Business School, 1970). Other sources that are illuminating in this context are P. R. Lawrence and J. W. Lorsch, *Organization and Environment* (Boston: Harvard Business School, 1967), and Yair Aharoni, *The Foreign Investment Decision Process* (Boston: Harvard Business School, 1966).

5. The next few paragraphs draw heavily on the works cited in note 4, as well as A. D. Chandler, *Strategy and Structure* (Garden City, N.Y.: Doubleday, 1966); L. E. Franko, *Joint Venture Survival in Multinational Corporations,* (New York: Praeger, 1971), and J. M. Stopford, "Growth and Organizational Change in the Multinational Firm," unpublished D.B.A. thesis, Harvard Business School, June 1968.

6. Mira Wilkins and F. E. Hill, *American Business Abroad: Ford on Six Continents* (Detroit: Wayne State University Press, 1964); William Rodgers, *Think: A Biography of the Watsons and IBM* (New York: Stein & Day, 1969), esp. chap. 5.

7. N. K. Bruck and F. A. Lees, "Foreign Content of U.S. Corporate Activities," *Financial Analysts Journal,* September–October 1966, pp. 1–6.

8. C. L. Suzman, "The Changing Export Activities of U.S. Firms with Foreign Manufacturing Affiliates," unpublished D.B.A. thesis, Harvard Business School, January 1969, pp. 118–135.

9. The summary that follows is based on work that will appear in another book in this series: S. M. Robbins, R. B. Stobaugh, and D. M. Schydlowsky, *Money in the Multinational Enterprise: A Study of Financial Policy.*

10. The tendency for U.S. parent firms to learn by error and to respond by a sporadic tightening of controls over their foreign subsidiaries is observed in D. T. Brash, *American Investment in Australian Industry* (Cambridge: Harvard University Press, 1966), p. 120.

11. H. T. Jadwani, "Some Aspects of the Multinational Corporations' Exposure to Exchange Rate Risk," unpublished D.B.A. thesis, Harvard Business School, 1971.

12. J. H. Dunning, *American Investment in British Manufacturing* (London: Allen & Unwin, 1958), p. 112; A. E. Safarian, *Foreign Ownership of Canadian Industry* (Toronto: McGraw-Hill, 1966), pp. 88–93; R. S. Deane, "Foreign Investment in New Zealand Manufacturing," unpublished Ph.D. dissertation, Victoria University of Wellington, November 1967, p. 189.

13. Only the Australian study among the major studies fails to detect the tendency: Brash, *American Investment*, p. 119. But the statistical problem of controlling some important causal variables, such as the method of acquisition of the subsidiary, presents major measurement difficulties.

14. I owe the reference to Antony Jay, *Management and Machiavelli: An Inquiry into the Politics of Corporate Life* (New York: Holt, Rinehart & Winston, 1968), p. 65. His description of how coordination is achieved by conditioning in large organizations is one of the best in the literature.

15. Brash, *American Investment*, p. 228; and Deane, "Foreign Investment," p. 334.

16. For some suggestive data generally supportive of these generalizations, see R. J. Aylmer, "Who Makes Marketing Decisions in the Multinational Firm?" April 1970, mimeograph.

17. Rodgers, *Th nk*, p. 287.

18. *Ibid.*, p. 238.

19. Jack Baranson, *Automotive Industries in Developing Countries* (Baltimore: Johns Hopkins Press, 1969), p. 37.

20. C. V. Vaitsos, "Transfer of Resources and Preservation of Monopoly Rents," 1970, Development Advisory Service, Harvard University.

21. Brash, *American Investment*, pp. 217–220. A New Zealand study suggests that the prices paid by the subsidiaries for goods sold by parents may actually be lower than open market prices; but the sample was small and the underlying observations of uncertain quality on this point. See Deane, "Foreign Investments," pp. 236–243.

22. Brash, *American Investment*, pp. 215–216, cites a number of different motives.

23. For an elaboration of this point, see my "Conflict and Resolution Between Foreign Direct Investors and Less-Developed Countries," *Pub lic Policy*, 17 (Fall 1968): 339–342; see also Brash, *American Investment*, pp. 76–79, and Deane, "Foreign Investment," pp. 104–106.

24. Compare the finding in Safarian, *Foreign Ownership*, p. 93. Subsidiaries with product lines identical with their parents tended to be more closely supervised than subsidiaries with product lines that deviated from those of their parents.

25. Brash, *American Investment*, pp. 117–121, 257; Safarian, *Foreign Ownership*, pp. 97, 234; Deane, "Foreign Investment," pp. 165–167, 187; Dunning, *American Investment*, pp. 110–111.

26. Deane, "Foreign Investment," pp. 95–96, 268–269, 271, 273; Brash, *American Investment*, p. 257.

27. Brash, *American Investment*, pp. 95–98; Deane, "Foreign Investment," p. 502.

28. Brash, *American Investment*, p. 207; Deane "Foreign Invest-

ment," pp. 234, 473, shows higher relative imports for wholly owned subsidiaries than for joint ventures, but attributes the difference to industry composition rather than ownership patterns.

29. Brash, *American Investment,* p. 233; Vaitsos, "Transfer of Resources," pp. 45–47; Reserve Bank of India, *Foreign Collaboration in Indian Industry* (Bombay: Examiner Press, 1968), pp. 106–110; Safarian, *Foreign Ownership,* p. 140; Deane, "Foreign Investment," pp. 342–343; de la Torre, "Exports of Manufactured Goods," chap. 5.

30. The order of magnitude is suggested by the fact that the market value of foreign holdings of U.S. corporate shares at year-end 1968 was reported to be $19.5 billion; U.S. Department of Commerce, *Survey of Current Business,* 49, no. 10 (October 1969): 24. On the same date, outstanding shares on the New York Stock Exchange were valued at $692.3 billion; *ibid.,* p. S–21. Though the figures do not appear comparable in a formal sense, their comparability is enhanced by the fact that for both figures there is a heavy weighting in favor of multinational enterprises.

31. See, for instance, F. G. Donner, in *Proceedings of the Eighth Annual International Congress of Accountants* (New York, 1962); see also A. K. Watson, paper presented to the Economic Club of Detroit, 1965.

32. See also Kenneth Simmonds, "Multinational? Well, Not Quite," *Columbia Journal of World Business,* 1, no. 4 (Fall 1966): 115–122, whose survey of 150 large U.S. corporations and their 3,847 top managers produced similar results.

33. See R. F. Gonzalez, *The United States Executive: His Orientations and Career Patterns* (East Lansing, Mich.: Michigan State Business School, 1967); J. C. Shearer, *High-Level Manpower in Overseas Subsidiaries* (Princeton: Princeton University Department of Economics and Sociology, 1960); Harlan Cleveland, C. J. Mangone, and J. C. Adams, *The Overseas American* (New York: McGraw-Hill, 1960).

34. For typical anecdotal materials, see a case study, IMEDE, *The Galvor Company R–2,* ICH 13G34 (Lausanne, 1967); see also Harvard Business School, *Trading with the Enemy,* ICH 13G252 (Boston, 1967).

35. T. F. M. Adams and N. Kobayashi, *The World of Japanese Business* (Palo Alto, Calif.: Kodansha International, 1969), p. 147.

36. Illustrative of survey results on this question are the findings of C. E. Watson, "Staffing Management Positions in U.S.-Owned Business Subsidiaries in Brazil," 1970, mimeograph, p. 10.

37. C. E. Watson, *op. cit.,* p. 9.

38. Adapted from Safarian, *Foreign Ownership,* pp. 56, 58.

39. Brash, *American Investment,* p. 108. For rich insights in an individual case, see Michael Baume, "Is General Motors Good for Australia," *The Bulletin* (Sydney, Australia), February 3, 1968, p. 18.

40. Council for Latin America, *The Effects of United States and*

Other Foreign Investment in Latin America (New York, 1970), p. 83.

41. E. A. McCreary, *The Americanization of Europe* (Garden City, N.Y.: Doubleday, 1964), pp. 269–270.

42. An excellent source on the handling of such conflict by local managers is Wilkins and Hill, *American Business Abroad.* Chapter 4 recounts the problems of the head of the British subsidiary of Ford from 1914 to 1917, when Henry Ford was a pacifist and Britain was at war; chapter 13 deals with the problems of the management of Ford's German subsidiary from 1933 to 1939.

43. The process is well described in E. V. Stonequist, *The Marginal Man: A Study in Personality and Culture Conflict* (New York: Scribner's, 1937).

CHAPTER 5

1. For typical analyses of this sort, see P. B. Musgrave, *United States Taxation of Foreign Investment Income* (Cambridge: Harvard Law School, 1969), pp. 9–25; Marvin Frankel, "Home versus Foreign Investment: A Case Against Capital Export," *Kyklos,* 18, no. 3 (1965): pp. 411–433; A. K. Severn, "Investment and Financial Behavior of American Direct Investors in Manufacturing," and M. F. J. Prachowny, "Direct Investment and the Balance of Payments of the United States: A Portfolio Approach," in "Universities-National Bureau Conference on International Mobility and Movement of Capital," 1970, mimeograph. For an effort to bridge the obvious inadequacies in the approach while retaining its basic framework, see R. Z. Aliber, "A Theory of Direct Investment," in C. P. Kindleberger, ed., *The International Corporation* (Cambridge: MIT Press, 1970), pp. 17–34.

2. H. G. Johnson, "The Efficiency and Welfare Implications of the International Corporation," in Kindleberger, ed., *The International Corporation,* pp. 35–56; R. E. Caves, "Foreign Investment, Trade and Industrial Growth," Royer Lectures, University of California (Berkeley), 1969, mimeograph, pp. 4–5; C. P. Kindleberger, *American Business Abroad* (New Haven: Yale University Press, 1969), pp. 1–36.

3. Detailed illustrations are found in *Continental Oil Company,* PP/170R, Harvard Business School case, 1969; and N. B. MacDonald, "A Comment: The Bladen Plan . . .", *Canadian Journal of Economics and Political Science,* 29, no. 4 (November 1963): 505–512; D. T. Brash, *American Investment in Australian Industry* (Cambridge: Harvard University Press, 1966), p. 69.

4. The point is infrequently recognized in explicit form. But see J. H. Dunning, "Further Thoughts on Foreign Investment," *Moorgate and Wall Street,* Autumn 1966, p. 13.

5. These estimates have been built up from two main sources. Total

asset figures represent an extrapolation of *Survey of Current Business* data on U.S. foreign direct investment in manufacturing and extraction industries, the extrapolation being based on a small sample of subsidiary balance sheets collected in the course of the present study. Resource flows from the United States came from the U.S. balance of payments series, published regularly in the *Survey of Current Business*.

6. These estimates are based on the "sources and uses of funds" analysis for 1958–1965, published in various issues of the *Survey of Current Business* and presented in summary in G. C. Hufbauer and F. M. Adler, U.S. Treasury Department, *Overseas Manufacturing Investment and the Balance of Payments* (Washington, D.C. 1968), p. 16. Later figures, covering 1967 and 1968, appear in U.S. Department of Commerce, *Foreign Affiliate Financial Survey, 1967–1968* (Washington, D.C. 1970), and in *Survey of Current Business,* November 1970, pp. 14–19.

7. These estimates are built up from U.S. Bureau of the Census, "American Overseas," Selected Area Report PC(3)-1C, *Census of Population* (Washington, D.C.: Government Printing Office, 1964), table 16; U.S. Department of Commerce, *U.S. Business Investment in Foreign Countries* (Washington, D.C.: Government Printing Office, 1960); Council for Latin America, *The Effects of United States and Other Foreign Investment in Latin America* (New York, 1970), pp. 84–89.

8. A. E. Safarian, *Foreign Ownership of Canadian Industry* (Toronto: McGraw-Hill, 1966), pp. 299–312, and *The Performance of Foreign-Owned Firms in Canada* (Montreal: Private Planning Association of Canada, 1969). His judgment is echoed in Royal Commission on Canada's Economic Prospects, *Final Report* (Ottawa: Queen's Printer, 1963), pp. 378–385, and in *Foreign Ownership and the Structure of Canadian Industry,* Report of the Task Force on the Structure of Canadian Industry (Ottawa: Queen's Printer, 1968), pp. 58–64 (but see the more equivocal comments on pp. 210–211).

9. Karel Holbik, "Canada's Economic Sovereignty and United States Investment," *Quarterly Review of Economics and Business,* 10, no. 1 (Spring 1970): 7.

10. J. H. Dunning, *American Investment in British Manufacturing Industry* (London: Allen & Unwin, 1958), pp. 290, 318–319, and "The Effects of United States Investment on British Technology," 1969, mimeograph, pp. 29, 32. Dunning observes wryly (*ibid.,* p. 28), that Britishers react ambivalently to the presence of American managers and technicians. On the one hand, they are the embodiment of a badly needed resource in Britain and, on the other, a challenge to British managers and technicians in their field.

11. Brash, *American Investment,* pp. 35, 52, 198; B. L. Johns, "Private Overseas Investment in Australia: Profitability and Motivation," *Economic Record,* 43, no. 102 (June 1967): 233, 252–254.

Notes

12. J. H. Dunning, "Technology, United States Investment and European Economic Growth," in Kindleberger, ed., *The International Corporation*, pp. 141–173. For data on Germany, see DIVO Institute for Economic Research, *American Subsidiaries in the Federal Republic of Germany* (New York: Commerce Clearing House, 1969). In addition, there are numerous studies of a less empirical character, covering especially France, with similar implicit or explicit judgments. See, for example, Jacques Gervais, *La France face aux investissements étrangers* (Paris: l'Enterprise Moderne, 1963), p. 198.

13. Commission des Communautés Européennes, *La Politique industrielle de la communauté* (Brussels, 1970), pp. 273–294.

14. For a summary of the evidence on this point, see Chapter 4.

15. J. H. Dunning, "Profitability, Production, and Measures of Business Performance," *The Investment Analyst*, 23 (June 1969): 22–34.

16. Brash, *American Investment*, p. 175; Dunning, *American Investment*, p. 186. See also R. S. Deane, "Foreign Investment in New Zealand Manufacturing," unpublished Ph.D. dissertation, Victoria University of Wellington, November 1967; he is even more guarded in his conclusion, p. 311, but entertains the possibility sympathetically.

17. Task Force, *Foreign Ownership*, p. 209; Safarian, *Foreign Ownership*, pp. 168–200.

18. Dunning, *American Investment*, p. 298, and "The Role of American Investment in the British Economy," PEP Broadsheet 507, London, February 1969. See Brash, *American Investment*, pp. 223–239, and DIVO, *American Subsidiaries in the Federal Republic*, p. 174. No such affirmative conclusion is reached for New Zealand, however; see Deane, "Foreign Investment," pp. 328–333.

19. Task Force, *Foreign Ownership*, pp. 203–207. On the other hand, note R. A. Matthews' rejoinder that these subsidiaries should be expected to export far more of their output than a purely domestic operation; address to the Canadian Institute of International Affairs, April 23, 1970.

20. Hufbauer and Adler, *Overseas Manufacturing Investment*.

21. This brief discussion simply scratches the surface of the difficulties that attend such measurements. For a more detailed presentation and critique, see my *U.S. Controls on Foreign Direct Investment— A Reevaluation* (New York: Financial Executives Research Foundation, 1969), pp. 39–64. See also R. N. Cooper's review of the Hufbauer-Adler study in *Journal of Economic Literature*, 7 (December 4, 1969): 1208–1209.

22. Allan Johnstone, *United States Direct Investment in France* (Cambridge: MIT Press, 1965), p. 14; Edward McCreary, *The Americanization of Europe* (New York: Doubleday, 1964), pp. 85, 183.

23. S. M. Robbins, R. B. Stobaugh, and D. M. Schydlowsky, *Money in the Multinational Enterprise: A Study of Financial Policy.*

24. H. T. Jadwani, "Some Aspects of the Multinational Corporations' Exposure to Exchange Rate Risk," unpublished D.B.A. thesis, Harvard Business School, 1971.

25. Commission des Communautés Européennes, *La Politique industrielle,* pp. 175–178.

26. Hufbauer and Adler, *Overseas Manufacturing Investment,* p. 16.

27. The figure on U.S. nationals is estimated from sources listed in note 7. The local employee estimate is extrapolated from data on U.S.-controlled subsidiary employment in Latin America, appearing in the Council for Latin America publication.

28. *Survey of Current Business,* 49, no. 10 (October 1969): 30.

29. Hufbauer and Adler, *Overseas Manufacturing Investment.*

30. R. B. Stobaugh, "The Product Life Cycle, U.S. Export, and International Investment," unpublished D.B.A. thesis, Harvard Business School, June 1968, pp. 110–111. Evidence on the same point is readily inferred from other analyses; see H. B. Chenery and Lance Taylor, "Development Patterns: Among Countries and Over Time," *The Review of Economics and Statistics,* 50, no. 4 (November 1968): 391, 395.

31 The evidence on this point is found in Chapter 3.

32 On the effect on import-substituting industrialization on internal prices see, for example, Jack Baranson, *Automotive Industries in Developing Countries* (Baltimore: Johns Hopkins Press, 1969), pp. 66–76; L. L. Johnson, "Problems of Import Substitution: The Chilean Automobile Industry," *Economic Development and Cultural Change,* 15, no. 2 (January 1967): 202–216. The citations on import-substituting industrialization overvaluing the nation's currency are voluminous. See B. A. de Vries, "The Export Experience of Developing Countries," in *World Bank Staff Papers,* no. 3 (Baltimore: Johns Hopkins Press, 1967); and S. R. Lewis, "Effects of Trade Policy on Domestic Relative Prices: Pakistan, 1951–1964," *American Economic Review,* 63, no. 1 (March 1968): 60–78.

33. Three careful quantitative studies of the balance-of-payments effects of foreign investment in raw materials are: for diamonds in Sierra Leone, A. J. Killick and R. W. During, "A Structural Approach to the Balance of Payments of a Low-Income Country," *Journal of Development Studies,* 5, no. 4 (July 1969): 274–298; for bauxite in Jamaica, H. D. Huggins, *Aluminum in Changing Communities* (London: Andre Deutsch, 1965), pp. 103–155; for oil in Nigeria, S. R. Pearson, "Nigerian Petroleum: Implications for Medium-Term Planning," in C. K. Eicher and Carl Liedholm, eds., *Growth and Development of the Nigerian Economy* (Lansing: Michigan State University Press, 1970), pp. 352–374. All conclude that the net balance-of-payments effects of the foreign investors are positive. The diamond and bauxite studies consider the possibility of even more attractive alternative arrangements. The alternatives, however, are based on the assumption that

the world price would remain unaltered and that access to downstream distribution facilities would be unaffected.

34. The economy of Venezuela, for example, is a classic case in point. See "Economic Developments in Venezuela in the 1950's," *Economic Bulletin for Latin America*, 5, no. 1 (March 1960): 21, 54–59; see also, Maurice Byé, "Self-financed Multiterritorial Units and their Time Horizons," *International Economic Papers*, 8 (1958): 173–174.

35. Summarized in J. R. Powell, *The Mexican Petroleum Industry* (Berkeley: University of California Press, 1956), pp. 15–32.

36. Jack Baranson, *Automobile Industries*, pp. 43–53; G. S. Edelberg, "The Procurement Practices of the Mexican Affiliates of Selected United States Automobile Firms," unpublished D.B.A. thesis, Harvard Business School, 1963, pp. 41–43, 54–84, 166–167, 187–190, 192–196; Lincoln Gordon and Engelbert Grommers, *United States Manufacturing Investment in Brazil* (Boston: Harvard Business School, 1962), pp. 55–59, 142–143.

37. J. M. Katz, *Production Functions, Foreign Investments and Growth* (Amsterdam: North Holland, 1969), pp. 149–154. One may question in which direction causation runs.

38. Compare A. O. Hirschman, *How to Divest in Latin America and Why*, Essays in International Finance, no. 76 (Princeton: Princeton University Press, 1969), p. 49.

39. Some interesting illustrations are provided in Norman Girvan, *Multinational Corporations and Dependent Underdevelopment in Mineral-Exporting Countries*, Economic Growth Center Discussion Paper (New Haven: Yale University Press, 1970), pp. 10–12.

40. Meir Merhav, *Technological Dependence, Monopoly, and Growth* (New York: Pergamon Press, 1969), pp. 6, 55–60; Roy Blough, *International Business: Environment and Adaptation* (New York: McGraw-Hill, 1966), pp. 312–313; R. S. Eckaus, "Technological Change in the Less-Developed Areas," in Robert Asher et al., eds., *Development of the Emerging Countries: An Agenda for Research* (Washington, D.C.: Brookings Institution, 1962), p. 134.

41. The issue is sometimes raised in Europe as well, although with much less emphasis. See Commission des Communautés Européennes, *La Politique industrielle*.

42. A characteristic statement on this score is V. L. Urquidi, "Tecnología, Planficación y Desarrollo Latino Americano," *Foro Internacional*, 10, no. 3 (1970): 229–236.

43. The debate is summarized in G. C. Hufbauer, "The Impact of National Characteristics and Technology on the Commodity Composition of Trade in Manufactured Goods," in Raymond Vernon, ed., *The Technology Factor in International Trade* (New York: Columbia University Press, 1970), pp. 145–231.

44. Edelberg, "Procurement Practices of Mexican Affiliates"; Jack Baranson, *Manufacturing Problems in India* (Syracuse: Syracuse University Press, 1967); W. A. Yeoman, "Selection of Production Processes for the Manufacturing Subsidiaries of U.S.-Based Multinational Corporations," unpublished D.B.A. thesis, Harvard Business School, April 1968.

45. W. A. Yeoman, "Selection of Production Processes," pp. 78–97.

46. There has been a great deal of speculation in the literature over such a possibility, but scarcely any empirical work. See R. S. Eckaus, "The Factor-Proportions Problem in Underdeveloped Areas," in A. N. Agarwala and S. P. Singh, eds., *The Economics of Underdevelopment* (London: Oxford University Press, 1958), pp. 348–378; Benjamin Higgins, *Economic Development: Principles, Problems, and Policies* (New York: Norton, 1959), p. 258; A. K. Sen, *Choice of Techniques* (Oxford: Blackwell, 1960), p. 89; U.N. Bureau of Economic Affairs, "Capital Intensity in Industry in Underdeveloped Countries," in K. E. Ettinger, ed., *International Handbook of Management* (New York: McGraw-Hill, 1965), pp. 235–259.

47. Strassmann, *Technological Change and Economic Development* (Ithaca, N.Y.: Cornell University Press, 1968), pp. 178–181, 200.

48. Christopher Clague, "The Determinants of Efficiency in Manufacturing Industries in an Underdeveloped Country," *Economic Development and Cultural Change,* 18, no. 2 (January 1970): 188–205.

49. See Chapter 6 for a broader discussion of this point.

50. One of the very few studies of income distribution over time in a less-developed country is I. M. Navarrete, *La distribución del ingreso y el desarrollo económico de México* (Mexico, D.F.: Universidad Nacional, 1960), pp. 72–73, tables 6 and 7. The data are equivocal on whether Mexico's income distribution was becoming less egalitarian; an upper middle income group seemed to be gaining from 1950 to 1957 relative to the richest and the poorest groups. For impressions on the same general point, see Nicholas Kaldor, "Economic Problems of Chile," *Essays on Economic Policy* (London: Duckworth, 1964); see also R. M. Bird, "Income Distribution and Tax Policy in Colombia," *Economic Development and Cultural Change,* 18, no. 4, pt. 1 (July 1970): 519–535.

51. Richard Weisskoff, "Income Distribution and Economic Growth: An International Comparison," unpublished Ph.D. thesis, Harvard University, 1969, pp. 57–74; "Income Distribution in Latin America," *Economic Bulletin for Latin America,* 12, no. 2 (1967): 38–60.

52. Jerry Della Femina, *From Those Wonderful Folks Who Gave You Pearl Harbor: Front-Line Dispatches from the Advertising War* (New York: Simon & Schuster, 1970), pp. 225–226.

53. D. S. Freedman, "The Role of the Consumption of Modern

Notes

Durables in Economic Development," *Economic Development and Cultural Change*, 19, no. 1 (October 1970): 25–48.

54. Hufbauer and Adler, *Overseas Manufacturing Investment*.

55. Report of the Economic Policy Committee to the AFL-CIO Executive Council, "International Trade," February 1970, mimeograph. For a recent summary of U.S. labor reactions, see R. L. Barovick, "Labor Reacts to Multinationalism," *Columbia Journal of World Business*, July–August 1970, pp. 40–46.

56. R. L. Barovick, already cited; also, statement of Heribert Maier, ICFTU representative, before U.S. Congress, Joint Economic Committee, July 28, 1970, reproduced in "The International Free Trade Union Movement and Multinational Corporations," ICFTU *Economic and Social Bulletin*, 18, no. 5 (August 1970).

CHAPTER 6

1. W. R. Crawford, *A Century of Latin American Thought* (Cambridge: Harvard University Press, 1961), esp. pp. 116–164; A. O. Hirschman, "Ideologies of Economic Development in Latin America," in A. O. Hirschman, ed., *Latin American Issues* (New York: Twentieth Century Fund, 1961), pp. 4–9; and Leopoldo Zea, *The Latin American Mind*, trans. by J. H. Abbott and Lowell Dunham (Norman, Okla.: University of Oklahoma Press, 1963), esp. pp. 77–86. Major Latin American works are Juan Bautista Alberdi, *Bases y punto de partida para la organización política de la República Argentina* (1852); José do Manoel Bomfim, *A América Latina* (1905); Carlos Octávia Bunge, *Nuestra América* (1905); Eucludes da Cunha, *Os sertões* (1902); and Domingo Faustino Sarmiento, *Facundo* (1845).

2. Raymond Vernon, *The Dilemma of Mexico's Development* (Cambridge: Harvard University Press, 1963), pp. 39–47.

3. Crawford, *A Century of Latin American Thought*, pp. 12–51; Hubert Herring, *A History of Latin America* (New York: Knopf, 1955), pp. 583–625; J. F. Rippy, *Latin America* (Ann Arbor: University of Michigan Press, 1968), pp. 274–281; Arthur Whitaker, *Argentina* (Englewood Cliffs: Prentice-Hall, 1964), pp. 20–64.

4. José Bello, *A History of Modern Brazil: 1889–1964*, trans. by James Taylor (Stanford: Stanford University Press, 1966), pp. 20–76; Crawford, *A Century of Latin American Thought*, pp. 190–198; J. F. Normano, *Brazil: A Study of Economic Types* (Chapel Hill: University of North Carolina Press, 1935), pp. 78–82; J. F. Rippy, *Latin America and the Industrial Age* (New York: Putnam's, 1944), pp. 26–27, 37–38, 96–104; George Wythe, "Brazil: Trends in Industrial Development," in Simon Kuznets et al., eds., *Economic Growth: Brazil, India, Japan* (Durham, N.C.: Duke University Press, 1955), pp. 29–77.

5. Herring, *History of Latin America,* pp. 543–555; Rippy, *Latin America,* pp. 259–264; Frederick Pike, *Chile and the United States, 1880–1962* (Notre Dame: University of Notre Dame Press, 1963), pp. 1–47, 159–169, and, *The Modern History of Peru* (New York: Praeger, 1967), pp. 56–180; Jonathan Levin, *The Export Economies* (Cambridge: Harvard University Press, 1960), pp. 27–123.

6. Percival Griffiths, *Modern India* (New York: Praeger, 1965), pp. 220, 282; V. A. Smith and Percival Spear, eds., *The Oxford History of India* (Oxford: Oxford University Press, 1958), pp. 710–713, 834–838; Matthew J. Kust, *Foreign Enterprise in India* (Chapel Hill: University of North Carolina Press, 1964), pp. 22–23; Percival Spear, *India: A Modern History* (Ann Arbor: University of Michigan Press, 1961), pp. 298–309.

7. See H. H. Smythe and M. M. Smythe, *The New Nigerian Élite* (Stanford: Stanford University Press, 1960), esp. pp. 74–92.

8. In addition to the sources cited in preceding footnotes, see Tomas Fillol, *Social Factors in Economic Development: The Argentine Case* (Cambridge: MIT Press, 1961), pp. 40–53; José Romero, *A History of Argentine Political Thought,* trans. by Thomas McGann (Palo Alto, Calif.: Stanford University Press, 1963), pp. 247–254; Werner Baer, *The Development of the Brazilian Steel Industry* (Nashville: Vanderbilt University Press, 1969), pp. 64–68; E. B. Burns, *Nationalism in Brazil* (New York: Praeger, 1968), pp. 29–127; Gilberto Freyre, *The Mansion and the Shanties* (New York: Knopf, 1963), pp. 203–229; Rollie Poppino, *Brazil: The Land and People* (New York: Oxford University Press, 1968), pp. 242–268; James Carey, *Peru and the United States, 1900–1962* (Notre Dame: University of Notre Dame Press, 1964), pp. 20–65; R. J. Owens, *Peru* (London: Oxford University Press, 1963), pp. 164–174.

9. Considerable anecdotal material can be mustered on this point but not much in the form of systematic studies. But see M. S. Wionczek, "Electric Power: The Uneasy Partnership," in Raymond Vernon, ed., *Public Policy and Private Enterprise in Mexico* (Cambridge: Harvard University Press, 1964), pp. 19–110.

10. Levin, *The Export Economies,* pp. 83–84, 115. To update the Peruvian case, see also Michael Roemer, *Fishing for Growth: Export-Led Development in Peru* (Cambridge: Harvard University Press, 1971).

11. H. B. Lamb, "The Role of Business Communities in the Evolution of an India Industrialist Class," *Pacific Affairs,* 28, no. 2 (June 1955): 102; A. I. Levkovsky, *Capitalism in India: Basic Trends in Its Development* (Bombay: Peoples Publishing House, 1966), p. 52.

12. Chi-ming Hou, *Foreign Investment and Economic Development in China, 1840–1937* (Cambridge: Harvard University Press, 1965), pp. 134–145, 165–188.

Notes

13. As illustrations, see Vernon, *The Dilemma of Mexico's Development*, pp. 163–169; Warren Dean, *The Industrialization of São Paulo, 1880–1945* (Austin: University of Texas Press, 1969), pp. 135–148.

14. Jean-Jacques Servan-Schreiber, *The American Challenge* (New York: Atheneum, 1969).

15. For example, Kari Levitt, *Silent Surrender: The Multinational Corporation in Canada* (New York: St. Martin's Press, 1970). S. H. Hymer and Robert Rowthorn, *Multinational Corporations and International Oligopoly: The Non-American Challenge*, Economic Growth Center Discussion Paper, no. 75 (New Haven: Yale University Press, 1969), pp. 23–24; J. H. Dunning, *American Investment in British Manufacturing Industry* (London: Allen & Unwin, 1958), p. 321; A. E. Safarian, *Foreign Ownership of Canadian Industry* (Toronto: McGraw-Hill, 1960), p. 312; "Foreign Ownership and the Structure of Canadian Industry," *Report of the Task Force on the Structure of Canadian Industry* (Ottawa: Queen's Printer, 1968), pp. 411–412. See also Jacques Gervais, *La France face aux investissements étrangers* (Paris: l'Entreprise Moderne, 1963), pp. 171–174.

16. A first class bibliography covering this point appears in Ralf Dahrendorf, "Recent Changes in the Class Structure of European Society," *Daedalus*, 93, no. 2 (Winter 1964): pp. 267–270. See also David Granick, *The European Executive* (Garden City, N.Y.: Doubleday, 1962) pp. 93–124.

17. John Porter, *The Vertical Mosaic: An Analysis of Social Class and Power in Canada* (Toronto: University of Toronto Press, 1965) pp. 444–446.

18. A. O. Hirschman, "Ideologies of Economic Development," pp. 12–17.

19. R. B. Stobaugh, "Systematic Bias and the Terms of Trade," *Review of Economics and Statistics*, 49 (November 1967): 617–619.

20. The ideology is well developed in Theotonio dos Santos, *El nuevo carácter de la dependencia* (Santiago, Chile: Centro de Estudios Socio-Económicos, Universidad de Chile, 1968), and *Dependencia económica y alternativas de cambio en América Latina* (Santiago, Chile: Centro de Estudios Socio-Económicos, 1970).

21. The early history of the corporation in the United States is drawn largely from J. S. Davis, *Essays in the Early History of American Corporations* (Cambridge: Harvard University Press, 1917); A. B. Levy, *Private Corporations and Their Control* (London: Routledge & Kegan Paul, 1950), vol. 1; and the dissent of Judge Brandeis in *Louis K. Liggett* v. *Lee*, 288 U.S. 517, pp. 548–564.

22. See especially R. T. Averitt, "American Business: Achievement and Challenge," *Daedalus*, 98, no. 1 (Winter 1969): 60–77.

23. S. P. Huntington, "Political Modernization: America vs. Europe," *World Politics*, 18, no. 3 (April 1966): 378–414.

24. For relationships in the nineteenth century, see the voluminous references in Mira Wilkins, *The Emergence of Multinational Enterprise* (Cambridge: Harvard University Press, 1970). For pre-World War II, especially the 1920s, see J. G. Wetter, "Diplomatic Assistance to Private Investment," *University of Chicago Law Review,* 29 (1962): 275–326.

25. Josephus Daniels, *Shirt-Sleeve Diplomat* (Chapel Hill: University of North Carolina Press, 1947), pp. 228–268; J. R. Powell, *The Mexican Petroleum Industry* (Berkeley: University of California Press, 1956), pp. 112–113, 158, 176.

26. A typical demonstration of division and confusion is provided by House Ways and Means Committee, *Hearings on H.R., 2652 . . .,* 79th Cong., 1st sess. (Washington, D.C.: Government Printing Office, 1945), pp. 1323–1363, 2195–2198, 2597–2601. For a broader analysis, see Raymond Bauer, Ithiel de Sola Pool and L. A. Dexter, *American Business and Public Policy* (New York: Atherton Press, 1963), pp. 107–153; J. F. Heath, *John F. Kennedy and the Business Community* (Chicago: University of Chicago Press, 1969), pp. 86–92.

27. Ralph Miliband, *The State in Capitalist Society* (New York: Basic Books, 1969). Also James Petras, "The United States and the New Equilibrium in Latin America," *Public Policy,* 18, no. 1 (Fall 1969): 95–131; A. G. Frank, *Capitalism and Underdevelopment in Latin America* (New York: Monthly Review Press, 1967); Gar Alperovitz, *Cold War Essays* (New York: Doubleday, 1970), pp. 75–121; W. A. Williams, *The Roots of the Modern American Empire* (New York: Random House, 1969), *The Tragedy of American Diplomacy* (Cleveland: World, 1959), and *The Great Evasion* (Chicago: Quadrangle, 1964); Harry Magdoff, *The Age of Imperialism* (New York: Monthly Review Press, 1969).

28. G. D. Nash, *United States Oil Policy, 1890–1964* (Pittsburgh: University of Pittsburgh Press, 1968), pp. 238–251.

29. For a provocative exploration of these relationships, see S. P. Huntington, "The Defense Establishment: Vested Interests and the Public Interest," in O. L. Carey, ed., *The Military-Industrial Complex and U.S. Foreign Policy* (Pullman, Wash.: Washington State University Press, 1969).

30. For an informed European view to similar effect, see Centre National du Calcul, *Le Contexte mondial de l'informatique française* (Rome, 1968), p. 18.

31. Among the sources used in the preparation of the U.K. materials are C. B. Gower, "Some Contrasts between British and American Corporate Law," *Harvard Law Review,* 69 (1956): 1369–1402, and *Modern Company Law,* 2d ed. (London: Stevens, 1966), p. 47; M. M. Postan, *An Economic History of Western Europe* (London: Methuen, 1967); Andrew Shonfield, *Modern Capitalism* (London: Oxford University Press, 1965); W. H. Scott, "Management in Great Britain," in

Notes

Frederick Harbison and Charles Myers, eds., *Management in the Industrial World* (New York: McGraw-Hill, 1959), and *The Constitution and Finance of English, Scottish, and Irish Joint Stock Companies to 1720* (Cambridge: Cambridge University Press, 1912), vol. 3, pp. 313–316; A. B. Levy, *Private Corporations and Their Control*, vol. 1, pp. 36–38; Noel Branton, *The Economic Organization of Modern Britain* (London: English Universities Press, 1966).

32. For instance, David Granick, *The European Executive* (Garden City, N.Y.: Doubleday, 1962), pp. 242–258.

33. Salvador de Madariaga, *Englishmen, Frenchmen, Spaniards* (London: Oxford University Press, 1929), p. 3. Among the sources used for this section are: A. L. Dunham, *The Industrial Revolution in France, 1815–1848* (New York: Exposition Press, 1955); Robert Gilpin, *France in the Age of the Scientific State* (Princeton: Princeton University Press, 1968); OECD, *Reviews of National Science Policy: France* (Paris, 1966); J. H. McArthur and B. R. Scott, *Industrial Planning in France* (Boston: Harvard Business School, 1969); Michel Crozier, *The Bureaucratic Phenomenon* (Chicago: University of Chicago Press, 1964); C. P. Kindleberger, *Economic Growth in France and Britain, 1851–1950* (Cambridge: Harvard University Press, 1964); John Sheahan, *Promotion and Control of Industry in Postwar France* (Cambridge: Harvard University Press, 1963); N. O. Henderson, *The Industrial Revolution on the Continent* (London: Cass, 1967); Stephen Cohen, *Modern Capitalist Planning: The French Model* (Cambridge: Harvard University Press, 1969).

34. Daniel S. Landes, "French Entrepreneurship and Industrial Growth in the Nineteenth Century," *Journal of Economic History*, 9, no. 1 (May 1949): 50–57.

35. The principal sources for this section are: Ministry of Finance, *Guide to Economic Laws of Japan* (Tokyo: Kobunsha, 1950) Ludwig Leonholm, *Japanese Commercial Law* (Tokyo: Eastern World Printing Office, 1895); U.S. Department of Commerce, *Investment in Japan* (Washington, D.C.: Government Printing Office, 1956); N. S. Smith, ed., *Tokugawa Japan* (London: King, 1937); J. C. Abegglen, *The Japanese Factory: Aspects of Its Social Organization* (Glencoe, Ill.: The Free Press, 1958); R. N. Bellah, *Tokugawa Religion: The Values of Pre-Industrial Japan* (Glencoe, Ill.: The Free Press, 1957); M. Y. Yoshino, *Japan's Managerial System: Tradition and Innovation* (Cambridge: MIT Press, 1968); G. B. Sansom, *Japan: A Short Cultural History* (New York: Appleton-Century, 1943); Ryusaku Tsunoda, W. T. de Bary, and Donald Keene, eds., *Sources of the Japanese Tradition* (New York: Columbia University Press, 1958); Johannes Hirschmeier, *The Origins of Entrepreneurship in Meiji Japan* (Cambridge: Harvard University Press, 1964); T. C. Smith, *Political Change and Industrial Development in Japan: Government Enterprises, 1868–*

1880 (Stanford: Stanford University Press, 1955); W. C. Lockwood, *The Economic Development of Japan: Growth and Structural Change, 1868–1938* (Princeton: Princeton University Press, 1954); Chitoshi Yanaga, *Big Business in Japanese Politics* (New Haven: Yale University Press, 1968); O. D. Russell, *The House of Mitsui* (Boston: Little, Brown, 1939).

36. For a revisionist view of Meiji entrepreneurship, at variance with this more orthodox account, see Kozo Yamamura, "A Re-examination of Entrepreneurship in Meiji Japan (1868–1912)," *Economic History Review*, 2d ser., 21, no. 1 (April 1968): 144–158.

37. This trend is documented in Uoshimatsu Aonuma, *Nihon no Keieso* ("The Managerial Class in Japan") (Tokyo, 1965), which is summarized in Yoshino, *Japan's Managerial System*, pp. 88–91. See also Kozo Yamamura, *Economic Policy in Postwar Japan* (Los Angeles: University of California Press, 1967), pp. 126–128.

38. One example is the pronouncements of the Doyukai, a group of young and progressive business executives established in the spring of 1946, during the initial phases of the occupation. The influence of the statements put out by this group since that time to the present is outlined in Yoshino, *Japan's Managerial System*, pp. 96–127.

39. H. F. Van Zandt, "Japanese Culture and the Business Boom," *Foreign Affairs*, 48, no. 2 (January 1970): 354: "The Ministries are apprehensive that foreign concerns would not accept the Government's extra-legal administrative guidance, thus endangering the political-economic establishment. There was also doubt that the majority of the westerners would show adequate understanding of Japan's norms, mores, and fear that they would eventually find themselves at odds with their employees, their bankers, their suppliers, their joint venture partners, their customers, their trade associations and the Government . . ."

CHAPTER 7

1. For a legal treatment of the problem as it relates to the multi-national enterprise, accompanied by an extensive bibliography, see D. F. Vagts, "The Multinational Enterprise: A New Challenge for Transnational Law," *Harvard Law Review*, 83, no. 4 (February 1970): 739–792.

2. *United States* v. *Aluminum Company of America*, 148 F.2d 416, 443 (2d Cir. 1945). For an authoritative discussion of the extraterritoriality issue in U.S. antitrust law, see W. L. Fugate, "The International Aspects of the United States Antitrust Laws," paper presented to the

International Conference on Monopolies, Mergers, and Restrictive Practices, London, September 1969, mimeographed.

3. An excellent summary of these reactions is contained in Kingman Brewster, Jr., *Antitrust and American Business Abroad* (New York: McGraw-Hill, 1958), pp. 45–51.

4. Indeed, a leading U.S. congressman has expressed concern that, in view of the British government's large minority stock ownership in British Petroleum, the company's acquisition of Sohio in the United States could create a Trojan horse in the U.S. economy. See "Europeans Irked by U.S. Trust Role," *The New York Times,* October 13, 1969, p. 71.

5. L. A. Litvak and C. J. Maule, "Conflict, Resolution and Extraterritoriality," *Journal of Conflict Resolution,* 13, no. 3 (September 1969): 306–315; J. R. Garson and H. J. Berman, "U.S. Export Controls—Past, Present and Future," *Columbia Law Review,* 67, no. 5 (May 1967): 791–890; n.a., "Extraterritorial Application of Antitrust Laws; A Conflict of Laws Approach," *Yale Law Journal,* 70, no. 2 (December 1960): 260–287; J. T. Haight, "The Restrictive Business Practices Clause in U.S. Treaties: An Antitrust Tranquilizer for International Trade," *Yale Law Journal,* 70, no. 2 (December 1960): 240–257; Kingman Brewster, Jr., *Antitrust and American Business Abroad,* esp. chap. 3, pp. 39–52; Kingman Brewster, Jr., *Law and United States Business in Canada* (Washington, D.C.: Canadian-American Committee, 1960); J. N. Behrman, *National Interests and the Multinational Enterprise* (Englewood Cliffs: Prentice-Hall, 1970), pp. 114–127.

6. Behrman, *National Interests,* pp. 104–113. The Canadian cases are elaborated in Litvak and Maule, "Conflict."

7. R. H. Cojeen, "Resentment Toward U.S. Direct Investment Abroad," *Michigan Business Review,* 16, no. 1 (January 1964): 25.

8. John Walsh, "France: First the Bomb, Then the 'Plan Calcul,'" *Science,* 156, no. 3776 (May 12, 1967): 767–770.

9. H. D. Willey, "Direct Investment Controls and the Balance of Payments," in C. P. Kindleberger, ed., *The International Corporation* (Cambridge: MIT Press, 1970).

10. Behrman, *National Interests,* pp. 93–98.

11. *United States* v. *United Fruit Company,* complaint no. 1203, Antitrust Division, Department of Justice, filed 1954, amended 1956, consent decree entered 1958, CCH 1958 *Trade Cases* 73, 790; complaint no. 1752, Antitrust Division, Department of Justice, filed 1963, terminated by plea of *nolo contendere,* 1963.

12. *In the Matter of General Foods Corporation et al.,* FTC docket no. 8198, filed 1960, 59 FTC 706 (1961).

13. For instance, Justice Department complaints against Sterling Drug, E. R. Squibb, and others (complaint nos. 1989, 1990, filed 1968). The most spectacular U.S. action against alleged international restrictive business practices by U.S.-controlled drug companies in recent years took the form of an investigation by the Committee on the Judiciary, Subcommittee on Antitrust and Monopoly, U.S. Senate, *Administered Prices, Drugs,* report no. 448, 87th Congress, 1st sess., 1961.

14. *United States* v. *American Smelting and Refining Company et al.,* complaint no. 1177, Antitrust Division, Department of Justice, filed 1953, Civ. 88–249 (SDNY 1953).

15. *United States* v. *Radio Corporation of America et al.,* complaint no. 1210, Antitrust Division, Department of Justice, consent decree entered 1958, CCH 1958 *Trade Cases* 74, 559; also *Hazeltine Research, Inc.* v. *Zenith Radio Corp.,* 239 F. supp. 51 (N.D. Ill. 1965); affirmed in part, reversed in part, 338 F. 2d. 25 (7th Cir. 1967); affirmed in part, reversed in part, 395 U.S. 100.

16. *United States* v. *International Ore & Fertilizer Corporation et al.,* complaint no. 1768, Antitrust Division, Department of Justice, filed 1963, terminated by plea of *nolo contendere,* 1964; *United States* v. *International Minerals & Chemicals Corporation et al.,* complaint no. 1769, Antitrust Division, Department of Justice, filed 1963, terminated by plea of *nolo contendere,* 1965; *United States* v. *The Concentrated Phosphate Export Association Incorporated et al.,* complaint no. 1839, Antitrust Division, Department of Justice, filed 1964, 273 F. supp. 263, rev. 89 U.S. 361, consent decree entered 1969, CCH 1969 *Trade Cases* 86, 568.

17. 15 U.S.C. 18.

18. For summary of antitrust programs in other countries, see C. D. Edwards, *Control of Cartels and Monopolies* (Dobbs Ferry, N.Y.: Oceana, 1967). H. M. Blake, ed., *Business Regulations in the Common Market Nations,* 3 vols. (New York: McGraw-Hill, 1969).

19. D. O. Swann and D. L. McLachlan, *Concentration or Competition: A European Dilemma?* (London: Chatham, 1968), pp. 46–50.

20. Stephen Cohen, *Modern Capitalist Planning: The French Model* (Cambridge: Harvard University Press, 1969), pp. 73–75, 139.

21. Chitoshi Yanaga, *Big Business in Japanese Politics* (New Haven: Yale University Press, 1968), pp. 173–176.

22. "Trustbusters Challenge U.S. Firms' Dealings with Concerns Abroad," *The Wall Street Journal,* July 30, 1970, p. 1.

23. *Petroleum Press Service,* December 1968, pp. 447–449; November 1969, pp. 407–409; December 1969, p. 465. Also *United States* v. *Standard Oil Co., et al.,* complaint no. 2076, Antitrust Division, De-

partment of Justice, consent decree entered 1970, CCH 1970 *Trade Cases* 87, 869.

24. *United States* v. *CIBA Corp., Geigy Chemical Corp., CIBA Ltd., and J. R. Geigy S.A.,* complaint no. 2118, Antitrust Division, Department of Justice, consent decree entered 1970, CCH 1970 *Trade Cases* 89, 065.

25. For summaries of these limitations, see Symposium sponsored by International and Comparative Law Center, Southwestern Legal Foundation, *Rights and Duties of Private Investors Abroad* (New York: Matthew Bender, 1965). Also see Herman Walker, Jr., "Provisions on Companies in the United States Commercial Treaties," *American Journal of International Law,* 50, no. 2 (April 1965): 373–393; S. H. Hymer, *Transatlantic Reactions to Foreign Investment* (New Haven: Economic Growth Center, Yale University, 1968), Discussion Paper No. 53, pp. 5–12; D. F. Vagts, "United States of America's Treatment of Foreign Investment," *Rutgers Law Review,* 17, no. 2, (Winter 1963), pp. 374–404. Individual country limitations are described in detail in various sources, See, for example, M. J. Kust, *Foreign Enterprise in India* (Chapel Hill: University of North Carolina Press, 1964 plus a 1966 supplement); S. W. Wurfel, *Foreign Enterprise in Colombia* (Chapel Hill: University of North Carolina Press, 1965); P. O. Proehl, *Foreign Enterprise in Nigeria* (Chapel Hill: University of North Carolina Press, 1965).

26. J. H. McArthur and B. R. Scott, *Industrial Planning in France* (Boston: Harvard Business School, 1969), pp. 353–356.

27. A. W. Johnstone, *United States Direct Investment in France: An Investigation of the French Charges* (Cambridge: MIT Press, 1965), pp. 78–79.

28. A detailed description of how the licensing of foreign investment actually works is found in Leon Hollerman, *Japan's Dependence on the World Economy* (Princeton: Princeton University Press, 1967), pp. 262–279. See also M. Y. Yoshino, "Japan as Host to the International Corporation," in C. P. Kindleberger, ed., *The International Corporation* (Cambridge: MIT Press, 1970), pp. 345–372. Japanese regulations were liberalized somewhat in 1970; see "Japan Agrees to Open 323 More Businesses Directly to Foreigners," *The Wall Street Journal,* August 26, 1970, p. 13.

29. See *The Trinidad Oil Company: Proposed Purchase by the Texas Company,* Cmd. 9790 (London: Her Majesty's Stationery Office, 1956); "Chrysler Bid for Share in Rootes is Approved Conditionally by Britain," *The Wall Street Journal,* July 30, 1964, p. 2.

30. Bilateral treaties of establishment between the United States and other countries commonly carry broad guarantees of "national treatment." For an analysis of the French case, see Charles Torem and

W. L. Craig, "Control of Foreign Investment in France," *Michigan Law Review*, 66, no. 4 (February 1968): 669–720.

31. In Japan, foreign-owned suppliers were "virtually excluded" from making sales to the Japanese government; only "designated companies" were permitted to submit bids. This general approach applied to fourteen categories of goods that collectively make up most Japanese government procurement. See Hollerman, *Japan's Dependence*, p. 260.

32. See, for instance: "Computers: Buy British, Sell American," *The Economist*, March 7, 1970, p. 63.

33. For a statement of the policy of the Industrial Reorganization Corporation, see "IRC Statement on the U.K. Ball and Roller Bearing Industry," *The Economist*, May 24, 1969, p. 76.

34. Behrman, *National Interests*, p. 98.

35. U.K. Monopolies Commission, *The British Motor Corporation Ltd. and the Pressed Steel Company Ltd.: A Report on the Merger* (London: Her Majesty's Stationery Office, 1966), p. 16; see also "What Sir Frank Is Up To," *The Economist*, January 18, 1969, p. 55.

36. S. T. Weiner, "Investment Incentives in Mexico," *Texas International Law Forum*, 4, no. 1 (Winter 1968): 64–78. See also E. L. Wheelwright, *Industrialization in Malaysia* (Melbourne: Melbourne University Press, 1965), p. 34.

37. For a good discussion of the issue, see C. F. Díaz Alejandro, *Direct Investment in Latin America*, Economic Growth Center Discussion Paper, no. 170 (New Haven: Yale University Press, 1970), pp. 337–339

38. About half the large U.S. enterprises with subsidiaries in Latin America claim to be engaged in integrated planning that assumes the existence of the Latin American Free Trade Area. Business International, *Report to the Interamerican Development Bank: Study of Multinational Companies*, New York 1968, mimeograph, p. 37. The report provides numerous illustrations of intraregional sourcing. Though no similar data exist for indigenously owned Latin American firms, there is not much doubt that their perspective is far more limited. José de la Torre, "Exports of Manufactured Goods from Developing Countries: Marketing Factors and the Role of Foreign Enterprise," unpublished D.B.A. thesis, Harvard Business School, 1970, chap. 6, p. 35.

39. Indications that the issue was very much alive in 1970 are to be found in the Commission des Communautés Européennes, *La politique industrielle des communautés européennes* (Brussels, 1970), pp. 247–257.

40. Two documents illustrate the approach: Commission of the European Communities, "Première Orientation pour une Politique Energétique Communautaire," Brussels, December 1968, mimeograph, p. 23; and European Coal and Steel Community, "Protocol of Agreement," *Official Gazette*, 69 (April 30, 1964).

41. CCH, *Common Market Reporter*, 1970, paras. 5509, 9298, 9381.

Notes

CHAPTER 8

1. S. P. Huntington, "Political Order and Political Decay," in W. P. Glade, *The Latin American Economies* (New York: American Book, 1969), p. 3.

2. Attributed to the U.S. Department of Defense in *ibid.*

3. For more on this subject, see Raymond Vernon, *U.S. Controls on Foreign Direct Investments—A Reevaluation* (New York: Financial Executives Research Foundation, 1969).

4. Ralph Cordiner, "Managerial Strategy for International Business," Speech to the National Foreign Trade Council Convention, New York, November 16, 1960; Sidney Rolfe, *The International Corporation* (Istanbul: International Chamber of Commerce, 1969), pp. 141–144; statement of John J. Powers, Jr., Chairman of Charles Pfizer and Company, in *Hearings* before the Subcommittee on Foreign Economic Policy of the Joint Economic Committee, 91st Cong., 1st sess., Dec. 4, 1969, pp. 129–133; Eno Hobbing, "The Good Corporate Guest Helps Build the House," *Columbia Journal of World Business,* 2, no. 5 (September–October 1967): 39–46; G. H. Clee, "Guidelines for Global Business," *Columbia Journal of World Business,* 1, no. 1 (Winter 1966): 97–104; Lynn Townsend, "The Multinational Corporation: A New Force for Economic Development," *Vital Speeches,* 31, no. 14 (May 1, 1965): 444–448.

5. A. O. Hirschman, *How to Divest in Latin America, and Why,* Essays in International Finance no. 76 (Princeton. Princeton University Press, 1969); P. N. Rosenstein-Rodan, "Multinational Investment in the Framework of Latin American Integration," paper presented to a round table of the Board of Governors of the Interamerican Development Bank, Bogota, April 1968, pp. 66–78. For a more qualified endorsement of the approach, see C. F. Díaz Alejandro, *Direct Foreign Investment in Latin America,* Center Discussion Paper no. 150 (New Haven: Economic Growth Center of Yale University, 1970), pp. 334–336.

6. C. S. Burchill, "The Multi-National Corporation: An Unsolved Problem in International Relations," *Queen's Quarterly,* 1970, pp. 15–16; Roy Ash, "The New Anatomy of World Business," *Columbia Journal of World Business,* 5, no. 2 (March–April 1970): 90–93; G. W. Ball, "Toward a World Economy," *Dun's Review,* 91, no. 2 (February 1968): 19; D. P. Kirscher "Now the Transnational Enterprise," *Harvard Business Review,* 42, no. 2 (March–April 1964): 6–10, 172–176.

7. "U.S. Easing of China-Trade Rules Will Help Overseas Units: Direct Exchange Still Out," *The Wall Street Journal,* December 22, 1969, p. 6.

8. H. J. Steiner and D. F. Vagts, *Transnational Legal Problems* (Mineola: The Foundation Press, 1968), pp. 419–424.

9. *Ibid.*, pp. 360–363.

10. D. F. Vagts, "The Multinational Enterprise: A New Challenge for Transnational Law, *Harvard Law Review*, 83, no. 4 (February 1970): 789.

11. For example, P. M. Goldberg and C. P. Kindleberger, "Toward a GATT for Investment: A Proposal for Supervision of the International Corporation," *Law and Policy in International Business*, 2, no. 2 (summer 1970): pp. 295–323; also statement of Heribert Maier, ICFTU representative, before U.S. Congress, Joint Economic Committee, July 28, 1970, reproduced in "The International Free Trade Union Movement and Multinational Corporation," ICFTU *Economic and Social Bulletin*, 18, no. 5 (August 1970).

12. See, for instance, Louis Turner, *Politics and the Multinational Company* (London: Dec. 1969), Fabian Research Series 279; the Maier testimony, already cited; and R. I. Barovick, "Labor Reacts to Multinationalism," *Columbia Journal of World Business*, July–August 1970, pp. 40–46.

Index

adaptation of productive processes, 181ff

advanced countries, *see* France; Germany; Japan; United Kingdom; *see also* less-developed areas

advertising, outlays for, 11, 12, 185

Africa, élites in, 194, 195; U.S. investment in, 62

agreements, *see* intergovernmental agreements; international agreements; petroleum; taxation

aircraft, 12, 84–86, 95, 105

Algeria, 52

Allende, Salvador, 51

aluminum, 37–45, 106, 110

Alusuisse, 44

Andean *altiplano*, 49

Andean group, 246

Anglo-Iranian Oil Co., 35

Anglo-Persian Oil Co., *see* Anglo-Iranian Oil Co.

antitrust policies, 237, 238, 240, 278

ARAMCO, 44, 49, 55

Argentina, 35, 56, 99, 179; tensions in, 193, 195, 196

Arrow, K. J., 115

Asia, élites in, 194, 195; U.S. investment in, 62, 104, 110

"as-is" oil agreement of 1928, 31, 33

Australia, 135, 149, 237; business-government relations in, 207; generation of exports in, 162; R & D in, 162; resource transfer to, 159

automobiles, 12, 20, 24, 84, 95, 100, 105, 179, 240; growth pattern of, 250, 252; pricing practices of, 138

balance-of-payments question, 17, 162, 186, 261; in advanced economies, 163–166; in less-developed areas, 172–178

bauxite, 41, 44, 45, 177

Bayer, Farbenfabriken, 81

Belgian Congo, élites in, 196

Belgium, 79, 193

Bendix Corporation, 107

Berle, Adolf A., Jr., 145

Bolivia, 31, 258

Brazil, 98, 184, 256, 259; tensions in, 193, 195, 196, 200; U.S. investment in, 20, 149

British East India Company, 215

British Petroleum Co. Ltd., 27, 34, 35, 110, 234, 240

bureaucrats, 197, 265

Burma, élites in, 196

business-government relations in the U.S., 205ff; *see also* individual countries

business schools, as transfer resource, 160

businessmen, attitude of, 197, 198, 265; professionalism of, in U.S., 217